IMAGES OF

Muhammad

IMAGES OF

Muhammad

Narratives of the Prophet in
Islam Across the Centuries

TARIF KHALIDI

DOUBLEDAY

NEW YORK   LONDON

TORONTO   SYDNEY   AUCKLAND

DD
DOUBLEDAY

Copyright © 2009 by Tarif Khalidi

Published in the United States by Doubleday Religion,
an imprint of the Crown Publishing Group,
a division of Random House, Inc., New York.
www.doubledayreligion.com

DOUBLEDAY and the DD colophon
are registered trademarks of Random House, Inc.

Book design by Ellen Cipriano

Library of Congress Cataloging-in-Publication Data

Khalidi, Tarif, 1938–
Images of Muhammad / Tarif Khalidi. — 1st ed.
p.   cm.
Includes bibliographical references and index.
1. Muhammad, Prophet, d. 632 — Biography. 2. Muhammad, Prophet, d.
632 — Biography — Sources. 3. Muhammad, Prophet, d. 632 —
Appreciation. I. Title.
BP75.K4935 2009
297.6'3 — dc22
2008036477

ISBN 978-0-385-51816-1

Printed in the U.S.A.

1 3 5 7 9 10 8 6 4 2

First Edition

Contents

CONTENTS

Preface

This is a book that exacts a lengthy toll of apologies and disclaimers from its author, a litany of excuses longer than the norm. Its subject is the evolution of the images of Muhammad as portrayed by his community across the centuries. It may be that the introduction that follows will clarify what is meant by this, but what I thought worth attempting was a kind of map of a literary tradition, from its origins to the present. I also suggest that there is a certain symmetry to that tradition. Although numerous studies exist on disparate aspects of that biographical tradition, I know of no study that casts an eye on the landscape as a whole. There may therefore be some value in having a large map, even if somewhat wrinkled and inaccurate in projection.

The sources are truly vast. There is hardly any work in any branch of Islamic studies written by Muslims, ancient or modern, that does not refer to Muhammad and his sayings or actions. He is simply everywhere in the literature, prose or verse, of his community. So I decided to confine myself by and large to the genre called the *Sira,* that is to say the genre of formal biography of Muhammad. Alas, here too the bulk, especially in the premodern period, is immense, and several primary works of the *Sira* will go unmentioned. I hope I have not done great violence to the *Sira* in omitting them, though other students of the genre will surely put matters right. Again, the *Sira* written in Arabic during the premodern period occupies center stage in this work, although the seminal modern contributions of Indian Muslims and Iranians are highlighted as well.

In telling the story of the *Sira,* and of other portrayals of his life that are not strictly *Sira,* I have kept away from historicity, from issues that have to do with their value as a factual source of information on Muhammad's life, although much history can of course be learned from historiography. Instead, I have concerned myself primarily with social ideality, by which I mean the manner in which a religious society gradually builds up images of ideal conduct for its central figure or figures. I like to think of ideality as a subset of the "social imaginary," that which drives a religious society to construct and reconstruct the ideal lives of its early heroes.

A question I sometimes used to set my students in early Arabic/ Islamic history and culture went as follows: "Muslims generally object to being called 'Muhammadans.' With what justification?" I no longer remember exactly what I expected from my students as an adequate answer, but this may have included a discussion of the tension between the human Muhammad and the Muhammad of miracle. Was he simply a messenger of God or was he more? And if more, how much more? This book is partially concerned with the answers to this question provided by the *Sira.*

But the social ideality of Muhammad is underlain by the love of his community. In 2006 Muhammad was the subject of a series of cartoons in the Danish press. The furor caused by that incident, like almost all similar furors, managed to obscure the raw nerve that these cartoons had touched. I am referring to the fact that little was said throughout that controversy about the love of Muhammad among his community, although much was said about respect for religious beliefs versus the primacy of free speech. At the heart of that incident was the love of Muhammad, which, in the phrase of Muhammad Iqbal, "runs like blood in the veins of his community." It was Muhammad as comforter, friend, intercessor, family member that these cartoons seemingly demeaned. A cliché has gained currency in recent years to the effect that the equivalent of Christ in Islam is not Muhammad but the Qur'an. That is not entirely true. The images of Muhammad collected in this book, from the *Sira* and other literary sources, may help to show how close the Prophet has been to his community, how much he remains at the center of their affection, and how vividly he still stands among them.

This book was first suggested by Trace Murphy at Random House. For his patience and constant encouragement, my heartfelt thanks. My thanks also to Darya Porat for her able shepherding of this work and to Maggie Carr for her perceptive and elegant copyediting.

Two colleagues at the American University of Beirut read parts of this work and made numerous suggestions, almost all of which I immediately incorporated, with gratitude for their concern and critical acumen: Maher Jarrar and Muhammad 'Ali Khalidi. I exonerate them from any responsibility for what remains.

It was Magda who isolated me from my surroundings while I wrote, sent me back again and again to my labors, and firmly and lovingly insisted that I finish what I started. This makes her the *maraine* of all that follows.

TARIF KHALIDI
Center for Arab and Middle Eastern Studies
American University of Beirut
March 10, 2009

Introduction

REFLECTIONS ON MUHAMMAD AND BIOGRAPHY

The name "Muhammad" means "worthy of all praise." For fifteen centuries or so this name has reverberated around the world so that today one in every five human beings calls down daily praises and blessings upon him, feels secure in his faith and intercession, holds him up as a model of virtue and good manners, and goes on pilgimage to the holy sites he designated, treading the same ground he once trod. And what of the rest of humanity? One might assume a wide range of attitudes, all the way from curiosity to admiration to dread. This book is not a "straight" or "objective" biography of Muhammad—there are more than enough of these. It is instead a book about his Islamic images. To be more precise, it is a biographical account that attempts to explore the manner in which his life has been constructed and reconstructed, designed and redesigned, over the last millennium and a half. How has his community narrated his biography? And why is Muhammad still such a commanding and fascinating figure in the twenty-first century?

To introduce the subject, I begin with the core story, which I shall confine to one paragraph. Muhammad, son of 'Abdullah son

of 'Abd al-Muttalib, was born in Mecca around the year 570 A.D.
He began to receive revelations around the year 610 A.D. and
shortly thereafter started to preach his faith. During his early
years as a preacher he seems to have achieved only a limited success in his hometown, and he had even less success in winning over
converts from outside Mecca. The turning point in his career came
in the year 622 A.D., when he abandoned Mecca for Medina, a
town where he had established a small base of converts who were
ready to protect him. This move to Medina *(hijra)* was later
adopted by Muslims to mark the first year of the Muslim, or *Hijri,*
calendar. From Medina Muhammad organized and often led a series of expeditions whose aim was ultimately to conquer Mecca,
"God's sacred precinct," and thereafter spread the religion of Islam
inside and outside Arabia. Mecca fell in 630, another landmark
year. His followers increased rapidly throughout his years in
Medina. The Prophet himself died in Medina in 632.

This or a similar core story would I think be accepted by the majority of scholars, Muslim and non-Muslim, who concern themselves with Muhammad's life. However, the early Muslim
biographical tradition peopled this core story with thousands upon
thousands of named and often sharply drawn personalities, men
and women whose life stories were intertwined with Muhammad's
own. Muslim biographers seem from an early date to have decided
to include in their biographies of the Prophet the names of every
single man or woman whose life in some way or another touched
upon or intersected the core narrative. It is as if some early
Christian Gospel writer had decided to fill out the Sermon on the
Mount and the feeding of the five thousand with the names and life
stories of every single one of those who were present, together
with some account, long or short, of their life and subsequent fate.

Until about the nineteenth century, the traditional Muslim biographies of Muhammad always place him within a large crowd of humanity. He towers over these multitudes, an object of adoration, and yet does not escape their harm, their ridicule, their disobedience, and even their active or secret hostility. "Muhammad died but his community lives on" is a widespread Muslim conversational phrase, invoked to stress that life goes on, that no human being is ever indispensable. It is perhaps an echo of that early biographical view that constructed and reconstructed his life as part and parcel of the life of his community. This image of Muhammad amidst his community may also be a reflection of his images in the Qur'an, to which I shall later return.

Given this early biographical conception of a prophet embedded in his religious community, or *umma,* it makes sense to try to determine what lay behind that conception. To begin with, biography in almost all literary traditions has been seen as the most vivid sort of history one can write. It personalizes history, it centers history on individuals, it encapsulates history in a number of individual lives. One might call biography a form of synecdoche, a substitution of the part for the whole. In this sense, biography stands for or substitutes for history. The smaller life of an individual stands for, symbolizes, prefigures, the larger history of a people, nation, city, community, or whatever. In fact some cultures at certain moments—for example, the premodern Islamic—identified biography with history. To them history *was* biography.[1] Hence, in that conception of biography, the life of Muhammad is inextricable from the history of his *umma.* But there are other considerations, chief among which is the perennial appeal of biography to a deep-seated but not fully explored human curiosity. One recent writer calls biography "a healthy form of voyeurism," a sense of intrigue about a life of achievement. Quite apart from voyeurism, however, is the desire, again perennial, to see through the lives, expected to be transparent, of great leaders. They ought to have nothing to hide. We want to know, almost by right, the intimate details of their lives. We want from a biography not only what the person was like *in public* but what he or she was like *in private.* Some measure of "voyeurism" may be involved here, but at issue too is the need to know how the prominent man or woman did something that we all have to do, that is, live from day to day with other people. We all have to get up in the morning, go to work, face a domestic crisis and cope with our daily problems. We would like to know how these great figures coped with these same problems of everyday life.

In traditional or premodern Islamic biographies of Muhammad, the need to know both the public and private person was overwhelming. Standing in the very midst of his community, Muhammad cannot and should not escape the community's closest scrutiny. His public persona, it was felt, must be joined to an examination of his life behind closed doors in order to endow his life with complete transparency. Everything he did held some example, some lesson or another for the believers. Indeed, his biography *(Sira)* was sometimes used as a synonym for his normative example *(Sunna).* 'A'isha, the favorite wife of Muhammad, was once asked: "Mother of the Believers, what did the Prophet do when he was at home?" She answered, "What any of you will normally do at home. He would patch his garment and repair his sandals. Most of the time, he sewed."[2] And so we have this marvelous image of the great prophet of Islam sitting cross-legged at home and, with thread and needle, sewing happily away—and what a feast this tableau is for the imagination! Did he whistle softly as he sewed? Was he good at threading the needle? But there he is, sharing the domesticity of his followers and in his daily life he was indistinguishable from the masses among whom his prophetic career ran its course.

But to turn once again to the dilemmas of biography, let us assume for a moment that the main task of biography is to answer the question What was he or she like? What were they *really* like? And let us suppose that in answer to this question a biographer takes a grid and proceeds to place it on the life of the biographee. This grid might then reveal a sort of graph, perhaps, of youth, maturity, old age, a chronological graph wherein the subject's life becomes readied for narrative. But being a grid, one can bisect it in all sorts of ways. The biographer can, for instance, divide it into themes such as the politician, the exile, the writer, the social reformer, the farmer, and so forth. Or the biographer can combine the two strategies. But whatever strategy is adopted, the question "What was he or she *really* like?" still looms large, inescapable. We have not really solved the problem by cutting the subject's life up into manageable or comprehensible units or categories and themes. We have not resolved the dilemma. Is life so tidy that we can draw it as a graph? "A biography," writes Virginia Woolf, "is considered complete if it merely accounts for six or seven selves, whereas a person may well have as many as a thousand."[3] Julian Barnes uses the image of a fisherman's net: "The trawling net fills, the biographer hauls it in, sorts, throws back, stores, fillets and sells. Yet consider what he doesn't catch: there is always far more of that."[4] I like to think that between them these two writers shattered the illusion of biography as a tidy and well-structured life. One can no longer ask what a person was *really* like. We are now in an age where a biography, instead of being called *The Life of X,* will almost as often be entitled *The Invention of X.* Hence, given both the untidiness of the outward and contingent events impinging on a life, and the untidiness of inward behavior, how can one possibly write a tidy biography? If a biography is to be an accurate, truthful reflection of a life, should it not itself be untidy, cluttered, disorganized, muddled, unfathomable?

The early biographies of Muhammad will often seem to a modern (postmodern?) reader to be as disorganized and untidy as any follower of Woolf or Barnes might wish them to be. In their early days the writers of these biographies remind one of Julian Barnes's fisherman, frantically hauling in every conceivable incident in Muhammad's life and heaping them one on top of the other in a motley assemblage of facts. For the pious biographer, no incident, however trivial, must ever escape his net. The overall impression is one of immense density of detail, confusing to all but the experts. Aware perhaps of the dangers of this untidiness, later Muslim biographers who reflected more deeply on the uses to which Muhammad's biography could be put imposed a grid upon his life, seeing in it certain neat patterns, certain divisions that appeared to reflect divine dispensation and order. There was no question in the mind of any biographer, early or late, that Muhammad's life was traceable and knowable. However, a tidy framework had to be found within which the innumerable and often contradictory versions of what the Prophet said and what he did could be fitted. Many, especially later, biographers were to criticize with great severity some early biographical accounts as unworthy of the Prophet or as interpolations by heretics. His life had to be pruned of myth or parti pris in order to reveal what Muhammad was really like. All the details of that life had to be made to cohere with his prophetic persona.

But let us pass now from the theoretical dilemmas of biography to examine some of the uses to which biography has been put. These reflections are cast in general terms but will highlight Islamic and Muhammadan biography in particular. To what end was biography used? What function, individual or social, did it serve? To answer these questions, it might perhaps be best if we adopt a broadly historical approach. I shall not attempt anything other than a very general sketch of the history of the use to which biography has been put, desiring merely to contextualize the many images of Muhammad that this book will eventually examine.

If we cast our eyes over the long history of biography, we may be able to detect three or four principal uses or aims of biography:

1. To provide inspiring examples to be imitated,
2. To celebrate famous men and women of a particular nation,
3. To exalt the self-image of a particular profession or group, and
4. To show how a particular life took on a meaningful shape (bildungsroman).[5]

I have alluded already to one or two of these uses of biography, and I propose now to say a few things about each. In most cases I will try to give one prominent example from the classical or Christian European tradition of biography and one or more from the Muslim, which remains my main focus. Needless to add, these uses of biography are not exclusive; one use will often include another.

In the history of the Western European tradition of biography, most influential in the beginning were the biographies of the Roman historian Plutarch (first century A.D.) and his *Parallel Lives* of famous Greeks and Romans, forty-six in number, arrayed in pairs; the aim here is to give a true portrait of the biographee, and the truth of the portrait makes the human lesson to be learned all the more valuable. These portraits are moral stories in miniature and so are told in such a way that their subject can best be imitated. A superman cannot teach a man much of value. Thus we get the "warts and all" approach to biography, the man or woman with all his or her human virtues and vices, who draws near enough to us in humanity so that we can imitate that person. The humanistic approach to biography remains to the present day one of the major purposes or uses of biography. I shall call it the "humanistic" purpose of biography, for short. The Muslim tradition of biography also contains a distinct humanistic purpose or approach. There are many elements in the traditional life of Muhammad that his biographers have used to bring him near to us by picturing him as an ordinary, frail, fallible human being, thus making his life easily followed and imitated. Muhammad, not being privy to the secrets of men's hearts, says the great Andalusian biographer al-Qadi 'Iyad (d. 1149), may well have delivered some wrong verdicts, but this merely makes it more urgent for his community to strive to imitate his endeavor to arrive at the truth.[6] We see him at many moments of his life as lonely, injured, afraid, doubtful, and weak as any of us; as anguished, troubled, and uncertain of where he is going as the rest of humanity. There is the famous story in the Muslim biographical tradition in which the farmers of Medina seek his advice about whether or not to pollinate their palm trees. He advises them not to pollinate. They obey his advice and the result is the total ruin of the date season in Medina. When the farmers complain gently to him about this misadventure, he replies, {You are more knowledgeable about your worldly affairs than I am.} And there are instances where, when Muhammad pronounces some opinion on something, he is asked, "O Prophet of God, is this God speaking through you [that is, does this have binding legal force?] or are you giving us an ordinary human opinion?" The implication is that we will obey you unquestioningly in the first case, but we might not obey you in the second. We will return to some of these issues later, but it seems fairly clear that the contrast drawn between the divinely inspired pronouncements of the Prophet of God and the portrait of Muhammad the man was seen by his biographers as an important distinction, a pointer to the use of his life as a model of conduct.

Now for the second use of biography, namely to commemorate

or celebrate famous men and women of a particular nation. This use of biography is also of perennial prevalence; the emphasis is on celebrating a community, a nation, a people through the lives of its outstanding men and women. One might call it the nationalist-heroic use of biography. The principal aim is not so much imitation, although this is not excluded, but communal celebration. Here the biography resembles a long obituary or a eulogy delivered at a memorial service. In other words, the biography sets out to show how an individual human being embodied the virtues or achievements of a larger group, and so the work is as much a celebration of the group as it is of the individual biographee. In the classical tradition, the *Agricola* of Tacitus (d. ca. 122 A.D.) is one of the earliest and most influential of this genre. Agricola was a Roman governor, a model of how the Roman Empire can best be ruled. His life by Tacitus embodies the best attributes of Roman rule such as wisdom, the ascendancy of law, civilization, peace: Rome is thereby portrayed as the worthy mistress of the civilized world.

The Islamic tradition of biography displays a similar use, that is, biography used for commemoration or celebration. Thus, in the life of Muhammad one finds a celebratory element, a nationalist-heroic approach when we encounter Muhammad in the midst of his community. It is as if he stands at the very center of an ever-expanding series of concentric circles of believers. An interesting debate can be heard among Islam's earliest historians: How is a Companion *(Sahabi)* of Muhammad to be defined? Who qualifies for this honor and how? Are all contemporaries of Muhammad to be counted as Companions or only those who actually saw him and/or submitted to his faith? To celebrate Muhammad as he should be celebrated one must also celebrate his earliest *umma*, the community of the faithful who heard his message and followed it heroically, and against overwhelming odds. Conversely, Muhammad himself embodies the virtues of his *umma*. He is divinely selected from among the best of nations, and he himself is the best of his nation, of his tribe, of his clan, and of his family. His life will also of course personify the religious message to his nation. When 'A'isha was asked, "What was Muhammad's moral character like?" she responded, "His moral character *was* the Qur'an."[7] Muhammad's life epitomized the virtues of his nation as well as his own religious message.

The third use of biography, the exaltation of a particular group or profession, can be dealt with more briefly since it is not directly relevant to Muhammad. In the early Christian tradition, the genre of biography called the Lives of the Saints is an early example of this exaltation of a group. In the Muslim tradition, the Companions of Muhammad were among the earliest biographees. Biography here serves to designate and exalt a group whose members gain their elevated status from their association with the original sacred figure. These Companions became the earliest spiritual heroes of Islam. The shadow that Muhammad cast was eventually to generate many biographies whose purpose was to exalt his family, for instance, or else other groups who in one way or another most piously followed his example. Out of these works would evolve a genre of biography called the *Manaqib*, or "Virtues," of these groups. A well-known exponent of this genre, Muhibb al-Din al-Tabari (d. 1294), puts it as follows: "The Almighty has elevated in rank all who have any relationship or kinship to Muhammad, all who aided or followed him, and made it incumbent on His creatures to love all his near relations, his family and their progeny."[8]

The bildungsroman is usually defined as a novel that deals with a person's formative years or spiritual education. When we apply this term to biography, we get a kind of biography that aims to show how early formation or development helped to explain spiritual evolution, and how the biographee gained in wisdom as life carried him or her forward. This element can be seen in biographies of Muhammad in which his early life and his preparation for the prophetic mission are shown to be essential to his later career. For instance, there are elements like the fact that he was born an orphan, the fact that he was born trustworthy (but not perhaps sinless, a theme to be dealt with later), the fact that he was from the beginning a meditative individual, the fact that he endured so much suffering and ridicule—as well as indications that these early episodes of his life prepared and educated him for his calling and were an essential prelude to his mission.

I end these reflections with a historical sketch of Western biographical concepts followed by a similar sketch of Islamic concepts. The object is to keep in view certain trends in biographical writing that are relevant to the images of Muhammad and to their conception and reconception across the centuries. In the Western tradition one notices a fairly constant conception of biography from Plutarch to the nineteenth century. Biography was throughout this period largely dominated by the model type, inspiring imitation, and was largely nationalist-heroic and celebratory in style. Biography is defined in terms of the public life, and if there are occasional glimpses of the private life, these glimpses are secondary or auxiliary to the public life: they reinforce the public image. In all cases, biography teaches by personal example. Instead of reading about, for example, the sense of duty, you read a life of someone who embodies the true meaning of duty. And instead of reading about a nation, you read the life of someone who embodies the life of the nation. Biography is a vivid moral lesson. Instead of the dry and boring sermon, you listen to or read the story of an individual, a far more interesting proposition.

Beginning, however, with the romantic movement of the late eighteenth and early nineteenth century, Western European biography underwent an important transformation. The practitioners of romantic biography advanced the notion that a life is often far too complex to be a true model for others; that we are all a mixture of virtue and vice; that biography to be true and useful must reflect the whole personality of a man or woman, both reason and emotions, both the rational and the irrational, both moments of nobility and courage and moments of cowardice and nastiness. Romantic writers undermined the ideal of a model by postulating that a life full of virtue only is not a life at all but a fantasy. The greatest practitioner in the nineteenth century was Thomas Carlyle, whose influence on biography in the West was considerable, and who of course attempted a biographical sketch of Muhammad.[9]

The next big step in Western biography is represented by the great biographical enterprise called the *Dictionary of National Biography* in the late nineteenth century, under the editorship of Leslie Stephen. The principles adopted by that enterprise were heavily influenced by dominant scientific ideas of the age, the age of the spectacular triumph of sciences such as geology, biology, and evolution. And so, where biography is concerned, we demand of it that a life should be as factual and accurate as possible, and that aspects of a life should be put in their rightful compartments or drawers. A life therefore should be categorized, it should have a taxonomy, it should be classified. For example, the thinking or thoughts or philosophy or whatever of an individual should be treated separately from his or her life. So too should the military exploits, the professional career, and so forth. If judgment is to be passed on a life, it should be balanced and moderate; the biographer must not pretend to be God and know all about the biographee. So here are the biographical facts all nicely packaged and classified like exhibits in a museum: one might call it biography as a scientific exhibit. The moral or lesson of the life is no longer a prominent feature. The model to be imitated is no longer a central issue in biography.[10]

The next big step in Western biography was to serve as an instrument for psychoanalysis, associated with Sigmund Freud.[11] Freud wrote only two biographies in the strict sense of the term: his lives of Leonardo da Vinci and of Woodrow Wilson. In the first biography, which concerns us more directly, much is made of Leonardo's dream of the vulture, an early cradle memory. Leonardo is reported to have recollected that a vulture had come down, opened his mouth with its tail, and struck his lips with the tail many times. Freud then uses this vision to psychoanalyze Leonardo, although the details of this analysis do not concern us here.[12] What is clear is that Freud wanted to explore biography as an analytic tool, as a procedure for probing the personality, a way of uncovering what is hidden or forbidden or taboo in a life. So for Freud the biographee becomes a patient. We start with a person's dreams, visions, early memories, fantasies (the manifest content) and we work inward to the real content, to what the person is hiding. This procedure has had a great deal of influence on modern biography. It was Freud who first dealt with an individual psyche as deeply unpublic. We are all of us to varying degrees neurotic, unstable, contradictory. And in the traditional Muslim biographies of Muhammad, Freud would have found in the accounts of the Prophet's life, had he bothered to examine them, a very large number of visions, early memories, dreams, and so forth, most notably the incident of the opening of Muhammad's breast as a child, which would have kept Freud happy for many years. Indeed, a Freudian biography of Muhammad would be much appreciated. In his *Muhammad* the French scholar Maxime Rodinson attempted something that may vaguely be called a Freudian approach, but with results too timid to qualify as pathbreaking. The influence of Freud on biography is still strong in the West. Freudian biography has been attacked from many quarters, for example, because the biographee cannot act as a living patient. Nevertheless, much biographical writing today includes a section on the childhood experiences and visions of the biographee and the attempt, Freudian or à la Freud, to discover in that childhood an important key to later developments. To that extent Freud was an advocate of the bildungsroman.

Of later developments I will not say much. But after Freud the fragmented personality, the mixture of fact and fancy in any human life, takes on a new meaning in modern biography. Is any human life really knowable? Can we really ascertain all the whys and wherefores like the laws of chemistry? Can we ever write a truly complete life in an orderly fashion? If a human life has no pattern, how can biography have a pattern? If a life is a sort of heap of facts, emotions, accidents, and so forth, then biography, as we have seen in the remarks of Virginia Woolf, should perhaps look like a heap also. What we are witnessing nowadays in Western biographical writing is the advent of what one might call postmodernist biography, or perhaps the application of the uncertainty principle to biographical writing. A recent and telling example is Mary Beard's *The Invention of Jane Harrison*. This biography steadfastly refuses to replace uncertainty with speculation. Biography fascinates us precisely because it cannot pin a person down. Beard's *Harrison* raises the following questions: Why should continuity be the mark of a life and not discontinuity? Can one really distinguish within a life between major and minor events? Can we really compartmentalize the life of a human being? Are we one person or many? Can we ever know what happens behind bedroom doors?

But let me turn now to the Muslim side of the question, to a sketch of the history of Muhammadan biography in Islamic culture. One might note that at several points the problems and challenges of biography will appear to be similar in the Islamic and in the Western Christian cultural traditions. I have already given some examples previously in discussing the use of biography, for example, humanistic, nationalist-heroic, and so forth. The earliest Muslim biographical writing ran along two parallel lines: the *Sira* of Muhammad and the *tabaqat* of his companions.

The Sira of Muhammad

A *sira* is a path through life and so by extension a biography, but *the Sira* (with a capital *S,* as it were) is the life of Muhammad. The *Sira* contains *sunna,* the latter setting out in a systematic fashion the Prophet's customary or normative behavior, that which must by and large be imitated or obeyed. The *Sira* narrates and charts the outward facts of his life, whereas the *sunna* is its ethical/legal content. The two, as stated above, are sometimes confused and spoken of in the same breath. This mixture of the two elements is not surprising, given that we are dealing with a prophet who teaches by personal example. Every detail of his personal and public life is potentially of legal or ethical interest for the believer.

But while the *Sira* of Muhammad continued over time to be an independent genre of narrative biography, the *sunna* of Muhammad was eventually collected in standardized *Hadith,* the name given to the "Traditions" of Muhammad, his pronouncements or his actions that have moral or legal content and that function as a guide to the believers. In sum, the *Sira* is the narrative biography of Muhammad, while the *sunna* is the record of his legal or normative example and action. The *Sira* takes its earliest shape with the celebrated *Sira* of Ibn Ishaq (d. 767); the *sunna* begins to cohere in collections of the mid-ninth century.[13] No longer a narrative, the hadith marked out, systematized, and sacralized *sunna,* arranging it under the principal features of the good Muslim life (faith, prayer, fasting, pilgrimage, and so forth). The *Sira* on the other hand pursued the path of narrative. There is a great deal of overlap in biographical content between the two genres, but in style, presentation, and objectives they are wholly different.

The Tabaqat

The second early genre of biography is the *tabaqat*. *Tabaqa* means "a generation," and the *tabaqat* (plural) that occupied early Muslim biographers were first of all the Companions of Muhammad, the *Sahaba,* then those who followed them *(Tabi'un),* then the followers of the followers *(tabi'u al-tabi'in),* then the religious scholars and men of learning of later generations. The first systematizer of the *tabaqat* genre was Ibn Sa'd (d. 845). These biographies are arranged more or less by religious importance: the major Companions get large biographies, the minor ones less so. Ibn Sa'd's introduction is made up of an important *Sira,* still considered, with those of Ibn Ishaq, al-Baladhuri (d. 892), and al-Tabari (d. 923), one of the four major early *Siras* of Muhammad; let us call them the four founding fathers of early Muhammadan *Sira.* We will have occasion to take a closer look at them later.

What Islamic biography in the strict sense do we have in Islam's first three centuries or so? The *Sira* and the *tabaqat.* The first concentrated on Muhammad's life as narrative, the second on Muhammad's community. These two biographical genres have run concurrently to the present day, that is, biography alongside the biographical dictionary. This latter was to become a distinguishing feature of Islamic culture, an immensely rich source on premodern Muslims and their lives. No premodern civilization has ever produced so many biographies or biographical sketches of its men and women. Up to about the nineteenth century it was the *tabaqat* genre that typified Islamic biographical literature, carrying forward that early conception of Muhammad standing in the midst of an ever-expanding community.

Meanwhile, and for many centuries, the *Sira* of Muhammad overshadowed all other biographies. Whose *Sira* could possibly have a remotely similar value? This early or formative period of Islam is the one that the great Ibn Khaldun (d. 1406) dubbed the "Age of Awe and Amazement" *(Dhuhul)*. This "awe" might partially explain why the Muhammadan *Sira* was the predominant *sira* in the strict sense in this early period, even though other early Muslims were commemorated in biographical notices of varying lengths in the dictionaries. It was only with the coming of the age of the great warrior-sultans of the eleventh century onward that the *Sira* genre began to expand to include other great heroes of Islam. Not only the great sultans were given separate and distinct biographies but also, for instance, great mystics were held up as models of spirituality, as well as other ancient Islamic heroes, for example, the caliphs 'Umar I and II. Many of these biographies were designed to show how the biographee conformed to or otherwise re-created through glorious exploits the example of Muhammad.

If, at this point, my readers require some rough and ready periodization of the trajectory of Muhammad's images, I will venture the following. We have, to begin with, the four founding fathers of the *Sira*. Between them Ibn Ishaq, Ibn Sa'd, al-Baladhuri, and al-Tabari laid down the basic framework of Muhammad's life and much of its narrative content. Theirs is a *Sira* of primitive devotion, a *Sira* that stands so much in awe of its subject that it gathers in its net all the reports that fall into it, paying little or no heed to their consistency. The guiding principle is inclusion rather than exclusion, and if there are stories or anecdotes about the Prophet that may offend the sensibilities of Muslims, the idea is that it is better for them to remain where they are than be excised because of any pretensions to piety. Next comes an age during which the Muhammadan *Sira* was subjected to critical assessment in order to prune it of superstition and heresy. From primitive devotion, we move to an age in which the *Sira* of Muhammad can be described as canonical, moral, exclusivist, and rationalizing. It is only through such pruning that the *Sira* can become usable by the believer as a guide to moral conduct. I would nominate the famous *Sira* of the Andalusian al-Qadi 'Iyad (d. 1149) as typifying this development in the image of the Prophet. Muhammad's superhuman qualities—his pre-eternity, miraculous powers, and sinlessness—are asserted in order to fortify the faith of his followers, but as an object of love and devotion he remains humanly imitable. Other examples of this new genre of *Sira* might include the *Sira* entitled *al-Rawð al-Unuf* by Abu al-Qasim al-Suhayli (d. 1185), in essence a running critical commentary on the *Sira* of Ibn Ishaq, one of the founding fathers. Examples might also include the later *al-Sira al-Halabiyya* by Abu'l Faraj Nur al-Din al-Halabi (d. 1635), which sets out to demonstrate how one can introduce consistency and coherence into the divergent historical versions of the *Sira*.

Finally, in the late nineteenth century and early twentieth century a new breed of the *Sira* of Muhammad began to appear: the polemical *Sira*, written largely to defend Muhammad's reputation against the attacks of European Orientalists. The first direct encounter between Muslim scholars and the new breed of European Orientalists over the life and personality of Muhammad took place during the heyday of European colonial rule of large regions of the Muslim world. Muhammad had been attacked consistently in European and/or Christian circles since at least the eighth century, but these attacks were either unknown or ignored in the Muslim world. In seventeenth-century Europe, Orientalism began to appear as a scientific discipline, and biographies of Muhammad based directly and "scientifically" on Islamic sources were published. It was against this backdrop of a "scientific" European assault on Muhammad, which reached its peak in the late nineteenth and twentieth centuries, that a new breed of Islamic biographies of Muhammad began to take shape, first perhaps in Muslim India and later in Egypt, Iran, and elsewhere. These works can broadly be described as defensive, polemical, and global in structure and argument. Typical of this new type of *Sira* is *Hayat Muhammad* (The Life of Muhammad) by the Egyptian Muhammad Husayn Haykal (d. 1956), which was addressed at least as much to the Orientalists as to the ordinary Muslim believer.

I come to the end of these reflections on Muhammad and biography. These reflections were meant to be suggestive, to evoke the kind of subject matter to which this work is dedicated. If they are found to be incomplete or overgeneralized, I can only plead that the rest of what I have to say might introduce some of the refinements and details that such a study must obviously entail. From the great Andalusian biographer al-Qadi 'Iyad, once again, comes the following passage on prophets, by way of concluding these introductory reflections and preparing for what is to come:

Prophets and Messengers, peace be upon them, are intermediaries between God and His creatures. They transmit to them the commands of God and His prohibitions, His promise of salvation and threat of damnation. They acquaint them with what they do not know of Him, of His creation, majesty, sovereignty, omnipotence and realm. The outward appearance of prophets, their bodies and their physiques possess the characteristics of humans and are subject to what humans undergo by way of contingency, disease, death, dissolution and other attributes of humanity. Their souls and inward existence, however, are characterized by super-human attributes which link them to the heavenly spheres, making them resemble the angels. They are therefore free from change and error, and not normally subject to human incapacity and weakness.[14]

The Turning Point

MUHAMMAD IN THE QUR'AN

Before I turn to the images of Muhammad in the Qur'an I shall begin with a few general observations on the Qur'anic portrait of the human psyche, a portrait that has remained central and influential, very much part of the tradition of Islamic biography. There are many verses of the Qur'an that describe man in the abstract, man's soul, and these verses, if put in one basket, reveal the contours of a likeness that in some respects is nearer the modern than the premodern portrayal of man. This portrait of man may be summarized as follows: man is forgetful, inconstant, impatient, fickle, frivolous (Q 4:137). Without belief, man is *jahili,* a creature of whim, running after shadows and illusions. Man is quick to call on God in misery and quick to abandon Him when he is at ease (Q 41:51). Man is by nature argumentative (Q 18:54), boisterous, torn in different directions, divided in desires. In a striking image, the human soul is compared by the Qur'an to a personality {in whom quarreling partners share} (Q 39:29). Man is habitually prone to factionalism, and is often hypocritical. The believer's soul, by contrast, is steadfast, patient, remembering. In fact, one of the major roles of Satan in the Qur'an is to get man to forget the goodness of God.

Man fluctuates between these two states of the soul. This portrait of man highlights not *sinning* man but *frivolous* man. It does not pass a blanket psychological judgment on man as does, say, the doctrine of original sin. Rather, it views man as a fragmented and deeply divided personality in need of discipline, the discipline of patience, of communal prayer in ranks, of obedience to God, of steadfastness, of reflection. If the test of discipline and patience is passed, then God will carry man from darkness to light, from error to truth, from poverty to riches, from the many divided personalities into the one concordant personality of the true believer.

If we draw a quick comparison here between Qur'anic man and Homeric man, we note an interesting contrast. In the Homeric view, one could argue, the human soul or character is represented as a substance: the *anger* of Achilles, the *cunning* of Odysseus, the *faithfulness* of Penelope, the *greed* of Agamemnon, the *filial piety* of Telemachus, and so forth. The same may be said of the *pietàs* of Aeneas in Virgil. These are defining traits of character, dominant and largely stable conditions of the soul, identifying characteristics of behavior. The Qur'anic view, by contrast, posits man as a mass of unruly and chaotic contradictions, as torn in shreds by illusory desires, at one time one thing, and at another its opposite. One might almost speak of man-as-child, constantly in need of the disciplined harmony that faith instills. It might be useful to keep in mind this or some such portrait of the human soul before we turn to the images of Muhammad.

It will become plain to anyone who reads even a little of the Qur'an that it addresses its readers in a number of voices, moods, or musical keys. There is to begin with an *apocalyptic* voice or mood, accompanied in certain passages by dramatic images of hell and paradise; scenes of the Last Hour and the end of the world; scenes involving the activity of angels, *jinn*, and other mysterious creatures; a cosmic drama of stars, mountains, and seas heaving; the pangs of creation. These passages can often be called poetic, although not according to strict rules of Arabic prosody, even though rhyming is very frequent. Man is often addressed directly and asked to contemplate all these natural phenomena, to be duly impressed and so to believe in his Creator. These scenes are generally found at the end of the Qur'an and are said to be the earliest revelations to Muhammad.

Second, some passages of the Qur'an have a *narrative* voice or mood. These passages, in effect, relate the stories of earlier prophets and, less so, of kings and rulers, as well as make allusions to incidents that were happening near or in Muhammad's own day and age. But just as one might describe the first voice as poetic but not poetry, so here the narrative is storylike but not story. Thus, the tales of prophets and kings are narrated as if they are well known to the audience, and the emphasis is entirely upon the *moral* of these tales rather than on the tale itself. The Qur'an *reminds* its listeners of these tales and draws the moral of each tale at many points, leaving us in little doubt as to its significance. But it does not tell stories in the normal narrative mode.

There is, thirdly, a Qur'anic voice or mood that one might describe as the voice or mood of a moral sermon, interspersed with many verses that clearly have binding *legal* force. One could call it the *homiletic/legal* voice or mood. In such passages, the Qur'an addresses believers and unbelievers, specified and unspecified groups of people, enjoining upon its listeners a particular configuration of virtues and warning them against particular configurations of vice. In all of this God is described as being Merciful, Wise, Omnipotent, All-seeing, and so forth. God is, of course, the speaker throughout, not Muhammad.

There is, finally, the communicative or dialogic mood or voice in the Qur'an. This is best seen in the way in which passages in the Qur'an are constantly engaged in communication and exchange, in debate and drama, in responding or reacting to ad hoc circumstances. This mood or voice leads one of the Qur'an's ablest modern scholars, Angelika Neuwirth, to call this voice *situative*. In illustration, Neuwirth points to a passage such as Q 25:32: {Those who disbelieve say "If only the Qur'an had been sent down on him all at once" . . . to strengthen your heart, We have revealed it in stages.} There is a spontaneity of voice in the Qur'an that is perhaps unique among sacred scriptures; one encounters a revelation in the process of unfolding, which keeps pace with the ever changing circumstances of its community of listeners.

If we accept for the moment that these are the four principal voices or moods of the Qur'an, we might argue that there are four principal colors in which Muhammad's portrait is painted in the Qur'an: visionary, narrative, homiletic/legal, and situative. But before we turn to these portraits of Muhammad a few words are in order on the subject of naming and allusion in the Qur'an. This is directly relevant to Muhammad's images. The *name* "Muhammad" itself is mentioned only four times in the Qur'an—surprising when one considers that groups such as the *Muhajirun*, the Meccan Emigrants, and the *Ansar*, his Medinese Supporters, the two earliest Muslim "parties," are mentioned at least twice that number of times. On the other hand, there are hundreds of references to Muhammad described as Messenger/Prophet (*rasul* and *nabiyy*) and hundreds of other allusions to someone unnamed who most probably is Muhammad. What is the significance of this? It looks as if, from the Qur'an's viewpoint, the personality of Muhammad takes second place to his role; the personal name retreats behind the divinely appointed universal missionary. Behind this stands another curious feature, namely that there are hardly any names of *contemporary* people in the Qur'an. There is Abu Lahab, Muhammad's uncle and chief enemy; there is Zayd, Muhammad's adopted son; and that is all. Abu Lahab is the family member who became the hostile outsider; and Zayd is the outsider who became the beloved family member. But all other contemporaries are anonymous. Yes, the Qur'an constantly *alludes* to people ("and those who did this or that" or "he or she who said this or that") but it never names them. This is one reason that many readers find the Qur'an to be such a difficult text: it seems impersonal, impenetrable, and written throughout in one tense, which one could call the "eternal present." The *moral* of the story is foremost, not the story itself with its names and dates and details.

Accordingly, the portrait of Muhammad in the Qur'an, like all other contemporary Qur'anic portraits, is, in its outer surface or aspect, almost uniformly anonymous. It is not the person Muhammad but the "Messenger of God"/"Prophet" who is at the center of the portrait. Earlier prophets have names; Muhammad has a title. Now the designation of Muhammad in the Qur'an almost wholly by his title gives him a special status. He is *the* Prophet of God, the final and ultimate Prophet, the Prophet who summarized and concluded prophecy and the prophetic line, the "Seal of Prophets," and so above all normal intimacies of human conversation. In Qur'an 33:40, we encounter the following divine admonition: {Muhammad cannot be called "Father of So-and-So" but only "The Messenger of God" and "The Seal of Prophets."} He is the final, supreme, and crowning prophet in a long line of prophecy that stretches all the way back to the beginning of creation, or at least back to Abraham. It follows, of course, that what he brings from God is the final and most authoritative revelation of all. God has finally spoken. And the impact of this speech of God is like an earthquake, as in Qur'an 59:21: {Had we sent down this Qur'an upon a mountain, you would have seen it humbled, shattered by the fear of God.} Such a messenger one should not in familiarity address as "Abu'l Qasim," which was his patronymic, and which his enemies sometimes used in order to stress his ordinariness rather than his prophethood.

In addition, a few words should also be said about what one might call Qur'anic prophetology, the theory of prophecy or, if you prefer, what all prophets have had in common. This is because the

Prophet of God's primary self-reference or spiritual genealogy is to a line of prophets who preceded him, all of whom, on the whole, had similar experiences. Their story is the story of a lonely voice crying out against the injustice or indifference of his community, and suffering ridicule and disbelief, arrogance, physical harm, and even death (or apparent death), but ultimately being vindicated or saved or justified, or else avenged by God. One version of this is in Qur'an 40:5: {Every nation resolved to seize their prophet and disputed with falsehood in order to refute God's truth. Then I seized them, and what a punishment it was!} Another is in Qur'an 23:44: {Then We sent Our messengers, one after another. Whenever its messenger came to a nation, they called him a liar. So We caused them to follow one another and made them parables. Away with a people who do not believe!} A third version in Qur'an 27:52 runs as follows: {There stand their dwellings, empty ruins because of . the evil they committed. Here indeed is a sign for a people who understand.} This last evokes the splendid ruins that surround Arabia from north and south, powerful reminders of God's revenge upon previous unbelievers.

It is possible that the designation "The Prophet of God" and the linkage with earlier prophets was not fully articulated during the earliest Qur'anic revelations but came somewhat later. Thus we will find that the earliest designators of Muhammad describe him as *bashir* and *nadhir* as in Qur'an 34:28: {We have sent you to all mankind, a bearer of glad tidings and a warner}; or else in Qur'an 98:2: {A messenger from God, reciting sacred scrolls.} What interests us here is the cumulative image rather than the history of its constituent parts. For, given the "eternal present tense" of the Qur'an, and if there is no time with God, then past, present, and future are all equidistant from the God of the Qur'an. Nevertheless, it is quite possible to argue for an increase in the status of Muhammad's image from the earlier to the later portions of the Qur'an, following the increase of his worldly authority. We thus notice a shift from *a* messenger *from* God to *The* Messenger *of* God. The visionary Muhammad gives way gradually to the divinely inspired leader and legislator of the community.

But the images of Muhammad should also be framed within a master narrative of prophecy. Given the typology of prophecy outlined above, Muhammad in many of his images in the Qur'an conforms to this master narrative. Like all other Qur'anic prophets, Muhammad suffers the disbelief and ridicule of his community but eventually is victorious. Therefore, many of the chief events of his life will follow the prophetic pattern. Thus, for example, *all* earlier prophets have met with ridicule as in Qur'an 36:30: {Alas for Humanity! Never did a messenger come to them but they ridiculed him.}[1] And so also Muhammad, even more pointedly, must pass under the same arch of tribulation as in Qur'an 21:41: {Messengers before you were ridiculed. But that which they ridiculed soon engulfed those who ridiculed them.} It is his fate, as it was theirs, to face charges of falsehood and unbelief and to be patient throughout that immensely trying ordeal of prophecy. To further emphasize this linkage with earlier prophets, Muhammad is instructed to say that he was not *bid'an* among prophets, a term that may mean either "first" or "originator" or even "innovator," as in Qur'an 46:9: {Say: I am not the first among [a novelty among] messengers. I do not know what will be done to you or me. I only follow what is revealed to me. I am merely one who brings a clear warning.}

Enough said, for the moment, about Muhammad in his public image/s as Prophet and the close biographical parallels with other prophets. I now turn to Muhammad as a human being in the Qur'an. In this regard let us deal first of all with what the Qur'an says he is *not*. This is often a fruitful way of approaching the question of identity. And determining what he is *not* is a fairly straightforward thing to do because the passages in the Qur'an that say

Muhammad is *not x, y,* or *z* are limited in number and are more or less consistent in image and significance, thus analytically manageable.

We could begin with the very last verse cited above: Qur'an 46:9. This is an image of a human being who is unsure of his fate or destiny. Yet this image is modified considerably, and some Qur'an commentators say it is "abrogated" by another image of a person all of whose sins, past and future, are forgiven, as in Qur'an 48:1–2: {We have granted you a decided victory, so that God may forgive you your past and future sins, and complete His blessings upon you, and lead you along a straight path.} In this second passage, there is no longer much doubt as to his moral destiny. Rather, he will clearly be forgiven all his sins and will definitely be saved as his mission moves on to victory. And yet implied in all this divine vindication is that Muhammad had committed sins at some point or other in his life. What these sins were is not clear from the Qur'an. There is one incident in his life that is often cited as an example of God's anger or frustration with him. This is the famous rebuke addressed to someone unnamed but widely assumed by Muslim tradition to be Muhammad, in Qur'an 80:1–10 {He [Muhammad] frowned and turned away when the blind man came to visit him. How do you [Muhammad] know? Perhaps he came seeking to cleanse his soul, or else to remember, and remembrance might benefit him. As for the wealthy man, it is to him you [Muhammad] turn your attention. And you do not care if he does not seek to cleanse his soul. And yet he who came to you in haste, and fearing God, you took no notice of him.}

What should we call this sin? Perhaps a form of snobbery. Muhammad is behaving like a political leader trying to build up his cause or party by cultivating influential people rather than behaving like a prophet whose mission is to serve mankind irrespective of social rank or prestige or power. But the Qur'an, so far as I can determine, cites no other explicit example of Muhammad sinning.

Clearly this sin of snobbery is not anything major, and in any case the forgiveness verse (Q 48:1–2) would strongly suggest that Muhammad is not a sinner or, at the very least, that he is on his way to complete forgiveness of all his sins, past, present, and future.

What else is he not? The most frequent charges levelled against him, which the Qur'an records and strenuously denies, are that he is (1) a sorcerer or *sahir*, (2) *Majnun* or possessed by *jinn*, that is, mad,[2] (3) tutored by someone, (4) a poet or *sha'ir*, (5) a soothsayer or *kahin*, (6) a spinner of fables, or combinations thereof. A good example of numbers (1) and (2) is Qur'an 51:52: {Likewise, never was a messenger sent to any previous people but they said about him "A sorcerer or a man possessed."} An example of (3) and (2) is Qur'an 44:14: {But they turned away from him and said, "He is being tutored; he is a man possessed,"}, where Muhammad is described as a man being tutored by someone else and also as a man possessed. The charge of being tutored by someone should give some pause. It is specifically related to Qur'an 16:103: {And We know that they say, "A mere mortal is teaching him." The speech of him to whom they allude is foreign, but this is clear Arabic speech,} where the charge receives a rather curious rebuttal: at issue is not the *existence* of the tutor, presumably very learned, but merely his native tongue. The charge that he was a poet (4) is of special interest because of its relevance for the later history of Islamic literature. The Qur'an is explicitly hostile to poets. The verses in question, Qur'an 26:224–26, run as follows: {As for poets, the demons of temptation are their disciples. Do you not see how they wander aimlessly in every valley? How they brag but do not act?} These verses appear to be almost a blanket condemnation of poetry. Accordingly, not only is Muhammad *not* a poet; it is not fit or proper for him to even engage in poetry as per Qur'an 36:69: {We did not teach him poetry, nor does it become him. This is a Reminder, nothing else, and a manifest Recitation.}[3] This intense

Qur'anic dislike of poets seemed however to have had very little impact on the course of Arabic/Islamic literature, and Qur'anic dislike was later moderated in the Hadith. The charge that he was a soothsayer or *kahin* (5) is levelled at Muhammad twice as in Qur'an 52:29: {So remind mankind! For you are not, by the grace of your Lord, a soothsayer or a man possessed.} A *kahin* appears to have been a familiar figure in Muhammad's Arabia, a fortune-teller of some standing, someone to whom people turned in times of decision, and who, like other oracular figures in other cultures, apparently delivered his or her verdict in rhymed speech. It seems that the Qur'an reminded some people of this oracular style, hence the denial that Muhammad is a soothsayer or Arabian *kahin*. The charge that he was a spinner (6), or a secondhand transmitter, of ancient legends occurs in Qur'an 25:5: {And they say: "These are fables of the ancients, which he transcribed in writing. They are dictated to him morning and evening." Say: It was revealed by One who knows the secrets of the heavens and earth, Forgiving and Merciful.} This charge is countered by the assertion of the truth of the messenger and the divine nature of the revelation.

These, then, are the most salient charges that the Qur'an denies with respect to Muhammad. One might call to mind how annoyed people can become if they are repeatedly mistaken for someone for whom they care little. Perhaps one should regard that experience as constituting one element of a psychological theory of the "double" but one that could nevertheless be of help in determining the contours of self-identity. In other words, in building up our portrait of Muhammad in the Qur'an, it is important for us to note what Muhammad *hated to be mistaken for.* If we translate this into contemporary speech, it would be as if someone were telling us in a rather angry tone of voice: "Listen, I'm not a magician, I'm not crazy, I'm not someone's flunky, I'm not a poet, I'm not a fortune-teller, and I'm not a spinner of ancient fables." If we turn these thoughts inside out, we might hear him say: "Listen, I am for

real, I am sober, I am my own man, I'm not trying to entice or en-
chant you, I cannot predict your future, and I'm telling you real
history. And let me add: all prophets before me have been like this
and all of them have preached for free." This last sentiment is
found in Qur'an 12:104: {Do not ask them for a payment for it.}[4]
This, or something similar, we might wish to regard as major aspects of Muhammad's self-identity or self-representation in the
Qur'an. It is in the context of such self-identity that the phrase in
Qur'an 7:157, {The illiterate prophet,} acquires its significance.
This is a phrase that has drawn a large literature of commentary,
both Muslim and non-Muslim.[5] In the Muslim tradition at large,
however, it has been understood as a crucial, even miraculous, element of his prophetic authenticity. Taught by none but God,
Muhammad cannot possibly be inspired by any human being or by
any religious or literary texts.

Moving now to other images of Muhammad's personality and
behavior, we find two passages that relate directly to his moral
character and to his personal conduct and manners. The first occurs in Qur'an 68:4: {You are truly of a character most sublime.}
Muhammad's character fully deserves the mission entrusted to him
by God and is absolutely necessary for a legislator. The second is
Qur'an 3:159: {Had you been a coarse or cruel man, your followers would have dispersed and left you.} This latter verse has to do
with Muhammad's daily dealings with the humanity around him.
Together these two Qur'anic images establish for Muhammad a
clear moral ascendancy on the one hand coupled, on the other,
with a sweetness and leniency of character in his role as leader and
preacher among men: he is a figure who inspires affection rather
than fear. The ordinariness of Muhammad, his nearness or proximity to the man in the street, is further emphasized in, for example, Qur'an 25:7–8: {And they say: "What is it with this Messenger
who eats food and strolls in the marketplace? Why was an angel
not sent down to be with him and act as a warner alongside him?

And why has a treasure not descended upon him from heaven, or at least he owned a garden from which he could eat?"} verses which contain some sarcasm at his expense. As expected from the typology of prophecy discussed above, this charge is answered in Qur'an 25:20: {We never sent any Messengers before you but they ate food and strolled in the marketplace.}[6] Further instances of sarcasm are found at, for example, Qur'an 9:61, where some supposed followers make fun of Muhammad by calling him {an ear,} that is to say, someone who gives his ear to all, or even someone who believes everything he hears. There are also moments of tormenting doubt, as per Qur'an 11:12, where he wishes some revelations could be rescinded.

All messengers despite their elevated status have in fact been intensely, painfully human, prone to the doubts and crises and misfortunes that befall the rest of us. Consider the following passage in Qur'an 93:1–8: {Your Lord has not forsaken you nor hates you. The afterlife is better for you than this life. He will give you of His bounty and you will be well pleased. Did He not find you an orphan and gave you shelter? And found you in error and guided you? And found you a dependent, and made you self-sufficient?} Here we have the full range of crises that Muhammad encountered, and, mixed with it, more than a hint of doubt on his part, more than a hint of being in error, the error being almost certainly inconstancy of belief. Again, one wonders: Was Muhammad an unbeliever before his mission? Did he at certain stages of his life experience the temptations of this world, preferring this life to the next? Was he, like all of us, an occasional victim of a sense of helplessness, of inadequacy, or even of despair? And yet this is a narrative of humble and difficult beginnings ending ultimately in triumph as in Qur'an 10:103: {And then We save our Messengers and those who believe. Indeed, it is only right that We should save the believers.}

The frankness, spontaneity, and human frailty of these images are prominent. Together with this, there continue to appear in the Qur'an certain images of Muhammad that highlight his fears for the inconstancy of his community and his anxiety about their future as in Qur'an 3:144: {Muhammad is merely a Messenger, and before him many Messengers have come and gone. If he were to die or is killed, will you revert back to your old ways?} There are persistent anxieties about his own vulnerability as in Qur'an 4:113: {And were it not for God's grace and mercy upon you, a group among them were about to lead you astray. But it is themselves that they lead astray.} Joined to this is his inability to effect miracles as in, for example, Qur'an 3:183: {There are those who say: "God has commanded us not to believe any messenger unless he brings us an offering which is then consumed by fire." Say to them: "Messengers before me have come to you with miracles and also with what you asked for. Why then did you kill them if you are sincere in what you say?"} We glimpse his irritation at the bad behavior of some of his followers in Qur'an 49:2: {Believers, do not raise your voices above the Prophet's voice and speak not loudly to him as you speak loudly with one another,} or else in Qur'an 33:53: {Believers, do not enter the chambers of the Prophet unless you are invited to a meal. And do not enter early and await mealtime. If invited, enter. Once fed, disperse, without lingering for idle talk. Your behavior annoys the Prophet, who is too embarrassed to tell you so. But God is not embarrassed to tell the truth.} At times we surmise his anger with those who hurt him deeply, as in Qur'an 9:61: {Those who hurt the Messenger of God will be punished most painfully.} He encounters disobedience from his followers even on the field of battle as in Qur'an 3:153: {Remember how you fled, heeding no one, while the Messenger was calling you from the rear?} All of this would suggest that Muhammad is a painfully human prophet who stands and listens *with* his community to the

words of God, and who is in constant need, like all of God's creatures, of God's guidance, reassurance, and mercy.

In sum, the images of Muhammad in the Qur'an we have explored thus far could be said to reside inside a sort of square: the
Revealer (God), the revelation (Qur'an), the medium (the Angel
Gabriel), and the recipient (Muhammad *and* his community).
Muhammad is linked to the divine through, first of all, visions as
in Qur'an 53:2–10: {Your countryman has not gone astray nor
erred. Nor does he speak fancifully. This is nothing but a revelation being revealed, taught him by one very mighty, very steadfast.
At first, he spread out on the highest horizon. And then he drew
near and hovered, and came within two bows' length or even
closer. Then he revealed to his servant that which he revealed.}
This vision of the horizon-filling Angel approaching him with the
Revelation links the four corners of the square, setting the stage
for the construction of prophetic authority. We will see later how
these verses in particular gained immense significance for the
Sufis, or mystics, of Islam.

Later, through direct divine speech, Muhammad is pronounced
an exemplary teacher of his community as in Qur'an 33:21: {In
God's Messenger you have a moral model}; and Qur'an 4:80:
{Whoever obeys the Messenger obeys God.} And yet between the
visionary prophet on the one hand and the moral model on the
other there stretches, as we have seen above, an utterly human personality, a man who repeatedly emphasizes his human limitations,
his nonmiraculous powers and inability to compete with Moses
and Jesus in this field, and his constant embarrassments, irritations, frustrations, and fears. True, we do not possess in the Qur'an
a narrative of Muhammad's life such as we have for Abraham,
Joseph, or even Jesus. There are no stories of Muhammad's birth,
youth, or mission. What we have instead are intensely vivid and
revealing psychological moments, a series of revelations unfolding
in constant dialogue with the community who listened to them,

moments that in their totality illuminate one man's struggles with the immensity of the prophetic burden. But the sense of divine victory is very strong in him: In the end all will be well. Every human being will receive his or her just reward. We shall all return to God.

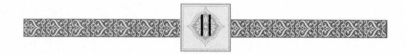

The Legislator

MUHAMMAD IN HADITH

A General Introduction to Hadith

Although relatively little doubt exists regarding the historicity of the Qur'an and the time in which it was revealed, collected, and so forth, the Hadith, or "Traditions" of Muhammad, is a very different text indeed. It is the second most important source after the Qur'an for establishing Muslim belief and practice. And yet among Muslims, the Hadith has never enjoyed the same sort of reception or consensus as the Qur'an. Here are some of the basic differences.

First, the text of the Qur'an exists in one more or less standard version for all Muslims. The Hadith exists in at least two versions: there are Sunni Hadith collections and Shia collections. Within each wing of Islam there are several famous Hadith collections, famous that is to say for the quality and wide acceptance of the collection among Muslims. For this select group of Hadith the term *ṣaḥiḥ*, or "authoritative," is reserved. Second, the Qur'an is God's book. The Hadith is, by and large, Muhammad's book, detailing his words and actions and organized under the main topics of Muslim ritual and belief. The first source is divine but the second is prophetic, even if divinely inspired. Third, most Muslim jurists down the ages have argued that the Qur'an and the Hadith are complementary texts, that the Hadith makes explicit what in the Qur'an is implicit, as for instance in its detailing of prayer, alms-giving, pilgrimage, and so forth.

Nevertheless, the Hadith from its very beginnings was the subject of a great deal of criticism from Muslim scholars who questioned the authenticity of certain individual hadiths, their tendentious or obviously partisan character, or else their *isnad*, which is the methodology of the Hadith. This critique of the Hadith was taken up by European scholars in the nineteenth and twentieth centuries, by scholars such as Ignáz G. Goldziher or Joseph S. Schacht who argue that *most* Hadith are fabricated. But even some contemporary Muslim leaders, for example, Qaddafi, have suggested abandoning the Hadith altogether and following only the Qur'an. The hadith has even been the butt of Muslim jokes in the form of fabricated hadiths produced for private scholarly amusement. And yet the Hadith remains of immense importance for Islamic belief and ritual in addition to being the first Muslim literary discourse. I cannot go into any detailed history of the Hadith here. A brief sketch will have to suffice to situate the images of Muhammad to be found in the Hadith.

It is likely that in origin the Hadith as a corpus resembled a ball of many colored threads. There was of course the hadith from Muhammad, but there were also hadiths, individual units, from his prominent Companions, and quite a lot of them, in addition to ancient Near Eastern wisdom and lore. Many individual hadiths flatly contradict one another. They differ greatly in legal import. Thus the earliest Hadith contained a mass of legal injunctions, ritual practice, ethical conduct, correct manners, admonitions, homilies, fragments of Muhammad's biography, hadiths about the Last Hour, virtues of various individuals, and so forth. In the course of the ninth century, and coinciding with the bureaucratization of

Muslim scholarship under the 'Abbasids, the Hadith was systematized in standard collections that remain unchanged to this day.
Six of these quickly gained authority and two gained special prestige: those of Bukhari (d. 870) and Muslim (d. 875). My remarks
are based largely on Muslim's collection.[1]

The collection of Muslim is one of the best examples of the
Hadith as it was systematized in the ninth century. The first problem for Muslim (and indeed for Bukhari) was choice. Muslim had
millions of hadiths to pick and choose from, and he chose only
what he considered authentic: some seven or eight thousand. The
material is arranged *under* major topics of practice and belief, and
Muhammad's sayings and actions are classified under each topic.
This setup was a pedagogical device, facilitating ease of reference
for scholars and students. If a believer wanted to know about
prayer, pilgrimage, almsgiving, or whatever, he or she would go to
the relevant chapter to find out what the Prophet said or did in that
regard.

The Hadith belongs overwhelmingly to Muhammad's Medinese
period, not his earlier Meccan period, the former being a period of
umma building, military expeditions, and growth of power. And
by the time of Muslim, the Hadith had become almost exclusively
the Hadith of Muhammad alone: the hadiths of Companions,
Followers, and so forth had all been recycled elsewhere, normally in pious or literary works other than Muhammadan Hadith
books—this was not a culture that threw anything away! Only
Muhammad was the binding model for the community, even if his
Companions are given full respect and affection. The Hadith is
therefore almost exclusively doctrinal and ethical in character: the
stories of earlier prophets or kings, much of Muhammad's *Sira*,
and Arabian or Near Eastern lore ("what our ancestors said or
did"), had all been pruned away. The ball of many colored threads
had now unraveled to become one or two colors only. In the
Hadith, the concept of *sunna*, or Muhammadan example, is pre-

eminent: this is what Muhammad said or did regarding this or that Muslim practice or belief. No one else is a binding model. Thus, following an early period when the net was cast wide in pursuit of moral edification, Muhammad is now exclusively at center stage: the only authority, the Hadith with a capital *H*, as it were. Rising to the defense of the Hadith against its numerous rationalist critics, and at about the same time that it was being systematized in the ninth century, was the famous scholar Ibn Qutayba (d. 889):

> Scholars of *Hadith* have sought to establish the truth from its proper sources, pursuing it back to its very origins. They seek nearness to God by following the normative practice *[Sunan]* of the Prophet of God. They track down his example and the reports about his life to the point where they can now distinguish true reports from false. Detractors accuse *Hadith* scholars of transmitting much unsound material and of pursuing the bizarre and the exotic, arguing that heresy issues from the bizarre. However, *Hadith* scholars do not transmit this material because they regard them as authentic; rather, they collect the sound and the unsound, the true and the false, in order to distinguish between them and to point them out.[2]

Before we come to the portraits of Muhammad in Hadith, a rapid survey of the table of contents of Muslim's Hadith collection may be helpful for the general reader. This table of contents is about the same in most Hadith collections and is normally arranged under the following chapter headings: faith, ritual purity, prayer, almsgiving, fasting, pilgrimage, marriage, divorce, buying and selling, judgments, jihad, rulers, food and drink, clothes and furniture, good manners, greetings and public behavior, virtues, virtues of the Companions, mercy to parents and others, knowledge, invoca-

tions and other rituals, repentance, paradise and hell, the Last
Hour and apocalyptics, tender mercies, and asceticism.

As might be imagined given this table of contents, the exemplary sayings and actions of Muhammad are spread out over a
wide spectrum of his public and private life. But there is no story
line in the Hadith: to that extent it is not a biography in the normal
sense of the term. For the story line one would need to go to the
Sira. In the Hadith, by contrast, what we have at center stage is
Islamic belief and practice, with Muhammad as the model teacher.
The portrait is, by design, ideal.

So, if the Hadith is not in the strict sense a biography of
Muhammad, how can we use it to construct a portrait of him?
First, there is great density of detail. Unlike the Qur'an, the
Hadith is jammed to the ceiling with contemporary names: personal names, place names, and events, both momentous and not so
momentous, together with the countless names of transmitters,
men and women who, by and large, were the earliest scholars of
the community and guardians of its lore. Second, the Hadith reveals not only what Muhammad commanded or forbade, but what
he personally liked and disliked, his personal tastes and the most
intimate actions of his life. We see Muhammad surrounded by his
followers, speaking, acting, interacting, teaching, but also going
about his daily business like any ordinary human being, that is,
eating, drinking, sleeping, and so forth. Even if not a biography in
form, the Hadith is full of biographical fragments. Third, the
Hadith, as we have seen above, was designed primarily to guide
Muslims to the good life; it was designed to answer the questions
of the ordinary Muslim believer who wishes to learn what
Muhammad's teaching is on any particular issue. But Muhammad
also taught by his actions and personal example. So every detail of
his life is considered exemplary and worthy of imitation. Hence the
Hadith contains a lot that a biographer or portrait-builder would
find of interest. We need not be concerned with historicity at this

point. Suffice it to say that the Hadith portrays what his early community imagined him to have been. Hadith experts and transmitters were doubtless concerned to establish accuracy. Nevertheless, some Hadiths were retained by the classical collectors despite doubts regarding their historicity because it was felt that they were, as it were, worthy of Muhammad or *could have been* spoken by him or otherwise constituted praiseworthy behavior.

Let us begin with his physical appearance and his personal likes and dislikes about which we are told nothing in the Qur'an. During his miraculous Night Journey from Mecca to Jerusalem, alluded to in the opening verse of Qur'an 17, Muhammad in the Hadith is taken on a tour of the afterlife, where he meets the other great prophets before him; later on he gives a physical description of each prophet he met. Muhammad affirms that in physical appearance he most resembles Abraham. This of course reflects the Abrahamic theology of the Qur'an, Abraham being the Prophet who antedated Judaism and Christianity, and was thus the prophetic ancestor of Islam. There are other bits and pieces of physical description; for example, he had the "Seal of Prophecy" on his back, between his shoulder blades (described in the *Sira* as an unusually large mole), he had hardly twenty white hairs on his head, his hands were soft and cold, his body odor was more sweet smelling than musk, his skin was soft as silk, his thighs were white, and his sweat was like pearls and was collected in bottles by devoted followers. The water with which he performed his ablutions was often drunk by devoted followers, and when the barber cut his hair, people would eagerly collect it. He often went hungry and would tie a belt around his waist to assuage hunger. And, in a domestic tableau, we see him having his head deloused by a pious woman servant, Umm Haram, and he predicts in a dream that she will join a military expedition.[3]

These physical descriptions are multiplied in *Sira* literature, so we will return to this topic when we come to the *Sira*. Suffice it to say for the moment that these physical characteristics are clearly symbolic in character. We cannot fully appreciate this symbolism because we are separated from the world of the Hadith of Muslim by about twelve hundred years. And we cannot assume that people living then are really just like us in mentality, given that they lived in a different environment. Their mental world, I would argue, was radically different from ours. Accordingly, we cannot today fully unlock the significance of these physical descriptions, but we can perhaps try. One might argue that most of these physical attributes appear to point to his immaculateness and his freedom from physical blemish. Many are allusions to the descriptions of beautiful women in pre-Islamic poetry. But we must also remember that the age of the Hadith of Muslim was far more sensitive to physiognomy than we are: to them, the physical exterior of a human being was intimately linked to his or her moral character.

Next, Muhammad's personal likes and dislikes, tastes and distastes, are a salient topic in the Hadith. This is not a moral issue but perhaps has more to do with aesthetics. If we arrange these likes and dislikes in a list we would get the following:

1. He liked sweets and honey.
2. He liked horses and little children.
3. He liked bread dipped in vinegar.
4. He disliked false wigs and very bushy beards as in the Hadith {Cut moustaches but leave beards alone.}
5. He disliked the torture of humans and domestic animals or slaughtering these latter with anything other than a very sharp knife.
6. He disliked leaving any food behind in a bowl or plate: the eating bowl should always be wiped clean.
7. He disliked voracious eaters.
8. He disliked gold and silver rings and bowls; also silk.
9. He disliked purple garments.

10. He disliked long garments that trail behind their wearer.
11. He disliked idle chatter by the wayside.
12. He disliked certain ugly or blasphemous names and gave their owners new ones, and disliked certain titles.
13. He disliked snakes and lizards.
14. He disliked poetry.
15. He disliked cursing, swearing, and swaggering.

This is a rough list of some of his more prominent personal likes and dislikes. Given the impact of his example on later Muslim generations, these likes and dislikes still affect Muslim taste today. Many conservative Muslim households, for instance, will not admit garlic into their kitchen, and many pious Muslims today go around with moustaches shaved and beards left to grow.[4] But many of these tastes are problematic, even in the Hadith itself. Thus, did he really dislike silver rings? There is a hadith that has him wearing a silver ring, which was later worn by his first two successors but lost by the third caliph, 'Uthman. Or take the wearing of silk. One hadith regards it as reprehensible while another says it is acceptable if one has a skin rash. Again, one hadith lays down the injunction that no angel will enter a home in which there is a picture of a dog, but another allows designs on clothes, and the owning of dogs if kept for the hunt. If one wants to, one may paint inanimate objects, for example, flowers, trees, and so forth. As for poetry, one hadith allows it if its object is to instill virtue.

If we care to, we could place all these personal tastes under a psychological microscope. What do they tell us about Muhammad the man? We might build up a quick portrait of someone who was almost obsessed with cleanliness on the one hand and simplicity in personal appearance and habits on the other. Whether his dislike of snakes and lizards, for instance, or else of painting and sculpture can be given a distinct psychological interpretation is an open question. Overall, we detect a certain predilection for beauty and abhorrence of ugliness and stench.

Moving to other aspects of his portrayal, let us examine his style of speaking. This one might call his "signature pattern." Just as Jesus in the Gospels had a distinct style of address ("Verily, verily I say unto you") so also Muhammad has his own style of addressing people and of teaching. It is captured in the way he formulates many of his commandments or prohibitions: "I order you to do four things and I forbid you to do four things." Another formula is "He who says or does x, y, or z enters paradise." Another is [Muhammad]: "Do you know what x, y, or z mean?" Answer: "God and His Messenger know best." Muhammad: "They mean a, b, or c." Another is [Muhammad]: "Do you know which part of Islam is best? You must do x or y." Another is to call out three times the name of the person addressed, for example, "O Mu 'adh, O Mu 'adh, O Mu 'adh"—followed by a very solemn pronouncement on some topic regarding faith or practice. Another is the giving of three attributes to, for instance, the hypocrite: he lies, he betrays trust, he breaks promises. Another is "Shall I guide you to that which will save you? Do a, b, or c." Another is "Every Muslim who does a, b, or c will necessarily merit Paradise." Another is "I once asked you not to do a, b, or c. Now I tell you that you can do them." Another is a question from a believer: "What if I can't perform this or that Muslim duty?" Muhammad suggests something less onerous. The believer asks: "What if I can't?" Muhammad suggests something even less onerous. "What if I can't?" is the further question. The obligation then becomes minimal, for example, "Simply refrain from committing an evil act."

In this matter of teaching style, the portrait of the Prophet appears somewhat forced. It sounds like a form of rhetoric designed specifically for instruction and preaching. Whether Muhammad actually used this style of speaking is debatable. At least as likely an explanation is that this style was invented by later legal scholars as a device for instruction or as aide-memoire. Commandments and prohibitions are much better learned or memorized if they are encapsulated in formulaic speech. There are in any case no parallels to this style of speaking in the Qur'an. This is Muhammad being constructed as a memorable teacher of the community.

We turn next to the status of Muhammad. In the Qur'an, as we have seen above, while his status is exalted as *The* Prophet of God, we nevertheless detect a figure who is sometimes uncertain, whose knowledge of the future is limited, and who denies any miraculous powers. In the Qur'an he was still subject to the irritations and annoyances of his community and to continuous enmity from inside and outside the company of his followers. In the Hadith, on the other hand, and as expected from a model teacher, Muhammad appears more self-assured, giving little or no sign of doubt or uncertainty, and able to give himself a status or attributes that seem at times inconsistent with his Qur'anic portrait. Thus, in the Hadith he declares:

{I was preferred above all other prophets for six things: (1) I was given perfection of language [that is, the Qur'an] (2) I was aided through the enemy's fear of me (3) Booty was made licit to me (4) All the earth is made pure for me as a place of prayer (5) I was sent to the whole of mankind (6) The line of prophets ended with me.}

His assertions of his own uniqueness and superiority are pronounced: {I am the Lord of humanity on the Day of Resurrection.} He seems far more confident about who will enter paradise and who will not, a choice usually left to God in the Qur'an. Thus he declares authoritatively: {He who dies believing in one God enters paradise.} He is asked: "Even the adulterer and the thief?" He replies: {Even the adulterer and the thief.} He declares: {Every Muslim who performs his ablutions and then prays in sincerity will

necessarily enter paradise.} This sort of knowledge is usually ascribed to God alone in the Qur'an. Again, he affirms that the last
day of the world will be a Friday, whereas only God knows when
the world will end in the Qur'an. He confidently arranges the scenario of the Last Day: {We are the last community to receive revelation but will be first to appear before God on the Last Day.} He
observes and then reveals the supernatural order, which is in intimate contact with Muslim ritual. Thus he tells his community that
{Angels stand at mosque doors, writing down names of the faithful arriving at mosques in order of their arrival, so that the earliest
to arrive are the most pious.} He claims he can lighten the darkness of the tomb by praying upon it; that is, he claims the ability to
lighten the burdensome interrogation of the newly dead person by
the angels. He will dispense medical advice regarding preservation
of health as in {He who eats seven dates in the morning will not be
harmed by poison or magic} or {Water of truffles is good for the
eyes.} He practiced some form of faith healing, passing his hands
over sick people and uttering a special prayer for the sick. He has
advice for how to behave during times of plague: {Do not enter a
plague region and do not leave it if you are already there.} He gives
an explanation for how astrologers and fortune-tellers can sometimes get predictions right. Thus, God decides upon a matter. The
angels sing its praises all the way down the ladder of creation.
Occasionally, the *jinn* overhear a garbled version of this divine
command and relay it to their friends, the astrologers and fortune-
tellers, who sometimes get it right. He considers his own generation to be the best, but steady deterioration is sure to follow. There
is a special category of hadiths called *Hadith qudsi,* in which it is
God who speaks but not in Qur'anic mode. There are, finally, detailed descriptions of the events of the future and of the last days.
Thus, the world will be plunged in ignorance, wine drinking, for-
nication, civil wars, violence, and mayhem. This is balanced by im-

ages of paradise and detailed descriptions of the appearance of the people of paradise, one of which runs as follows:

> {They shine like the full moon; they do not urinate or defecate; they do not blow their nose or spit; they smell like musk; they are like Adam in size, sixty feet tall; they are transparent: their bones are visible; they are all of one heart; they are eternally young.}

These hadiths, when taken together, project quite a different image and status for Muhammad. We see a more assertive, more emphatic Muhammad, especially with regard to his claims to know for sure how a human being will be saved. This is Muhammad in his image as prophet, with a small *p*, someone who can actually see and predict the future, and predict the salvation or damnation of an individual. There are equally emphatic pronouncements about the future of Medina and its status: {Neither plague nor the antichrist will enter it. One prayer in my mosque in Medina is worth 1,000 prayers anywhere else save Mecca.} There may be hints about these qualities or predictive powers in the Qur'an, but in the Hadith they are far more emphatic, detailed, and specific. Classical as well as modern Hadith scholars have often been able to detect beneath many hadiths the activity of later generations of Muslims who disguised their own particular theological and moral views beneath the aegis of the Hadith.

This image of Muhammad as one who predicts what is to come is fortified by two other portrayals of his personality: his miracles and his contacts with the world of the unseen and the supernatural. In the Hadith of Muslim, Muhammad's miracles are given a special subsection in the chapter entitled "Virtues." There is, for example, the incident of the water that is poured from a jug on his hands and then flows from his fingers, enough to allow sixty to

seventy people to perform their ablutions; the bowl in which butter is sent to the Prophet, which is found by its owner to be always
full of butter; food offered to guests by him, which is multiplied;
springs that he causes to overflow after having been dry. These
miracles are mostly to do with feeding and drinking. Many more
examples of miracles will be found in the *Sira* literature.

The other aspect is Muhammad's contact with the unseen and
supernatural. This is a facet of his image that is related to the
prominence of his status and the expansion of his prophetic powers. The scholarly world that assembled this image of Muhammad
was permeated with the invisible, the hidden, the unseen, the hand
of God. Their world was peopled with creatures like the *jinn*, with
spirits and demons. It was a world that believed in things like the
evil eye, magic spells, and the supernatural significance of dreams.
It was also a world that had witnessed the dramatic victories of
Muhammad's people. So history, as it were, had justified his
claims, had proved beyond doubt the veracity of his mission and
its divine source.

In Hadith, Muhammad is shown to have rejected some supernatural manifestations of the pre-Islamic Arabian period but accepted others. He declared that there is {No transmission of skin
disease among animals or humans; no divination through bird
flight; no ill omen in the month of Safar; no *hamah* [or bird that
leaves the head of a dead or murdered person and screams for re-
venge]; no *ghul* [a demon that assumes various forms in the desert,
leading travelers to their death]; no *kahana* [or fortune-telling]; no
good or bad omens}.

On the other hand, Muhammad is said to have believed in the
evil eye, in magic spells, in *maskh* (the metamorphosis of humans
into animals), in auspicious and inauspicious personal and place
names, and in *ruqya* (incantations against the evil eye). He provides an explanation for shooting stars, and for noises like cocks
crowing or donkeys braying. Thus, {If you hear cocks crowing,

ask God for a favor for they have seen an angel; if you hear a donkey braying, call on God for support for it has seen a demon.} There is also an explanation for dreams: {Good dreams come from God; bad dreams come from the devil. If a person sees a bad dream, let them call on God for help. The dream will not harm them}; or {He who sees me in a dream has actually seen me. Satan cannot impersonate me.} As in the Qur'an, so in the Hadith, the presence of Satan is pervasive. But whereas in the Qur'an Satan is largely a moral tempter, in the Hadith he has become a daily reality and Muhammad is engaged in a perpetual struggle against his all-invasive presence, as in the following hadith: {The mention of the name of God before eating or sleeping drives away Satan who tells his followers: "It is impossible for us to eat or sleep here tonight."}

In these hadiths, Muhammad is seen to be revealing the supernatural order that lies just above the natural order, taking on a role hitherto largely the preserve of God in the Qur'an. Muhammad is thus not just the message bearer of God; he is also His active instrument, with full access to the world above and beyond this world, and himself now possessing a number of superhuman attributes. He can now unlock the secrets of nature. From the Hadith one gets an impression of the comprehensiveness of Muhammad's teaching. It leaves us in no doubt whatever that Muhammad, endowed with supra-human attributes, has given the Muslims a complete manual of belief and conduct. The message of Islam has been taught down to its minutest details. But much of its cosmos too is now revealed.

Of course, to summarize that Islamic message even in its broadest aspects would be something far beyond what interests us here. But permeating these ethical teachings are there certain overriding themes that have a special resonance for Muhammad, and that can be said to strike a deep chord in his own personality? What can we find out about Muhammad the man from examining his ethical teachings? We have seen above, when discussing his likes and dislikes, that if we draw a quick psychological portrait of Muhammad, we find someone obsessed with simplicity in speech and act and cleanliness, and with a distinct preference for beauty and an aversion to ugliness. We need now to see what can be further inferred about his personality from a very broad review of his ethical teachings.

There is to begin with a pronounced emphasis on the infinite mercy of God. This mercy has as its primary object the poor, the widows, and the orphans, the helpless in general. Of all the ethical virtues, Muhammad consistently teaches mercy to the poor and the helpless, and without any of the reservations that often accompany other ethical teachings. Thus the five principal religious obligations of Islam (the profession of faith, prayer, fasting, almsgiving, and pilgrimage) are all accompanied by mitigating circumstances, establishing maximum as well as minimum limits of fulfillment. These mitigating circumstances are even more apparent where questions of taste, manners, and decorous behavior are concerned. Yet mercy to the poor and helpless appears to be an absolute commandment: {The poor *Muhajirun* will precede the rich to paradise on the Day of Resurrection by forty years.} In fact it appears at times as if, given the infinite mercy of God, the only unforgivable sin is to show no mercy to others, humans or animals. The two following contrasting parables of mercy illustrate this: {A woman was sent to hell for keeping a cat locked up until it died. She had neither fed it nor given it to drink nor had she allowed the cat outside to eat what the earth provides}; *and* {A prostitute once saw a dog pacing around a well on a very hot day, its tongue lolling out from thirst. She drew water in her pail and gave the dog to drink. Her sins were forgiven.}

Accordingly, this obligation of mercy is pervasive, encompassing all God's creatures, even the ant:

{A prophet from among the prophets of God was sitting under a tree. An ant stung him. He ordered that the whole nest of ants be rooted out and burned in the fire. God revealed to him "Should you not have punished only one ant?"}

One particular object of mercy is parents, who are of course mentioned in the Qur'an. In the Hadith, taking care of parents is pronounced more important than going on jihad:

{A man came to Muhammad seeking his leave to go on *Jihad*. Muhammad asked: Are your parents alive? Yes, replied the man. Then go and perform *Jihad* by taking care of them, said Muhammad.}

From mercy flows the conception of Muslims as one body with different organs, all caring and tending for one another:

{The likeness of the believers in their mutual affection and mercy to each other is like the human body. If one organ falls sick the rest of the body summons the other organs to tend to it and share its pain.}

Muhammad's own personal behavior toward dependents is a prominent example. To illustrate this, his domestic servants are brought in as witnesses to his conduct. And although we are often reminded of the famous saying of Madame Cornuel (1605–1694), a French society hostess: "Il n' y a point de heros pour son valet de chambre" (No man is a hero to his valet), Muhammad is a prominent exception to this maxim. His servants adored him. His most famous personal servant was Anas ibn Malik, who served him throughout his Medina period, eventually becoming a major transmitter of the Hadith. His most detailed hadith about his master recounts how Muhammad was the easiest and most forgiving of masters. Anas was apparently ten years old when the following episode took place:

{One day, the Prophet sent me on an errand. I was torn between not wanting to go and wishing to perform his command. So I made my way deliberately towards a group of youngsters who were playing in the marketplace. Suddenly I felt the Prophet of God grabbing me from behind. I turned around and found him laughing. He said, "O little Anas, have you gone where I ordered you?" I said, "Yes, I am going right away." Anas added, "I served him for ten years. Never once did he tell me 'Why have you done this or that?' or 'Why have you not done this or that?' "}

Muhammad is shown as forgiving even his enemies who were intent on killing him and who managed in fact to wound his face and break his teeth during the crucial battle of Uhud, during which he uttered words that echo Christ's words on the Cross:

{At the Battle of Uhud, one of the Prophet's front teeth was broken and he was wounded in the head. Looking at him, it was as if I [the narrator] were looking at a previous prophet who was likewise wounded by his people. As the Prophet wiped away the blood from his face, he said, "Lord, forgive my people for they are ignorant."}

We are told that he never punished any injury done to him personally but only sin displeasing to God:

The Prophet never struck a servant or a woman with his hand except in the course of *Jihad* in the cause of God. He never exacted revenge for any injury done to him unless it was a case of a sinner transgressing the commands of God. He would then take revenge on behalf of God.

This anger for the sake of God was often used to defend his occasional acts of violence, e.g., after the Battle of Badr. We will return to this theme in later chapters. In short, he was described as being "as humble and shy as a virgin in her bedroom. If he disliked something, we saw it in his face." Thus mercy and its attendant virtues such as kindness, patience, ease of temperament, and forgiveness appear in the Hadith to have emanated from Muhammad's own personality and pervaded his ethical teachings. In consequence, the door of repentance was wide open to the believers, and available to almost all sinners. God is always happy to receive back the repentant sinner. Here, too, the images echo Jesus' parable of the lost sheep:

{God is happier when a believing servant repents than a man travelling through a barren land with his mount, upon which is carried his food and drink. The man sleeps and upon waking finds his mount has disappeared. He goes in search of it until he is exhausted by thirst. He then tells himself, "Let me return to my original place and sleep until I die." So he places his head upon his arm, preparing to die. He then wakes up to find that his mount has returned, still carrying his food and drink. God is happier with the repentant believer than that man with his mount and his food.}

Hell is filled mostly with tyrants, paradise mostly with the wretched and poor:

{Paradise and Hell disputed with one other. Hell said, "I was specially chosen to receive the arrogant and the tyrannical."

Paradise replied, "Look at me. Only the weak, the wretched and the simple-minded enter me."}

As a corpus of writings, the Hadith is what one might call the official and ideal portrait of Muhammad the teacher and model. The various Islamic beliefs, rituals, and regulations occupy the front of the stage. Muhammad is their ideal teacher. In the Hadith we have the Islamic curriculum as taught and established by its founder, *and* as all this was seen by people living during the first three centuries of Islam. The Hadith is thus a selective anthology, a representative sample of Muhammadan speech and act. But underneath lies its template, the Qur'an. I have argued above that the Qur'an has four main moods or styles: narrative, legal/homiletic, apocalyptic, and situative. The Hadith in contrast has only one main mood: legal/homiletic. Narrative is by and large missing in the Hadith, and the apocalyptic and supernatural occupy a distant second place, playing only a minor role. The situative is almost totally absent: the Hadith is at all times under the direct control of its collector/transmitter. Like the Qur'an, however, allowances are made in the Hadith for progress in religious regulations and obligations and for the principle of abrogation, that is, a later Muhammadan practice canceling an earlier one. In the Qur'an, one of the most famous instances of abrogation is the change in the direction in which believers pray—from Jerusalem to Mecca; another is the gradual prohibition against wine drinking. In the Hadith we are told that Muhammad's Companions always followed his very latest practice. Yet these regulations could not always be reconciled, for example, Muhammad *both* fasted *and* broke the fast during a journey. In general, we sometimes detect in the structure and layout of Hadith transmission a progress from the bare to the detailed. Although this cannot be considered a general guide to the appearance of hadiths over time, the coexistence of shorter and longer versions is intended to show that Muhammad himself did not remain static in his teaching but frequently developed that teaching in reaction to events and circumstances. The hadiths show a legislator who is ready to change or modify, to abrogate earlier or outdated practice, to respond creatively to the demands of his times. Sometimes this task of modification falls to his Companions: 'A'isha, for instance, will scornfully modify a hadith that invalidates prayer if the believer comes into contact with women.

There are two characters in the Hadith who have considerable impact on his biography. These two are 'A'isha, his favorite wife, and 'Umar, a senior Companion. 'A'isha's role as a devoted wife and major transmitter of the Hadith nevertheless includes an astonishing amount of outrageous or insolent or discourteous remarks she made to Muhammad. 'A'isha said:

> "I used to be jealous of women who offered themselves to the Prophet and say, 'How can a [self-respecting] woman do this?' When God revealed the verse {You may defer any of them you wish or take in any of them you wish} I said to the Prophet, 'By God, I cannot help but notice how quickly God acts to sanction your desires.' "

There was also the *Ifk* incident when 'A'isha was falsely accused of adultery. The Prophet maintained his distance from her to await revelation. Her innocence was finally proclaimed by God in Qur'an 24:11. Her mother urged her to go to Muhammad. 'A'isha responded, "By God, I will not go to him nor will I thank anyone except God for it was He who revealed my innocence."[5]

'Umar on the other hand often appears as a more strict Muslim than Muhammad himself; Muhammad frequently restrains or softens his religious zeal and severity. 'Umar will often request permission to cut off the head of an offender or an insolent person and Muhammad will refuse to do so. 'Umar will show excessive severity toward any show, any entertainment, any frivolity:

{'Umar entered while a group of Ethiopians were playing with their spears in the presence of the Prophet. He bent down to pick up some pebbles to throw at them. The Prophet said, "Leave them alone, 'Umar."}

These two figures, 'A'isha and 'Umar, stand in close proximity to the figure of the Prophet: the woman whom he loved most and who was allowed to take excessive liberties with him to the point even of questioning his prophetic sincerity; and the Companion who sometimes interpreted the religion even more strictly and severely than did its founder. It may be possible to find precedents for these two figures in other prophetic narratives. In the case of Muhammad, however, 'A'isha and 'Umar probe deeply into the personality of the Prophet of Islam; they bracket his mission with liberties taken on the one hand and excessive zealotry on the other.

III

The Master Narrative

MUHAMMAD IN THE *SIRA*

The *Sira* of Muhammad, with its various subdivisions and spin-offs, for example, *Maghazi* (the military expeditions of the Prophet) and the *Tabaqat* (the biographical dictionaries of the Companions of Muhammad and their descendants), dominated the biographical horizons of early Islam. How did the *Sira* arise? How and why did this form become distinct from the Hadith? How was it structured or conceived? What was its ultimate purpose? Who brought it into existence? Some of these questions I shall attempt to answer and not necessarily in this particular order; others will remain only partially answered. The *Sira* continues to this day to be an endless source of fascination to both Muslim and non-Muslim readers, as attested each year by the proliferation of biographies of Muhammad as well as the detailed academic study of the sources and their authenticity. The *Sira* therefore is a very rich field and a very problematic one. How much of it we believe to be authentic, how much is legend and myth, are questions that will doubtless be debated into the foreseeable future.[1]

Let me begin with the easy questions. The classical *Sira* of Muhammad was basically fixed, as we saw earlier, by four authors:

Ibn Ishaq (d. 767) / Ibn Hisham (d. 833), al-Waqidi (d. 822)/ Ibn Sa'd (d. 845), al-Baladhuri (d. 892), and al-Tabari (d. 923).[2] These four I have called the founding fathers of the *Sira*. Although later *Siras* appeared and gained immense popularity, these later biographies, while adding many important details and adopting very different perspectives, did not alter the basic structure first put in place by the founding fathers. The four founding fathers fixed the order of the *Sira* and determined much of its content for all later biographers of Muhammad.

Turning our attention now to the founding fathers, the first characteristic common to all of them is that they were authors and not, like the Hadith masters, transmitters and collectors. In other words, it is clear that these four took the biographical materials about Muhammad and put them in a particular shape or form. Unlike the Hadith masters such as Bukhari and Muslim with whom many *Sira* writers were contemporary, and who can be described as collectors/anthologists, the *Sira* writers were more like *authors*, whose intentions and strategies were often clear and explicit. Yes, the *Sira* looked like the Hadith with its *isnad* and *matn*,[3] but the *Sira* was clearly a narrative, a story with a beginning, middle, and end, told by an author whom we often glimpse at work. We might at this point recall how the Hadith pictured Muhammad essentially in a legal/homiletic mode or perspective, disregarding chronology and narrative. Now the *Sira* comes in to supply the narrative dimension.

Hence one might argue that the dominant portrait of Muhammad in the Hadith was "Muhammad the model teacher"; whereas in the *Sira* the dominant portrait is "Muhammad in history." Thus, a division of territory occurs. The Hadith takes care of one aspect of Muhammad, one image, while the *Sira* takes care of another. One might say that the Hadith and the *Sira* satisfied two different needs of the believers: Muhammad as lawgiver and Muhammad as a prophet who lived through and fulfilled a certain prophetic mission or ministry. Which of these two images came first? Did the Hadith grow out of the *Sira* or did the *Sira* grow out of the Hadith? If I am correct in suggesting that the Hadith began its life as a ball of many colored threads, it may be difficult to give a definitive answer to this question. The prudent answer might be to say that this many colored ball began to unravel into different threads about a hundred years or so after the death of Muhammad, and by the time of Ibn Ishaq, the first of the four founding fathers, the *Sira* and the Muhammadan Hadith were two quite distinct disciplines. This is illustrated by the fact that while Ibn Ishaq's *Sira* of Muhammad was held in very high esteem, Hadith experts held that his *isnads* were untrustworthy and his Muhammadan hadiths, especially those with legal import, should not be accepted. This is a strange situation. It is as if the Hadith experts are saying that Ibn Ishaq is good on narrative biography but not to be trusted for legal/homiletic Hadith. You can trust him for the main events of Muhammad's life but you cannot trust him for Muhammad's model statements or actions. Here then one detects a parting of the ways. The Hadith was taken over by the Hadith experts and lawyers of Islam while the *Sira* was taken over by the biographers and historians *(akhbaris)* and would become, as it were, chapter one in the history of Islam as written by Muslims.

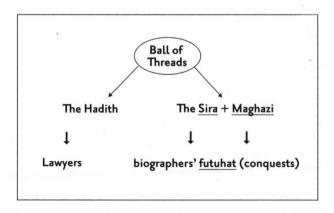

From its earliest days, the *Sira* included the military expeditions of Muhammad, his *Maghazi,* to the point where the two terms became inseparable and almost synonymous. Some have suggested that the *Maghazi* carry on a pre-Islamic tradition of battle literature *(Ayyam al-'Arab),* others that the *Maghazi* became an object of special interest *after* the dramatic conquests *(futuhat)* of early Islam; that is, they were the reconstructed prelude to the conquests and a model of how conquests should be carried out. Whatever the case may have been, the *Maghazi* present us with the image of Muhammad as a military leader, an image that complements his image as a religious reformer, and so a leader in both peace and war.

By and large, the *Sira,* as structured by its founding fathers, followed a certain chronological order. The first section one might call the "Prelude to Muhammad." This section normally begins with creation and the prophets, proceeds to the history and antiq-

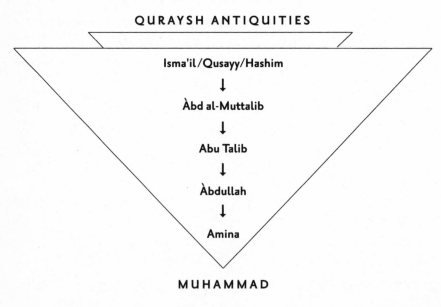

ADAM TO ABRAHAM

QURAYSH ANTIQUITIES

Isma'il/Qusayy/Hashim
↓
Àbd al-Muttalib
↓
Abu Talib
↓
Àbdullah
↓
Amina

MUHAMMAD

uities of the Quraysh, the tribe of Muhammad, with special attention devoted to his grandfather, 'Abd al-Muttalib, then narrows
down further to his father, 'Abdullah, his mother, Amina, and his
uncle Abu Talib. The treatment of this section reminds one of an
inverted triangle: the focus gradually narrows down as the scheme
of God zeroes in on Muhammad's immediate family.

The narrative in this section moves by divine plan toward its
predestined conclusion, providing a genealogical and political pro-
logue to the coming of Muhammad. In the early Christian tradition, this is referred to as the *preparatio evangelica.*[4] The second
section may be called "Birth and Infancy Stories." Here the child
Muhammad is the focus of attention, with many miracles attend-
ing his birth and early years. Section three is his youth prior to his
marriage to Khadija. This section portrays the young Muhammad
growing up pious, pure, and trustworthy, in preparation for his
mission. Section four details his marriage to Khadija, a crucial
event in his life, and then the beginning of revelations. Section five
includes Muhammad's preaching at Mecca and the tribulations of
Muhammad and his early followers, culminating in the disastrous
death of Abu Talib and Khadija. This is the lowest point of
Muhammad's life, the "Year of Sorrows." Section six encompasses
the Emigration from Mecca, the *Hijra,* and the early history of the
community in Medina, his *Maghazi,* the establishment of the community, the laying down of Muslim ritual and laws, and his increasing power and authority up to the conquest of Mecca in 630.
Section seven outlines his last days and death. These divisions can
be glimpsed in the *Sira,* even if the founding fathers did not explicitly give the *Sira* the divisions I have suggested.

The founding fathers of the *Sira* lived between 100 and 250
years after the events they described. In any discussion of authenticity, one ought to remember that this span of time lies well within
the capacity of a historian to record what he could have heard
orally from his grandfather and, by extension, from his great-

grandfather, to say nothing about the survival of written materials. During these two and a half centuries of Islamic history, a great deal happened. There were the great conquests that carried Muslim armies westward to Spain and eastward to the frontiers of China. But there were also very divisive civil wars, during which Islam broke up into two major wings, Sunnism and Shiism, and in which conflicts often emanated from radically different interpretations of certain events in the life of Muhammad and of his immediate successors. If we confine ourselves only to the Sunni-Shiite divide, we could define the Sunni mood as being one that emphasized the unity of the community as the most important ethical/social value. The Shiite mood, on the other hand, can be described as one that emphasized the personal integrity of the ruler, and a member of the family of Muhammad was the best guide to following the prophet. And there were of course many possible shades of opinion in between. In other words, like the Hadith, the *Sira* also was a field in which ideological considerations and views were active. Therefore the *Sira* cannot be described solely as an "objective" historical account of what actually happened. True, these founding fathers clearly aimed at accuracy and often expressed doubt about the truth of the stories they relate. But that did not prevent them from including such stories all the same.

They did so because their conception of history was different from ours. They believed not only that history should relay the facts or events of the past but that the duty of the historian was to transmit what reached him from his predecessors, with minimal critical interference from the historian himself. Yes, the historian could and did say that this version of events was more trustworthy than that, but his duty remained to include, not to exclude, other versions. Generally speaking, Muhammad's biography, like his Hadith, was too important a subject to be left to the personal whims of a historian. In addition, history for the founding fathers had a moral and educational purpose. If a story was factually doubtful, it would still be included for its moral or ethical value — even for its entertainment value. Sometimes the historian would also want his history to lead to consensus or the agreement of Muslims on a divisive issue. Thus, some of the historians saw history as a means of healing the wounds of the community, much as in war-torn societies of today one hears pleas for a "unified history textbook" as a healer of the wounds of war.[5] In addition, the life of Muhammad was now perceived "under the aegis of eternity"; it had acquired cosmic significance. Thus "A man asked Muhammad: Since when have you been a prophet? The people standing around say: Shut up!" Muhammad said, {Leave him alone. I was a prophet when Adam was still halfway between soul and body.} It follows that Muhammad and/or his mission existed from the beginning of the world and that this is attested by previous prophetic scriptures. Furthermore, our modern understanding of what constitutes the natural and the supernatural is quite different from that among the founding fathers. While most historians today would not normally claim that God, the angels, demons, or *jinn* had caused this or that war or revolution or crisis or major event, the founding fathers clearly saw the hand of God constantly guiding the life of Muhammad and the later history of his community. In other words, the supernatural was far more in evidence as historical factor or cause than it is for us today.

Then again, their concept of what constitutes historical evidence was different from ours. The best example to illustrate this difference is their reliance on verse. Thus, when a biographer like Ibn Ishaq cites verse, he thinks of it as corroborative evidence of historicity. To him, as to Roman and medieval European historians, verse has documentary validity. This did not prevent other historians from attacking the verses transmitted by Ibn Ishaq as spurious. But verse remained an important source of authentication for them because they believed it was less likely, because of its strict rules of meter and rhyme, to be corrupted in transmission than prose.

Let us now turn our attention back to the chronological order of the *Sira* and the seven chronological divisions into which I suggested it could be divided, and let us consider how the founding fathers portrayed the first section of the *Sira* of Muhammad. This segment, which one could call the "Prelude to Muhammad," has been compared above to an inverted triangle. The upturned base of the triangle is made up of stories of origin. Muhammad is not solely the Omega of prophets; he is also their Alpha. Let us recall his self-description of how he originated when Adam was halfway between spirit and matter. These stories of origin are on the one hand biblical (Adam to Abraham/Ibrahim to Ishmael/Isma'il) and on the other hand Yemeni antiquities represented by figures such as Tubba' and his legendary exploits in Mecca and Medina at the time of Muhammad's grandfather 'Abd al-Muttalib. In other words, the whole of Arabia comes together to prepare for Muhammad's arrival: northern Arabs (Isma'il and his progeny) and southern Arabs (Tubba' and the Yemeni kings). In fact the arrival of Muhammad is the result of a cosmic selection process that he himself describes as follows:

{God divided the earth in two halves, placing me in the better half; that half was further divided into three and I was placed in the best third; God then chose the Arabs from among mankind; then chose Quraysh from the Arabs; then Hashim from Quraysh; then 'Abd al-Muttalib from Hashim; then me from 'Abd al-Muttalib.}[6]

This text spells out what has been called the inverted triangle of focus. This process of narrowing of choice also points to the arrival of Muhammad having occurred "at the best of times."

Now this divine selection process operates in the case of other prophets as well, each of whom is in each era of history the best available in his community. So each prophet is also the result of an inverted triangle of selection; but the Muhammadan mission or triangle coopts them all; it is larger and more universal than any before. The whole of human history, at least as known to the *Sira* writers, is enlisted to prepare for his coming. This being the case, it was clear to those founding fathers that the "Prelude to Muhammad" would find echoes, or be a mirror of, or repeat earlier preludes to earlier prophets; after all, it was basically the same story but with differing versions. For example, the biblical sacrifice of Isaac by his father Abraham, one of the great master stories of the Old Testament, finds its echo in the sacrifice of 'Abdullah, father of Muhammad, by his father 'Abd al-Muttalib. 'Abd al-Muttalib therefore plays the role of Abraham and 'Abdullah of Isaac.[7] The faith of 'Abd al-Muttalib and his loyalty to God serve to illustrate the purity of the Prophet's genealogy, while even older ancestors, for example, Hashim, are praised for these or similar virtues such as generosity, courage, and so forth. This pure genealogy represented by the virtues of 'Abd al-Muttalib is further fortified by the pure genealogy of Muhammad on his mother's side; his entire maternal line is cited by the *Sira* writers and pronounced pure. No impurity, sexual or moral, can be attributed to any of them.[8]

In the *Sira*, 'Abd al-Muttalib's greatest achievement was his rediscovery of the well of Zamzam, first dug by God for Isma'il and later neglected. What are we to make of this story? In rediscovering the sacred well, 'Abd al-Muttalib was perhaps rediscovering the fountain of life and, by extension, the primordial religion from which all earlier prophets had "drunk," and he gained from this discovery both honor and importance. His other great achievement was his recognition of Muhammad, his grandson, from his very earliest years as a person of exceptional significance.

In addition to the prefatory role of 'Abd al-Muttalib, the period covered in the "Prelude to Muhammad" is portrayed as an era of expectation, akin to the atmosphere of expectation that we see in the Gospels in the time surrounding the birth or ministry of Jesus.[9] Thus we are told that the priests of the Jewish and Christian communities foretold his coming from their books, and that Arabian fortune-tellers *(kuhhan)* also foretold his coming from the *jinn* eavesdropping on the commands of God. In addition there were strange or unusual occurrences, some having to do with showers of stars, others with odd reversals of natural or human custom or behavior, all of which foretold his coming in different ways. In fact, many of these strange reversals of natural order continued to occur, especially in the early period of Muhammad's life, to which we will return below.[10]

The last aspect of this "Prelude to Muhammad" is what one might describe as the stirrings of monotheism in Mecca before the coming of Muhammad. The most famous of these Meccan monotheists was Waraqa ibn Nawfal, cousin of Khadija, Muhammad's first wife. Waraqa was to play the role of spiritual mentor to Muhammad, a role of announcer and authenticator, validator or witness to the truth of Muhammad, similar to perhaps the role of John the Baptist to Jesus. The fact that Waraqa was a Christian would suggest a handing-over process, the Christian passing revelation on to the Muslim, the torch of prophecy changing hands. Later on, the stories of Ka 'b al-Ahbar, the Jewish convert, and Salman al-Farisi, the Zoroastrian convert, who made their way to Medina to embrace Muhammad's religion, complete the process of other major religions passing on the torch to Islam.[11] In sum, this "Prelude to Muhammad" is deemed necessary by the founding fathers of the *Sira* in order to situate Muhammad within the historical plan of God. All earlier divine scriptures point to Muhammad. The nation is selected. The genealogy is pure. The signs of his coming are echoed in nature itself, which begins to show signs of turmoil. The world is about to give birth.

Compared to his grandfather, 'Abd al-Muttalib, the father of Muhammad, 'Abdullah, plays only a minor role, perhaps because he died young. He is seemingly conspicuous only for his beauty and the light shining in his face. This theme of light is then incorporated into a curious story in which a woman attempts to waylay the newlywed 'Abdullah and seduce him. But he refuses and proceeds to consummate his marriage to Amina. Having done so, 'Abdullah again passes by the woman and asks her to renew her offer. This time it is she who refuses him because the light that had been shining from him had now disappeared. The woman had hoped that she would be the one to be impregnated with supernatural light but she lost out to Amina.[12]

The theme of light is carried on with Muhammad's mother, Amina, whose own ancestry, as we have seen above, was totally free of sexual impropriety. When pregnant with Muhammad, Amina did not feel her pregnancy or any of its usual discomforts. Like Mary, the mother of Jesus, she too had her Annunciation: a voice, sometimes identified as Gabriel, told her that she will be giving birth to the "Lord of this *Ummah* and its prophet." When Muhammad was born, Amina reported seeing a "flash of light which lit up the palaces of Busra and al-Sham."[13] This theme of light, eventually called *Nur Muhammadi*, was to play an important role in Shiite biography and theology. But the most immediate and perhaps the most crucial role in Muhammad's early life is assigned by the founding fathers to his uncle and guardian, Abu Talib, who lived well into Muhammad's ministry and acted as his protector. We will meet him again shortly, but let us pass now to the second section, the "Birth and Infancy Stories."

In this section of the *Sira* and in the following section also, what appears to be simple, factual, generally plausible although sometimes contradictory narration is overlaid by a thick carpet of supernatural stories. What one needs to imagine are basically two levels of biography intermingled together, dominant or recessive in turns. The first level is concerned to anchor the life geographically in real places and establish for it historically accurate dates, even addressing contemporaneous readers to point out to them where these places are to be found "today"; for example, "it is today on your left as you enter this or that place." At the other level Muhammad's life, especially his birth and infancy, is endowed with a strong miraculous element. These miracles are now receiving some attention from modern scholars, most of whom attempt to trace them back to similar prophets' miracles in Middle Eastern religions. So one might be tempted to conclude, at least tentatively, that the writers of the *Sira* may well have scooped up what they found in a large pool of Middle Eastern miracle stories and adapted them to Muhammad. Alternatively, these stories might be part of an even larger pool of human stories that belong to what Carl Jung called the "collective unconscious," the primeval metaphors of human culture as a whole. I am not concerned with the question of the origins of these miraculous stories but simply to describe their nature and significance, their form and purpose.

In Ibn Sa'd, Muhammad's birth is described by his mother Amina as follows:

{I [Amina] became pregnant with him but found his pregnancy to be free from difficulty until I gave birth. When he was detached from me, a light came out of me which lit the distance from east to west. He fell to the ground, using his hands to support him. He took a handful of earth tightly in his fist and raised his head to heaven.}

Another version: {He fell on his knees, raising his head to heaven. With him there shone forth a light which lit up the palaces of al-Sham and its markets, until I could see the necks of camels in Busra.}[14]

This is the best-known version of his birth, his birth as illumination.[15] His earliest years are equally attended by miraculous events, the most famous in the *Sira* being the opening of his breast by the two angels and the cleansing of his heart. This miracle has special importance. At about the age of four or so, and while he was spending his days in the care of a foster mother, Halima, who meanwhile was prospering because of her fostering of the Prophet, the boy was visited by two men in white. Muhammad himself tells it as follows:

{While I and my foster brother were out in the countryside, two men in white robes approached me. They were carrying a golden bowl filled with snow. They laid me down on the ground, cut open my chest, removed my heart, cut it open, removed a black spot therein and threw it away. They then washed my heart and stomach with the snow until thoroughly cleansed, and restored it to its place.}

Another version: {Two angels approached me in the form of two cranes *(kurkiyyayn)*. With them they had snow, ice and cold water. One of them opened my chest while the other emptied its beak inside my chest and washed it.}[16]

To a student of the Bible, mythology, or folklore, or even Freudian psychology, these miracles would doubtless be of interest. For example, is this only a cleansing story or does it also have to do with the absence of parents (his father is dead, his mother is away) as per the Freudian analysis of Leonardo? And why the cranes? Or are they storks, which have a special relationship with babies? The *Sira* does not comment on the significance of these stories; it simply narrates them, leaving its readers to conclude what they want. For us, however, they might belong to a category of miracles or supernatural events that we could call "light and purity miracles or stories," aimed at showing a pure and untainted birth.

Section three of his life depicts his youth before his marriage to Khadija. Here the two levels of narration continue side by side, the natural and the supernatural. In this part of his life the best-known story is that of the hermit or monk Bahira and the manner in which he came to recognize the boy Muhammad as the future prophet. This is a longish story that shows this holy monk examining the young boy whose exact age is not determined but is perhaps ten or so, testing him, finding him to be the one predicted in his scripture and prophesying a great future for him.[17] This story can be called an attestation story, a holy man of another religion attesting to the truth of Muhammad. There are several such attestation stories, the other most famous being the story, later on, of the Negus *(Najashi)* of Ethiopia. Waraqa, Bahira, and Najashi are, so to speak, the three wise and holy men of Muhammad's birth and youth. All three are Christian: the priest, the monk, and the king.

Alongside attestation stories there are also temptation stories. These depict Muhammad as a boy being exposed to what ordinary boys of his age are exposed to, and then being divinely guided or aided to resist these temptations. One such "temptation" story concerns him as young boy transporting stones on his head with other boys. Muhammad tells it thus:

{I was with some boys of my own age, and we had tied our cloaks up around our necks in order to better carry some stones with which to play when I received a severe blow from someone who called out to me: "Wrap your cloak tightly around yourself!"}[18]

This particular story is reinforced by many later accounts that depict his private parts as being invisible and also his invisibility when answering the call of nature. Even his excrement is invisible. There is an even more pointed temptation story about his facing the sexual seductions that teenagers face:

{I never lusted after women, as the people of the *Jahiliyya* used to do, except on two nights, on both of which God Almighty granted me chastity. One night I was with some Meccan youths herding our families' sheep. I said to my companion: "Will you look after my sheep while I enter Mecca and spend the night there as youths are in the habit of doing?" He agreed so I went into Mecca and in the very first house I came to I heard the music of drums and pipes. I asked about the occasion and was told that a wedding was in progress. So I sat and waited. God made me deaf to the music and I woke up when the sunlight touched me and returned to my companion. He asked, "What did you do?" "Nothing," I replied, and related my experiences. [Exactly the same experience takes place on another night and the Prophet continues:] I never desired or returned to the same sort of act thereafter and then God dignified me with His prophecy.}[19]

The crowning story of his youth is the story of how he acquired the sobriquet "trustworthy" *(al-Amin)* by solving the dispute among Meccan clans regarding the placing of the black stone in the rebuilt Ka'ba. This story is known to every Muslim school child today who is educated in a traditional Muslim school. It relates how, when the Ka'ba or sacred square structure was rebuilt by the Meccans, the clans disputed the honor of placing the black stone back in the structure. They finally agreed to allow the first person who entered their place of assembly to arbitrate their dis-

pute. Muhammad walked in and was asked to settle the dispute.
He proposed that the clans should place the stone on a piece of
cloth, each corner of which was held by a leading clan member.
The cloth was lifted up and he himself then carried the stone and
fixed it in its former place. The *Sira* writers use this story to emphasize his esteem among his people before he took on his mission.
But one might also detect in it elements of a sacred crowning ceremony, or ritual. Similar to some extent is the story of his partici-
pation, as a young man of twenty, in an alliance, called the Alliance
of the Virtuous, concluded apparently to guarantee fair dealing in
Mecca. This is how Muhammad recalled that alliance in later life:

{An oath of alliance I attended once . . . is dearer to me than to
possess the most precious of camels, nor will I ever betray it.
The clans of Hashim, Zuhra and Taym had banded together to
side with any man unjustly treated . . . If I am called upon again
to abide by it I will answer the call.}[20]

The intention here is to highlight the virtues of his clan, who
had instituted that alliance, as well his own ever-present readiness
to respond to the call of justice.

All these stories not only imply but also state explicitly that
Muhammad from birth was pure from the sins of *Jahiliyya* (the
name given by the Qur'an to the pre-Islamic period, best translated as "Age of Barbarism") and morally fit for the mission that
would be entrusted to him by God. Nevertheless, these stories
prompt one to ask: What were Muhammad's views about God before his mission? Was he a Muslim *avant la lettre*, as it were, a
Muslim with a small *m?* This question is not at all easy to answer.
The evidence is ambiguous. There is on the one hand the interrogation of Muhammad by the monk Bahira, which is alluded to
above. Among the tests that Bahira administered to the young
Muhammad was a question regarding the goddesses of Mecca.

The scene is set outside Bahira's cell, the young Muhammad having traveled to Syria in his uncle's caravan:

> When the people had eaten and dispersed, Bahira got up and said to him [the young Muhammad], "Young boy, I ask you in the name of al-Lat and al-'Uzza [Meccan goddesses] to please answer all the questions I ask you." Bahira used this formula because he had heard the Meccans using it in their oaths. They allege that the Prophet of God replied, "Do not ask me for anything in the name of al-Lat and al-'Uzza, for I swear by God there is nothing I hate more." Bahira said, "I ask you by God, then, to answer my questions." "Ask what you will," replied Muhammad.[21]

This of course suggests that Muhammad was a monotheist ab initio. But there are also some counter-stories, stories that suggest that Muhammad may not have been completely monotheist during the pre-prophetic period of his life. One story has him confessing: {I sacrificed a white lamb to al-'Uzza when I was still a believer in the religion of my people.}[22] The second story is more detailed and narrated by him as follows:

> {The first to forbid me from idol worship was Zayd ibn 'Amr ibn Nufayl [a Meccan monotheist]. I was returning from Ta'if with Zayd ibn Haritha [a servant of his wife Khadija]. We passed by Zayd ibn 'Amr on the slopes above Mecca. The Quraysh had condemned him for forsaking their religion to the point where he was forced to abandon the city and retire to the heights above Mecca. I sat next to him. With me was a meal of meat carried by Zayd ibn Haritha. I was a young man at the time. The meat was part of what we had sacrificed to our idols. I offered him food saying, "Eat of this food, uncle." He said, "What if, dear nephew, this meat is part of what you sacrificed

to your idols?" "It is so," I replied. He said, "If only you had asked the daughters of 'Abd al-Muttalib, they would have told you that I do not eat the meat of such sacrifice." He then condemned idols, idol worship and sacrifice, saying they are false, and do no benefit or harm anyone. Thereafter, I never consciously touched an idol nor sacrificed to any idol until God Almighty honoured me with prophecy.}[23]

There is finally the famous incident of the "Satanic Verses," an incident that belongs to the period *after* he announced his prophethood, when he momentarily reverted to what appears to be praise for the pagan goddesses, an incident we shall return to later.

How does a modern biographer account for the presence of these contrasting images of Muhammad's belief? If the intention of the *Sira* writers was to present an image of a completely pure prophet, why does it also preserve stories that throw doubt on this purity? Or could it be that Muhammad's life before his mission was a gradual process of preparation, in the light of a passage like the following from Ibn Ishaq, and one typical of the authorial voice of the *Sira* writers:

When the time came for revelation to descend upon the Prophet of God, he was already a believer in God and in what was to be revealed to him. He was, moreover, fully prepared to act accordingly and to suffer for his faith what God had imposed upon him, both the pleasure and displeasure of mankind. Prophecy imposes heavy burdens and responsibilities, which can only be shouldered by resolute prophets, aided and blessed by God. This is because of what prophets meet with from people and what God-ordained events might befall them.[24]

It would be best if these questions were left to the end, when we survey the full range of images found in the *Sira*. Let us simply note the existence of a number of counter-stories or counter-narratives that cast a shadow of doubt over the light, purity, attestation, and temptation stories that predominate in this section of Muhammad's life. The hagiography of Muhammad appears to be cracked in a few places.

We move now to section four, the Prophet's marriage to Khadija and the beginning of revelations. This is a period about which there is relatively little information in the *Sira*.[25] It is nevertheless a fateful period of his life and one that the founding fathers of the *Sira* clearly regard as crucial to his spiritual development. The same mixture of the miraculous and the factual obtains here as in the previous sections. Khadija, to begin with, is described as a prosperous and aristocratic widow and, like Amina, of pure, untainted stock on her mother's side. In addition, she is described as being honorable, strong-willed, and intelligent. The generally accepted version of their ages at marriage shows him to have been twenty-five years old and her to be forty years old, although other variant ages are also found, for example, twenty-eight for Khadija, perhaps to make it easier to believe that she produced four girls and two or three boys from that marriage. Khadija is the great comforter of Muhammad and indeed the first Muslim. 'A'isha's irritated reaction to her memory is something one can almost sympathize with, as in the following story:

The Prophet was once offered the gift of a cooked piece of meat. He tore out a leg of it and said, "Take it to so and so (a female)." 'A'isha said to him, "Why did you dirty your fingers with it?" The Prophet replied, "Khadija made me promise to do so." 'A'isha was jealous and said, "As if there was no other female on this earth except Khadija!" The Prophet rose up angrily and left. He was away for a while then returned. He was met by Umm Ruman [the mother of 'A'isha] who said to him, "Prophet of God, what happened between you and 'A'isha? She is only a

young girl and you are the most worthy person to forgive her."
He pinched 'A'isha by the corner of her mouth and said, "Didn't
you just say 'As if there is no other female on the face of this
earth except Khadija?' By God, let me tell you. She believed in
me when your own clan did not believe in me. She was granted
children from me and you were denied this."[26]

Khadija cast a long shadow over the rest of Muhammad's life.
While she lived, Muhammad was monogamous. After her death,
he became polygamous, suggesting two possible and contrasting
patterns or models of Muslim marriage. We are told that it was
she who offered marriage to him, that this was partly because of
her admiration for his honesty as her business agent and partly
after being informed by her servant Maysara that another monk
of Syria had made predictions about Muhammad while he
[Muhammad] was on another journey to Syria, this time as an
agent of Khadija. The first fifteen or so years of their married life
before the descent of revelation is a period about which virtually
nothing is related in the *Sira*. One highly dramatic incident, which
occurred soon after the prophetic call—Muhammad was then
forty years old or so—was recorded as an unusually vivid temptation story. This is a story about Muhammad, Khadija, and the angel Gabriel. To confirm his prophecy, Khadija asks Muhammad to
inform her whenever that "companion of yours comes to visit you,"
the angel Gabriel being invisible to all but Muhammad. The story
proceeds as follows:

One day, when Muhammad was with her, Gabriel came upon
him. The Prophet saw him and said, "Khadija, Gabriel is here
with me." She asked, "Can you see him at this moment?" "Yes,"
he replied. She said "Sit on my left side." He sat on her left. "Do
you see him now?" "Yes," he replied. "Sit on my right side." He
sat on her right. "Do you see him now?" "Yes," he replied.

"Come and sit in my lap," she said. He sat in her lap. "Do you see him now?" she asked. "Yes," he replied. She sighed and uncovered herself while the Prophet sat in her lap. "Do you see him now?" she asked. "No," he replied. "This cannot be the devil," she said. "It can only be an angel. Be firm in your conviction and of good cheer." So she believed in him and witnessed that he had brought the truth.[27]

The Prophet's marriage to Khadija is not without some disagreeable elements that are preserved by the *Sira*. Khadija is said in most versions to have been married to Muhammad by her uncle, but in another version it is her father who married her off after she and her sister conspired together to make him drunk, to get him to agree to the marriage. Once sober, he disavowed his action saying:

"No, I did not marry you off! How could I possibly marry you off to him when you have received proposals from the best men of Quraysh which I declined?"

Waqidi adds: Where we [historians] are concerned, this is all mistaken and inaccurate. Khadija's father had died long before . . . and it was in fact her uncle who gave her away in marriage.[28]

The question then arises: if historians like al-Waqidi considered these versions of the marriage wrong, perhaps even insulting and scandalous, why preserve them? We come back again to the problem of what one might call the "antibodies" in the *Sira*. I point them out here to be discussed when we have surveyed all the periods of Muhammad's life. A reader of the *Sira* will often be struck by its very rich texture, which preserves many reports about Muhammad without excising them even when they were considered false.

Further factual details about his life with Khadija and his age when he received his call from God are also not firmly or uniformly presented in the *Sira*. Even something as simple and straightforward as the number of children he had with Khadija differs in diverse versions. He had four girls, but was it two or three boys? And how old was he exactly when he received his call? Most authorities agree on forty but forty-three is also cited. We have seen above that Khadija's age at marriage was forty but twenty-eight is also cited.[29] If we were writing an "objective" biography of Muhammad, a decision would need to be made among these numbers. However, for those of us who are in pursuit of his images, these contrasting versions of events and dates enable us to see the writers of the *Sira* at work and to examine their attitudes to the raw materials of history. Is this ambiguity in facts and figures related to the "antibodies" alluded to above? Perhaps yes, in the sense that the *Sira* writers were inclusionist rather than exclusionist in their accounts of the past. A modern historian facing a similar problem would either disregard these other versions completely or would refer to them in a footnote. But he or she would not normally put them side by side with the accepted version. The *Sira* writers on the other hand put what they considered true and what they considered dubious on the same level. And they often expressed no specific or explicit preference. The primary loyalty or obligation of the *Sira* writers was to those from whom they transmitted the stories.

What did Muhammad do in these fifteen years between his marriage and his prophetic call? The *Sira*, as we have seen above, is largely and strangely silent. But as the call of God approached, Muhammad is said to have become inclined to solitary meditation for one month every year. Nature then intervened:

Some scholars relate that the Prophet, when God Almighty wished to honor him, and by way of commencing his mission, would not pass by any tree or stone without that tree or stone greeting him. The Prophet would turn his eyes left or right or behind him but would see nothing except trees and stones. He would hear them greeting him with the greeting of prophecy: "Peace be upon you, Prophet of God."[30]

Nature itself speaks his name. At this point in the account of the Prophet's life these miraculous or marvelous events become regular features in the *Sira*, and we will examine a few of them later. They will come to include animals speaking and natural objects such as the stumps of trees sighing aloud in yearning for him. At this point we should note that these miraculous elements do not correspond to or sit easily with the images of Muhammad in the Qur'an. In the Hadith, the miracles are normally allotted a separate chapter or section and are clearly testamentary in character. In the *Sira*, however, these miracles are woven into the very fabric of narration. What is the intention of the *Sira* in doing so? If we borrow the vocabulary of advertising, the *Sira* can be said to be "packaging" Muhammad to conform, I would argue, with the prophetic type, creating for Muhammad an image and a story as rich and full of the supernatural as the images and stories of Moses and Jesus.

Picking up a phrase from Q.46:35 about "resolute" prophets, {And so bear in patience, as did the resolute from among prophets before}, the *Sira* of Ibn Ishaq sets up a distinction between major and minor prophets. The major or "resolute" *[ulu al-'azm]* prophets are said to have been Noah, Abraham, Moses, Jesus, and, of course, Muhammad. These prophets, Ibn Ishaq tells us, were distinguished by their courage and decisiveness in bearing the heavy burdens of prophecy.[31]

The minor ones, on the other hand, often fail the test of resolution, for example, Jonah: "Jonah was a pious servant of God but he was impatient. When the burdens of prophecy—and prophecy is burdensome—were imposed on him, he cracked under the heavy strain. Jonah threw off this burden and fled."

In these comments on the narrative, the voice of the author, Ibn Ishaq, can be clearly heard, explaining, constructing, and arranging the materials he has in front of him.

The divine call of Muhammad is, once again, a very well known story to every Muslim schoolchild. Thus, the angel who wrestles Muhammad in his sleep and almost suffocates him, ordering him to "Read!"—coupled with the initial reaction of Muhammad, that is, disbelief and resistance to the overwhelming angelic presence—is captured in an agonizing moment of doubt Muhammad experiences regarding the true character of revelation and a brief contemplation of suicide because of this doubt:

{Of all God's creatures, the most hateful to me were poets and those possessed by *jinn*. I could barely get myself to even look at them. Am I to be thought a poet or a man possessed? No, the Quraysh shall never call me such. I shall go to some high mountain peak and throw myself down and be killed and so gain respite.}[32]

It is the vision of Gabriel filling the horizon that stops Muhammad from doing so by calling out to him as the Prophet. Final confirmation of the truthfulness of the experience comes from Khadija by way of her cousin Waraqa, who says to her:

I swear by God your husband is truthful. This is the beginning of a prophecy. To him shall be revealed the Great Law *(Al-Namus al-Akbar)*. Command him to harbor in his soul nothing but virtue.[33]

These constituents of the story of Muhammad's call to prophecy doubtless have parallels in the stories of other prophets, and this parallelism is intentional in the *Sira*. As with earlier prophets, so with Muhammad, certain aspects of the prophetic call are similar and repetitive. Other aspects of this call, for example, the immense vision of the angel, would later on have a particular appeal to Muslim Sufis, or mystics, as symbols of God's majesty and His overwhelming and universal reality, an experience that the Sufis taught could be recaptured in Sufi devotions. Yet other aspects of this call to prophecy are explicitly said to match the description of the prophetic function, for example, that Muhammad, like all earlier prophets, was a shepherd:

> The Prophet said: {Never was there a prophet who did not herd sheep. He was asked, "You too, Prophet of God?" "Me too," he replied.}[34]

Certain aspects of the call, however, seem to be peculiar to Muhammad, principally the confirmatory role of Khadija; her faith in him and his call to prophecy appear to be two closely related events, part of the same cluster of significance. Indeed, there are three women in Muhammad's life who seem to play a role of preponderant importance: Amina begets him in glory, Khadija confirms his prophecy, and 'A'isha later on wins his heart and records and transmits his ministry.

We move to the fifth section of the *Sira*, the Prophet's early preaching in Mecca. In this section Muhammad is tested to the absolute limits of endurance by the hostility of the Meccans but his resolve remains steadfast. When his uncle Abu Talib begs him to desist from saying things hateful to their tribe and divisive in their consequences, Muhammad stands firm:

> {O uncle, were you to place the sun in my right hand and the moon in my left, I would not give up this religion until God sends it victorious or I die in the attempt.}[35]

Abu Talib relents.

There is much on the suffering of both Muhammad and his Meccan followers in the *Sira*. The hostility of the Meccans slowly increases, as does the pressure they exert on the Muslims. These early Muslims are the earliest heroes of Islamic history. Against them are ranged the earliest villains of Islam. On the supernatural level Gabriel actively engages with Satan in a sort of cosmic battle overshadowing the earthly. The Prophet is ridiculed repeatedly and on at least one occasion he is physically assaulted while praying. He is given several nicknames and derogatory epithets, for example, *Sabi'* (star worshipper). He is also called in derision Ibn Abi Kabsha, Abu Kabsha having been a man of the Quraysh who abandoned the tribal religion for star worship.[36] He is accused of being taught by a man, or perhaps a god, from the region of Yamama (eastern Arabia) called Al-Rahman.[37] Nevertheless, despite all this suffering, the tenor of the *Sira* after the prophetic call is somewhat changed. The reader of the *Sira* begins to feel that things are now more under the direct hand or guidance of God, that events have begun to take a more predetermined course, that in opposition to all these unfolding events there is a new and vigorous salience in the activity of Satan, whose role is not only to tempt but to undermine the activity of Muhammad at every turn.

The preaching of Muhammad is pictured in the *Sira* as occurring in stages. At first, he preached to small groups and in secret. Later on, his preaching became public and so drew upon him increasing hostility. A man called 'Uqba stepped on Muhammad's neck while he was praying, causing him to choke. Nevertheless, the *Sira* injects an element of divine justice by making it clear that all the early Meccan enemies of Muhammad would die awful deaths, either from horrible diseases, or from thirst, or in battle against Muslims, or they were blinded or disabled in some way by Gabriel, or cursed by Muhammad and later killed, or killed by wild animals, or captured later on and killed by Muhammad himself.[38] Here Gabriel plays the role of the instrument of God in the fight against Satan, becoming not just the announcer of the word of God but the avenger of His messenger as well. This theme of the enemies of Muhammad dying horrible deaths is continued into the Medinese period of his life. Attempts on his life are divinely thwarted. The lowest point in this Meccan period comes when Abu Talib and Khadija both die in rapid succession. The traditional date corresponds to 618 A.D., the "Year of Sorrows." Muhammad loses both his tribal protector and his personal comforter. Abu Talib, while protecting Muhammad, nevertheless did not, like Khadija, embrace his religion, his excuse being that he didn't want to abandon the religion of his father, 'Abd al-Muttalib; otherwise he would have followed the religion of Muhammad. In another version, his excuse is that the Quraysh would think him cowardly if he were to embrace the new religion only at the point of death.[39] Yet it appears that he tolerated the conversion of his young son 'Ali to the new faith.

So here again, a highly revered personality such as Abu Talib does not escape the hostility of certain reports in the *Sira*. His image is not free from blemish, despite the utterly fearless loyalty he showed to Muhammad at a time when Muhammad desperately needed his protection. Nor indeed is Abu Talib's ultimate destiny, any more than that of Amina, entirely clear. Thus, one report in the *Sira* tells us that Muhammad asked God to forgive her but God refused:

> When the Prophet conquered Mecca, he went to the remains of a grave . . . then rose and left it, weeping. 'Umar . . . faced him and asked: "What caused you to weep, Prophet of God?" The Prophet replied {This is the grave of my mother. I asked God's permission to visit it and was allowed to do so. I asked God's forgiveness for her but this was not granted. I remembered her, I grew tender and so I wept.} He was never after seen to weep as much as he did that day.

Ibn Sa'd comments: This is a mistake. Amina's tomb is not in Mecca but in al-Abwa'.[40]

Even more significant was the deathbed scene of Abu Talib:

When Abu Talib was on his death bed, the Prophet of God came to visit him and found 'Abdullah ibn Abi Umayya and Abu Jahl ibn Hisham [two enemies of Islam] by his side. Muhammad said {O uncle, say "There is no god but God," a phrase I would hope to use as witness in your favor before God.} The other two said, "O Abu Talib, do you truly wish to abandon the religion of your father 'Abd al-Muttalib?" The Prophet continued to urge him in the same terms while the other two continued to ask him the same question but his last words were: "I am of the religion of 'Abd al-Muttalib." When he died, the Prophet said {I shall seek forgiveness for him provided I am not forbidden to do so.} The Prophet sought forgiveness for him until the following Qur'anic verse [Q. 9:113] was revealed {It is not proper for the Prophet or the believers to ask forgiveness for the polytheists even if they are close relatives, after it has been made clear to them that they are in Hell.}[41]

In the *Sira* a lot seems to depend on the interpretation of this Qur'anic verse, one that may well have predisposed the writers of the *Sira* to accept narratives damning in hell otherwise glorious relatives such as the mother of the Prophet or his protective and kindly uncle in order to maintain Qur'anic consistency. But then, why go through the trouble of inventing an immaculate genealogy for Amina when her ultimate destiny is hell? And why construct this marvelous portrait of Abu Talib only for him to end in the same place? This is yet another puzzle, intimately tied to the question of "antibodies" in the *Sira*.

The crowning moment of this period of Muhammad's life is his

Night Journey from Mecca to Jerusalem, alluded to in the opening verse of Qur'an 17 {Blessed is He who carried His servant by night from the Sacred Mosque to the Furthest Mosque, whose precincts We blessed, to show him some of Our signs. He hears all; He sees all.} This miraculous vision, or else a real journey in some versions, is said to have taken place one year before the Emigration to Medina. Muhammad narrates it as follows:

{I was carried upon a white animal, something between an ass and a she-mule with two wings on its haunches . . . When I came to ride it, it shied. Gabriel placed his hands upon it and said, "Are you not ashamed, O Buraq? By God, no servant of God has ever ridden you before more honorable in God's sight than Muhammad." The animal was ashamed and sweated profusely, quieting down until I rode her. She twisted her ears, and distances were contracted so that its hooves fell upon successive horizons. Its back and ears were long. Gabriel kept up with my flight until we arrived in Jerusalem. The Buraq reached a place whereupon it was tethered by Gabriel, a tethering place of earlier prophets. Earlier prophets had been assembled for me: Abraham, Moses and Jesus. I thought they needed a leader of prayer so Gabriel placed me in front. I asked them and they replied: "We were sent to preach the unity of God."}[42]

The second part of the account of this Night Journey is the ascent of Muhammad to heaven, where visions of heaven and hell are detailed, ending with a vision of the divine and detailed instructions regarding prayer. The *Sira* inclines to view belief in this vision as a test of the believer's faith: this is where, for example, Muhammad's close Companion Abu Bakr acquired his sobriquet of *Al-Siddiq*, the firm believer. In later biographies this journey to heaven looms large as a portent of Muhammad's preeminence and a harbinger of his coming mission to the world.

We move now to section six, the *Hijra,* the *Maghazi,* and the Medinese period up to the conquest of Mecca in 630 A.D. My estimate is that this period of Muhammad's life occupies some seventy-five percent of the *Sira,* and that the Meccan period occupies only about twenty-five percent or less. In other words, all that has been said so far about the images of Muhammad would make up barely a quarter of his biography in the *Sira.* We must necessarily be selective but remember that the Medinese period of his life is the one that occupied the major portion of the attention of the *Sira* writers, a period when the Muslims came to constitute a politico-religious community, a proto-state. With one major exception, the setback at the Battle of Uhud, the *Sira* depicts Muhammad as going from victory to victory, from Meccan preacher to Arabian and then finally to international leader.

And what can be said about the *Sira* in general with regard to this part of Muhammad's life? The miraculous element is, if anything, even more evident. God makes the Prophet victorious over his enemies inside and outside Medina. Angels appear to help him in his battles; there are miracles of feeding and of water gushing forth. He is now the "Prophet Armed" where before he was the "Prophet Unarmed." And by and large the material in this part of the *Sira* is less controversial with regard to things such as dates, numbers, and names. The *Sira* fills out with people, with hundreds upon hundreds of names. Muhammad is now fully in the public eye, and constantly on public show. This Medinese part of the *Sira* is a wide theater of events and personalities. It is biography on an epic scale, and a history made by Muhammad *and* his community; a transition has occurred from Muhammadan biography to Muslim history. Muhammad of course remains at the very center of things, but around him can be seen an ever growing body of followers who become an essential part of his story, both as actors and as witnesses. Muhammad is more self-confident, more sure of where things are going, less doubtful and persecuted. He still has many enemies, but the way he deals with them is more decisive and assured. We can almost speak of a new Muhammad.

Soon after his arrival in Medina in 622, war is declared against Mecca, a war that continues uninterrupted and culminates in 630, with the conquest of Mecca. This is a war *à outrance*. It is waged through propaganda, tribal diplomacy, poetry, as well as fighting—a war on all fronts. Accordingly, Muhammad's images as war leader predominate and deserve primary scrutiny. These roles afford him a new scope to exercise his abilities, with, of course, the active help of the divine and of his ever-increasing number of followers. One Arabian grandee after another tumbles into submission.

In war, Muhammad's various images combined project a leader who is both cunning in battle and relentless in pursuing his objectives. Nevertheless, he remains willing to compromise with the enemy if the need arises even at the cost of alienating or shocking some of his followers. The truce of Hudaybiyya, one famous incident in this period, illustrates his foresight in the face of strong opposition from Muslim zealots.[45] The glory he achieves both as a war leader and as a diplomat reflects not only on Muhammad but also on his followers, who now share in his divine favor or grace. Thus, the seventy camels upon which were mounted the 314 followers who agreed to fight with him at the Battle of Badr are henceforth called the Badrites; they were the earliest and most prestigious group of Muslims, guaranteed to enter Paradise.

The major battles, such as Badr, Uhud, al-Khandaq, and Hunayn, are narrated at considerable length in the *Sira*. There is a high sense of drama in the narrative of these major clashes and a considerable degree of conscious artistic creativity. The scene moves back and forth between the Muslim camp and the camp of the enemy. The building blocks of the narrative are little anecdotes, conversations, a great deal of verse, individual combats, acts of heroism or of treachery. At Badr and again at Hunayn, the angels intervene in support of the Muslims while Satan does his best to mislead, to sow discord, and to aggravate the tension. There are lists everywhere in the *Sira,* lists of names of participants, lists classified by clans, lists of hypocrites, lists of the battle dead, lists of prisoners. The number seventy is frequent. There are also many "firsts": the first to arrive at some locality, the first woman emigrant, the first to offer hospitality in Medina, the first to raise his sword in battle, the first Muslim child born in Medina, the first Ansari to die in battle, and so on. The dating of events is meticulous, or at least meticulousness is attempted by the *Sira* writers: which day of the week and which month and which year an event occurred preoccupy someone like al-Baladhuri, for instance. In several of these battles Muhammad seeks military advice from his more experienced followers. But his most potent weapon is his prayers to God for victory. He himself will occasionally join the battle and will even be wounded as at Uhud. More often, however, he urges the Muslims on with words of encouragement and promises of salvation. Occasionally he will curse a particular enemy, who will inevitably die. He is also the arbiter regarding booty and prisoners.

All in all, the Muhammad we now begin to encounter is a more stern, a more forbidding personality, one who forgives most of his enemies in victory but one who also unhesitatingly orders the execution of a few of them:

> The Prophet ordered 'Asim ibn Thabit to strike off the head of 'Uqba ibn Abi Mu'ayt, who had been captured in battle by 'Abdullah ibn Salama. 'Uqba began to protest: "Alas! Why, O Quraysh, should I be killed from among all these prisoners?" The Prophet answered: {Because of your enmity to God and His Prophet.} 'Uqba said, "Your forgiveness is best. Treat me like others of my clan. If you kill them, you kill me. If you forgive them, you forgive me. If you accept ransom for them, you

accept it for me. O Muhammad, who will take care of this young daughter of mine?" Muhammad answered: {Hell! O 'Asim, bend his neck forward and cut it off.} 'Asim cut his head off. The Prophet said, {You were the worst of men. By God I never met a man more disbelieving in God, His Prophet and His Book nor one more harmful to His Prophet. I thank God who killed you and gave me satisfaction.}[44]

In his capacity as political leader, he is bracketed by the soft-hearted Abu Bakr on the one hand and the overzealous 'Umar on the other. Abu Bakr always counsels forgiveness and leniency; 'Umar counsels rigid and merciless justice. A royal Muhammad is beginning to emerge in the *Sira*, a figure who dispenses both life and death. And it may well be that the writers of the *Sira* were aware of this new aspect of Muhammad's personality. So they introduce stories of Muhammad designed specifically to dispel the impression that Muhammad was behaving like a king:

Gabriel appeared to Muhammad when the latter was on the heights above Mecca, eating while reclining on his elbow. Gabriel said, "O Muhammad, this is how kings eat." Muhammad sat up straight.

It further reached us that an angel appeared to the Prophet, one he had not seen before, accompanied by Gabriel. The angel spoke as follows with Gabriel remaining silent, "Your God offers you the choice of being a prophet/king or a prophet/servant." The Prophet glanced at Gabriel as though waiting for instructions. Gabriel signalled to him to be humble. The Prophet then answered, {I would rather be a prophet/servant.}

The historian al-Zuhri says, "They allege that the Prophet never afterwards ate while reclining on his elbow until he departed from this world."[45]

By and large, the *Maghazi* are a melancholy affair, if occasionally punctuated by the black humor of battle:

> Advancing towards Badr, the Muslims met a bedouin *[a 'rabi]* from the region of Tihama [the coastal region of Mecca]. The Prophet's companions asked him about the caravan of Abu Sufyan, which they were pursuing. The bedouin denied any knowledge of it. They said, "Come and salute the Prophet of God." "Is he really among you?" he asked. "Yes," they replied. Arrived in his presence, he asked, "Which of you is the Prophet?" They pointed him out. He asked, "Are you the Prophet of God?" "Yes," the Prophet replied. The Bedouin said, "If you speak the truth, tell me what is inside the belly of my she-camel." A man called Salama ibn Salama ibn Waqash replied, "You had intercourse with your she-camel and she is now pregnant with your issue." The Prophet found the remark distasteful and turned away.[46]

The *Maghazi* of Muhammad provide rich material for a narrative that is often full of pathos, of the pity of things, of painful memories of happier times:

> When the prisoners from the Battle of Badr were brought in, Sawda, a wife of the Prophet, saw one of them called Abu Yazid with his hands tied behind his neck.
>
> *She continues:* "By God, when I saw him tied in this manner I could not help but cry 'O Abu Yazid, you who used to give with both hands! Should you not die in dignity?' No sooner had I said this than I heard the Prophet calling from inside the house, {O Sawda, do you wish to antagonize God and his Prophet?} I said, 'O Prophet of God, I swear by Him who sent you in truth I could not help saying what I said when I saw him tied up in that condition.' "[47]

For in many senses the *Maghazi* depict what was all too often a war of cousins and neighbors, of clans who were once allies before the days of Islam but were now divided by religion. Indeed, one could read the *Maghazi* as an Arabian civil war. This is the most bitter of wars, engendering a violent rearrangement of identities and loyalties. Muhammad's most prominent enemy throughout this period was a figure of immense cunning and influence, the virtual leader of Mecca, Abu Sufyan, together with his equally formidable wife, Hind. They are the Macbeth and Lady Macbeth of the *Sira,* although fate was eventually kinder to them. Abu Sufyan was a worthy opponent of Muhammad, a brilliant speaker and strategist and a determined enemy of Islam until the very last:

> When the Quraysh returned to Mecca after Badr, Abu Sufyan stood up and made the following speech: "O Quraysh, do not weep over your dead nor allow a female mourner to wail over them, nor a poet to lament them in verse. Display resolution and composure. If you mourn for them or lament them in verse, your anger will dissipate and this will make you less determined in your enmity towards Muhammad and his followers. On the other hand, if Muhammad and his followers hear about this, they would derive malicious joy *[shamata]* from it, and this would be the worse of our two calamities. Who knows, perhaps we will exact vengeance. I declare all perfume and women to be forbidden to me until I wage war on Muhammad."[48]

Abu Sufyan is the father of Mu'awiya, founder of the Umayyad dynasty (661–750). His prolonged enmity toward Muhammad seems not to have affected the rise of his descendants to supreme power.

Inside Medina, Muhammad had another formidable enemy, the enemy within, as it were, 'Abdullah ibn Ubayy, the head of the so-called *Munafiqun* or hypocrites. It is difficult to understand why

Muhammad and the Muslims tolerated his enmity for so long. Possibly these "hypocrites" had accepted Islam as a religion but not necessarily the absolute *political* authority of Muhammad. In any case, Ibn Ubayy was quite capable of making some very nasty remarks about the Meccan emigrants who had come with Muhammad to Medina. When an Emigrant got into a fight with a Medinese Ansari, and each appealed to his group for help, a clash among Muslims becoming imminent, Ibn Ubayy was heard to remark:

> "Have they really gone and done it? They [the Meccan Emigrants] compete with us and now outnumber us in our own town. By God, I do not see it any other way with these 'Quraysh belts' [a derogatory epithet] than the way it was put by someone long ago: 'Fatten your dog and it will eat you.' When we return to Medina, the low-born will drive out the high-born."[49]

Muhammad patiently endured the man's enmity and was even ready to pray over his grave. The man's son, however, was a staunch Muslim whose faith is contrasted with his father's hypocrisy.

In Medina, the *Sira* of Muhammad expands greatly in detail and becomes in large part political. But every one of the Prophet's private acts also has immediate visibility and, with time, imitability. Muhammad appears to us as a very busy man, and one whose most secret and private life is on public display. The *Sira* is cinematic, following him around wherever he goes, right into his bedroom. Although this is the story of a man who slowly but surely attained his objectives, we do not get the impression that he necessarily grew happier with time. Although we encounter him smiling and even occasionally laughing, there were many events that depressed him or made him unhappy: the death of his infant son Ibrahim; the death of his uncle Hamza; the horrific affair of the *Ifk*, when 'A'isha was accused of adultery; the many wives who brought him at least as much trouble as they did comfort; as well as of course the unending problems that attend the creation of new states or new communities, including his followers' frequent acts of disobedience.

Muhammad was both the founder of Islam and the interpreter of the message, an announcer and a legislator, Jesus-like in Mecca but Moses-like in Medina. In other words, in Medina Muhammad taught his followers how to live as a community whereas in Mecca he was preaching piety to individuals or small groups. This division between the Meccan Muhammad and the Medinese Muhammad was already well known to the founding fathers of the *Sira* as early as a hundred years or so after Muhammad's death. Indeed, some of them liked to detect a certain symmetry in these two periods: a neat division of years divided into ten years in Mecca and ten years in Medina.

We move now to the seventh section, the last two years of the Prophet's life. With the conquest and cleansing of Mecca in 630 behind him, Muhammad was now overlord of roughly the western half of Arabia. According to the *Sira,* that success established him as an Arabian and a regional leader of significance. He is portrayed as such by the *Sira* writers, who see the last two years of his life as years of submission by his enemies. One of these two years is called *'Am al-wufud* (Year of Delegations), when Muhammad sat in Medina receiving delegations from all over Arabia offering him various treaties of alliance or submission. This is the year of Islamic diplomacy, when the community under Muhammad felt strong enough not only to send long-range expeditions to the furthest parts of Arabia but also outside the confines of Arabia, into the greater Syria region. He also afterward supposedly sent letters to the great rulers of the world surrounding Arabia, to the Byzantine emperor, Persian shah, Egyptian Muqawqas, and so forth. Historians have expressed doubts about these letters.[50] But these doubts do not really concern us as we pursue images of Muhammad in the *Sira*. Accounts of these letters seem in any case to be intended to signify the expansion of his mission to the far corners of the earth.

The other major event is his last "Farewell Pilgrimage," *Hajjat al-Wadà*, and the speech he made upon that occasion, his last will and testament in the eyes of the *Sira* writers. Did he really have a premonition of his end or were the *Sira* writers being wise after the fact and therefore doctored that pilgrimage to make it appear as if he was bidding farewell to his community? Into his mouth the *Sira* writers put words that explicitly spell out that he felt his end was near:

{O People, listen to my words for I do not know whether I will ever meet you again on such an occasion after this year has passed.}[51]

It was of course only fit for a prophet to have a premonition of his end for prophets do not die suddenly or accidentally. Nor again do prophets die a protracted death. The usual time is a few days. And here too Muhammad conformed to prophetic type.

His illness began soon after he visited a cemetery in Medina, to ask forgiveness for its dead. Then he developed a splitting headache, went into 'A'isha's chamber, and had an extraordinary conversation with her, startling in its domesticity:

From 'A'isha: The Prophet returned from the Baqi' cemetery to find me with a splitting headache and crying out "Oh my head!" He said to me: {No, it is me rather who should cry "O my head!"} Then he said to me, {How would you like it if you were to die before me, so that I would stand over you and shroud you, pray for your soul and bury you?} I said, "Yes, by God, I can just see you, having done that, coming back to my own chamber and lying down with some woman of yours." The Prophet smiled. His pains increased as he made the rounds among his wives until the pain became unbearable when he was in the chamber of Maymuna. He called his wives together, asked their leave for him to be nursed in my chamber, and was given leave.[52]

He recovered briefly, and the hopes of his followers were raised, but then he eventually died either in the lap of 'A'isha or, in another version, in the lap of 'Ali. Since these two figures had very little liking for each other, it seems that the *Sira* writers wanted this honor to fall to both of them, we might say to satisfy all Muslim inclinations and to bring the Muslim community together.

Those who like the literary genre called "famous last words" may be curious to know what Muhammad's famous last words were. There are several versions but one leading version goes as follows:

From 'A'isha: Coming back that day from the mosque, the prophet lay down in my lap. There entered a man from the family of Abu Bakr carrying a green toothpick. The Prophet glanced at him in such a way that I knew he wanted it. I said, "Prophet of God, do you want me to give you the toothpick?" "Yes," he replied. So I took the toothpick, chewed it until it was soft and gave it to him. He cleaned his teeth with it more vigorously than I had ever seen him do before, and then put it aside. I felt him grow heavy in my lap. I looked down at his face and found that his eyes had glazed. He said, {Rather, the Friend on high.} I said to him, "I swear by Him who sent you in truth, you were given a choice and you chose." The Prophet died.[53]

The *Sira* explains that Muhammad was given a choice: either the company of God or earthly glory and immortality, and he chose the first. His last act on earth, the cleaning of his teeth, is patently a ritual cleansing act, an affirmation of the truth he spoke. It may also refer back to the opening of his breast when he was still a young boy. The two cleansing acts, one at the beginning and the other at the end, thus bracket his mission.

Before leaving the *Sira*, there remain two more subsidiary subjects to be discussed briefly: his personal appearance and moral character, and the long delayed discussion of what I have been calling the "antibodies" of the *Sira*.

Descriptions of Muhammad's physical and moral attributes *(Shama'il)* were an early biographical genre to which independent works were devoted.[54] In the *Sira* we have physical descriptions of the Prophet so detailed that if one were inclined to give this information to an artist, an accurate likeness of Muhammad could easily be drawn. It is best simply to list these physical characteristics, paraphrasing and conflating some original accounts: very dark hair; hair down to shoulders with a small parting in the middle; hair normally let down but if tied does not extend further than earlobes; white shining face; taller than medium height; large head; radiant skin color; broad and shining forehead; long eyelashes; full and arched eyebrows but not connected and between them a vein that fills up when angry; eyes appeared as if naturally dyed with antimony *(kuhl);* hooked nose; thick beard with hardly twenty gray hairs; smooth cheeks; strong mouth; white teeth with clefts in between; dark thin lips; thin chest hair; neck like that of a doll; inclining to fatness; thickset and broad-shouldered; broad-chested; large-boned; thin line of hair between upper chest and navel; no hair on stomach or nipples; hairy arms; long upper arms; big palms; shapely fingers; slender legs; short and thick palms and feet. He walked very fast, looking neither to left nor right. When turning, he turned with his whole body. He lowered his eyes; looked more to earth than to sky; was constantly in thought, never at ease, prone to long silences; did not talk except when necessary; when speaking he often struck with the edge of his right palm the inner part of the thumb of his left.[55]

To decipher this list of physical characteristics, we need to stress again that we are dealing with an age when it was widely believed that a person's inner character was reflected in his or her physical appearance; a whole science was later devoted to this, called the science of *Firasa*, or physiognomy, and perhaps there is even an allusion to this belief in Qur'an 48:29: {Their mark is upon their faces as a trace of prostration.}[56] So what we have here in the physical description of Muhammad is as much an ideal as it is a historical reality. The accent is not so much on physical beauty but on radiance and nobility of character.

Muhammad's moral attributes are gathered together in a series of descriptions of him by people who knew him intimately. 'A'isha, as we have seen earlier, says quite simply that his moral character *was* the Qur'an. We also learn such things as his aversion to vulgarity in speech, his generosity, his frequent smiling and laughter, his forgiving nature. Of any two legitimate choices he always chose the easier. He never struck anyone with his hand, except in the cause of God. He was "humble and shy as a maiden in her bower." He never said no to any request. He was furthest removed from the character of a tyrant. The following encounter illustrates his humility:

> A man came to see the Prophet. Standing before him, the man shook with terror. The Prophet said to him {Be at ease. I am not an angel. I am merely the son of a woman from Quraysh who used to eat dried meat.}[57]

My last theme is one that has been alluded to from time to time in this discussion of the *Sira* and its images. I am referring to the way in which the *Sira* preserves at several points in the story of Muhammad accounts and anecdotes, opinions and impressions that cannot be called favorable to the Prophet's overall image, or at least seem at odds with that image. I have called them collectively "antibodies," foreign substances inside a body of texts whose obvious objective is otherwise to celebrate and glorify the Prophet of Islam. The presence of these antibodies becomes all the more visible when we remember that another body of texts, the Hadith, gives us a far more uniform version of what Muhammad said or did, with far fewer antibodies.

Let us first of all recapitulate very briefly some earlier remarks on the historical horizons of the *Sira*. It has already been argued that (1) the writers of *Sira* considered history to be in essence transmitted material. The historian was primarily a transmitter, not a critic. Hence inclusion rather than exclusion was the dominant method. (2) Even if a story was unbelievable or inappropriate, it might still be included because it could have a moral or aesthetic aspect or value. (3) The *Sira* writers took for granted the preponderant role of the supernatural. Hence, strange causes of events were tolerated and, by extension, strange or unusual evidence could be admitted. There was in addition a different conception of evidence; for example, verse was regarded then as we might regard documentary evidence today. (4) The *Sira* writers operated within a prophetic framework. Muhammad's life needed to conform to the life of prophecy as understood by these writers, and needed of course to conform to the Qur'an. To recall some of the "antibodies" in the *Sira*, one might compress them into two or three questions: Why are there so many stories that cast doubt on such things as the purity of Muhammad's belief before his mission? Why do the writers of the *Sira* preserve the true and the false on the same level? Why does the *Sira* cast doubt on the ultimate destiny of highly revered characters such as Abu Talib and Amina? These "antibodies" can be multiplied to include, for example, bizarre reports about Muhammad's sexual prowess or about women who refused to marry him.[58]

The answer to these questions can be found partly in one or more of the four historical horizons set out above. And yet we do not feel that these historical horizons, so different from our horizons today, can account fully for the antibodies. Thus, if we take the principle of inclusiveness, this would partially explain the presence of antibodies. Writers of the *Sira* could not ignore what was transmitted to them. Indeed, accepting what was transmitted was a sign of trustworthiness in a historian. The best-known statement of this particular attitude to the transmission of historical reports comes in the introductory section of al-Tabari's celebrated *History,* which runs as follows:

Let him who examines this book of mine know that I have relied, as regards everything I mention therein which I stipulate to be described by me, solely upon what has been transmitted to me by way of reports which I cite therein and traditions which I ascribe to their narrators, to the exclusion of what may be apprehended by rational argument or deduced by the human mind, except in very few cases. This is because knowledge of the reports of men of the past and of contemporaneous news of men of the present do not reach the one who has not witnessed them nor lived in their times except through the accounts of reporters and the transmission of transmitters, to the exclusion of rational deduction and mental inference. Hence, if I mention in this book a report about some men of the past which the reader or listener finds objectionable or worthy of censure because he can see no aspect of truth nor any factual substance therein, let him know that this is not to be attributed to us but to those who transmitted it to us and we have merely passed this on as it had been passed on to us.[59]

This obligation to be faithful in transmission is even more strin-
gent when the subject is Muhammad's life. No matter how "objectionable" a story might be, since it concerns the Prophet, it could
not possibly be ignored or excluded. The subject was far too hallowed to be handled with anything other than total honesty in
transmission. This is perhaps one clue to the explanation of these
antibodies. Another clue may lie in the fact that the lives of earlier
prophets were also not entirely free of "lapses," as "lapse" is defined in their own narratives. Hence, if at certain points of
Muhammad's *Sira* one detects inappropriate or unpleasant elements, these too could be explained as prophetic "lapses," for
which parallels could be found in the lives of other prophets.

One last theme in the *Sira* is poetry and the images of Muhammad
purveyed therein. This is a subject to which we shall return in
other sections of this work, but it should be broached at this point
because it marks the starting point for all later Muslim discussions
of Muhammad *in* poetry as well as Muhammad *and* poetry. We
turn first to Muhammad *in* poetry, saving the problem of
Muhammad *and* poetry for later chapters.

Among the founding fathers of the *Sira*, Ibn Ishaq was the one
who included the largest volume of verse in his work. A great deal
of that verse is undoubtedly inauthentic. It was in fact Ibn Hisham
(d. 833), Ibn Ishaq's redactor, who, half a century or so after Ibn
Ishaq, first questioned the authenticity of much of the verse, citing
the opinion of "experts in poetry" *(ahl al-'ilm bi'l shi'r)*.[60] For our
purposes here, the genuineness of the verse is of little concern; fabricated or not, this verse purveyed certain images of Muhammad
that were current among Muslims as early as the early eighth century. This was the mid-Umayyad period, a time of immense poetic
productivity, and some pious, pro-Ansar versifiers may well have

wished to regale the Prophet with verse retrojected to his own age.[61] For us today the interest of these works lies in their being early attempts to fill out the *Sira* with the vividness and evidentiary authority of verse.

Muhammad seems to have retained two or three poets at a time, but his poet laureate was the Medinese Ansari Hassan ibn Thabit (d. ca. 659). From his poetry, as well from other poets in the *Sira*, certain stock images of Muhammad emerge. Muhammad is often described as a "light" *(nur)* from God, a shooting star *(shi-hab);* he brings with him justice and truth; he is aided by the Holy Spirit *(al-ruh al-quds* or *qudus);* his guidance saves the wayward; Gabriel and other angels are constantly by his side. He is a man of his word, generous, trustworthy. There is much pride in the fact that it was the Medinese Ansari who took him in when the Quraysh, his own tribe, had rejected him. The poetry becomes dense at certain high points in the *Sira,* especially in describing major battles and the deaths of Islamic heroes. Here Hassan and other poets lay into the enemy with the arrows of poetry, and much is heard of obedience to the Prophet leading to triumph and the disobedience of enemies leading to their destruction:

> *Amongst us stands the Prophet, a shooting star, followed*
> *By light, outstripping all shooting stars.*
> *Truth is his speech, justice his way of life,*
> *Whoso answers his call is saved from destruction.*[62]

Of all the poems in the *Sira,* by far the most famous is the "Banat Su'adu" (Su'ad has departed), these being the first words of the poem. This is an ode constructed in accordance with a standard pre-Islamic or *Jahili* model: an opening section bemoans the loss of love, a middle section is devoted to the toils of a journey, and a final section describes the encounter with the beloved's substitute, a lord or patron of some kind. The poet was Ka'b ibn

Zuhayr, the son of an equally famous poet. It was allegedly composed as an apology by Ka'b, who feared for his life because of
some earlier anti-Islamic verse that he had written. When the ode
reaches the third, or encounter, section it portrays Muhammad as
follows:

> *The Prophet is a light, illuminating the way to truth,*
> *An Indian blade, unsheathed, from the blades of God;*
> *Amidst a band from Quraysh, one of whom had said to them*
> *In the center of Mecca: "Be gone!" when they embraced Islam.*
> *They went; but did not retreat like weak men without armor*
> *When battle raged, or like men unsteady in the saddle, untrained.*
> *Haughty-nosed are they, heroes, wielding shields, decked in armor.*
> *They do not rejoice when their spears give them victory over a people,*
> *Nor do they panic if they are beaten.*
> *Their battle wounds are suffered only from the front;*
> *They tarry not from the pools of death.*[63]

Here is Muhammad in epic mode, about to do battle with the
enemy, his troops fully decked out and ready, fearless and steadfast. The ode is filled with awe of Muhammad and his power, an
awe reflected even in the verse of his enemies. Muhammad's victorious banner is also a frequent theme of Hassan's poetry, except
that in Hassan's work the banners of his own tribe are intertwined
with those of the Prophet:

> *God honored us through the victory of His Prophet;*
> *With us He built up the pillars of Islam.*
> *Through us He brought glory to His Prophet and His book;*
> *Us He glorified with fighting and courage.*
> *Gabriel visits our dwellings,*
> *Revealing Islam's duties and laws.*[64]

When the *Sira* of Ibn Hisham approaches its end, the author cites a few elegies of the dead Prophet by Hassan, none of which has ever been found worthy of inclusion in the Arabic poetical cannon.

This in brief is how the verse of the *Sira* attempted to depict Muhammad. Verse was thought necessary for historical authentication; it acted like a stamp of truth. More to the point, verse endowed the *Sira* with epic vividness: the Prophet as a shining hero, the warrior of God and the most gracious lord of the believers.

All in all, the *Sira* is a very rich mixture. It is a mixture of the natural and the supernatural, of prose and poetry, but within it lies a figure who is decidedly human, a man trying to become a model, not always succeeding, but all the more human because of these elements in his life, these incidents that underline both his strengths and his weaknesses as a human being.

The Teacher of Manners

MUHAMMAD IN *ADAB*

The theory and practice of *Adab* is central to the understanding of premodern Arabic/Islamic culture.[1] *Adab* may be defined, to begin with, as a curriculum of learning and courtliness, its end product being the *Adib*, the gentleman-scholar. This last is a social type with many guises, recognizable across a wide swath of time and cultures. *Adab* assumes that there can be no true erudition without the polished character that goes with it. The *Adib* was an ornament to any literary salon or *majlis*, a courtly gathering, holding forth with ease on all branches of learning but careful to keep himself aloof from the plebs and the contamination of the *mauvais goût*. He peddled his elegant learning to his own class but often under the patronage of the rich and powerful who were fond of staging debates between prominent *Adibs*. His scholarly baggage would typically have consisted of a formidable array of the arts and sciences of his age: the web of the religious sciences, poetry, philology, history, and literary criticism, together with a solid acquaintance with the natural sciences, from arithmetic to medicine and zoology.

Almost by definition, the practice of *Adab* militated against specialization in any one subject, opting instead for breadth of cultivation. To a cosmos whose various parts were thought to be so intimately linked, *Adab* was perhaps an appropriate literary and moral response, its emphasis being on the interconnectedness of things, their harmony and their divinely instituted design. Appropriately, the style of *Adab* was eclectic, variegated, full of asides. It was important for the *Adib* not only to educate the listener or reader with a very broad canvas but also to keep his interest engaged and avoid boring him with pedantry. Clearly, *Adab* does not correspond to literature in the strict sense; perhaps the happiest congruent term so far suggested is the classical Greek *Paideia*; its later manifestations during the Hellenistic age may well have percolated down to *Adab*'s earliest practitioners.[2]

One common literary product of *Adab* was the *Risala*, the literary epistle, or perhaps the essay, frequently addressed by its author to a patron and devoted to a particular theme. But the theme was only an excuse for the display of learning that followed. The *Adib* felt free to pursue his subject across a wide expanse of the scholarship that he commanded. It is here that *Adab* took on the world. Almost any subject, sacred or profane, was deemed worthy of lively scrutiny, which was often iconoclastic, always self-assured. Curiosity was infinite, and obvious pleasure was taken in the display or marshaling of argument. It was *Adab*, for example, that helped to define the relationship between Arabic/Islamic civilization on the one hand and other world civilizations on the other. On the home front, *Adab* was instrumental in establishing the parameters of the debate between reason and revelation. The literary canon as well as ethics, politics, society, and the world of nature were all regular and often skillfully interwoven *Adab* themes. Liveliest of all were the polemical essays directed at real or fictive enemies. These duels of reason, learning, and wit, some of which are still preserved, constantly broadened the horizons of what one might suggest as another congruent term for *Adab*: classical Arabic/Islamic humanism.

Another common product of *Aḋab* was the anthology. These anthologies enjoyed a heyday lasting from the ninth to the fifteenth centuries. In their various modern editions, they are still brisk sellers in bookshops throughout the Arab/Islamic world. Most of them have ornamental titles in which words like "meadow," "necklace," or "fountain" are frequent. Their introductions would normally begin with a bow in the direction of piety, the anthologist taking care to justify his activity first in strictly religious terms but then proceeding to include in his anthology, commonly divided into chapters, material that was often far from pious. One preeminent practitioner of *Aḋab*, the ninth-century al-Jahiz (d. 868), took particular delight in debunking the myth of the golden age by pointing out that the hallowed ancestors were no more nor less humanly frail than we are. If they could occasionally be outrageous, flippant, irreverent, even blasphemous, so can we. The *Aḋab* anthology becomes the mirror held up to life, and sermons, anecdotes, plenty of verse, proverbs, fables, and historical narrative, serious and ribald, are its building blocks. From these anthologies emerges the literary canon, the scripture of the secular spirit, for the anthologist of one age will frequently and lovingly copy some of the choice morsels of admired predecessors. As memorials of the tastes and fashions of a world civilization these medieval *Aḋab* anthologies are unrivaled in their richness and vitality.

Given the spirit of *Aḋab* and its well-defined pedagogical mission, style, and audience, it was natural for *Aḋibs*, anthologists and essayists alike, to view Muhammad as primarily a teacher of *Aḋab*, and to project an image of him that reflected their own concerns and preoccupations. In staking out a territory for *Aḋab* within their cultural field, the *Aḋibs* were well aware that their activity might be regarded as "secular" or at least as nonreligious. Therefore they

needed, at least in their early days, to pursue a dual strategy: to justify what they were about, and to claim Muhammad as an arche-
typal *Adib*. Most revealing in this context is the introduction to Ibn
Qutayba's (d. 889) *'Uyun al-Akhbar* (The Choicest of Narratives),
one of the most celebrated of early *Adab* anthologies:

> This work, while not devoted to Qur'an or *Sunna*, the laws of re-
> ligion or the sciences of the licit and illicit, is nevertheless a
> guide to sublime matters and noble character; it reprimands
> vileness, proscribes shameful deeds, and inspires proper man-
> agement of affairs and sound decision making, as well as le-
> niency in governance and earthly welfare. There is not one
> single path to God, nor does the whole of virtue consist in
> spending the night in prayer, continuous fasting, and knowing
> the licit and illicit. Rather, the paths to God are numerous, the
> gates of virtue are wide open, and the well-being of religion de-
> pends on the well-being of temporal matters. The well-being of
> temporal matters depends on the well-being of the ruler, which
> in turn depends, following God's grace, upon right counsel and
> sound advice. I have composed these "Choicest of Narratives"
> to act as an eye-opener for someone who is ignorant of *Adab*, as
> a reminder to scholars of religion, as an education to him who is
> in charge of people and as a relaxation to rulers.[3]

Given the mundane nature of *Adab* with its mirror held to life,
it was important for Ibn Qutayba, as it was for al-Jahiz before
him, to defend, amidst all the incitement to virtue and proper conduct, the occasional citing of profanities or obscenities of speech.
This is a prime example of how the practitioners of *Adab* insisted
upon their freedom to deal with topics far removed from the religious realm but that nevertheless reflected the variety of life accurately and candidly. Ibn Qutayba paints the following image of his
work:

This work is like a meal spread out where dishes of various tastes are displayed to satisfy the diverse desires of the meal eaters. If you encounter a report in which there is an explicit mention of a pudendum or the frank description of a debauchery, do not allow your piety, real or affected, to turn you away in contempt. Naming bodily members is not a sin. Sin resides in cursing the honor of others, in perjury and lying, and in backbiting. The Prophet, upon whom blessings and peace, said {If you hear someone consoling someone else with the consolation of the *Jahiliyya,* tell him to bite his father's thing [member], but do not mention the father's name.} When Budayl ibn Warqa' said to the Prophet, "If your followers feel the edge of steel they will surrender you," Abu Bakr said to him, "Go bite the clitoris of Al-Lat! How can we ever surrender him?!" 'Ali once said, "He who reaches the height of his father's penis will wear it as a belt" [understood to mean that a man with many brothers gains in strength].[4]

The point is then made that obscenity is sometimes unavoidable in order to serve the cause of literary naturalness, and that *Adibs* eschewed hypocrisy and affectation, but it should not be interpreted as license for the use of filthy language. It is a mark of the daring of the *Adab* practitioners that the Hadith of Muhammad quoted above was the very first to be cited by Ibn Qutayba. And while one should not perhaps make too much of this singular citation, it nevertheless serves to emphasize that *Adab* aimed at total frankness and honesty or, perhaps, at the freedom of literary "realism." In the view of these early *Adibs,* to suggest that "our pious ancestors" were a breed apart or were above all profane speech was to endow them with a status they did not possess.[5] In order to move freely in the present, there was much in *Adab* that desacralized the past.

Of the many themes and categories of *Adab,* the subject of good manners and proper conduct was of course in the forefront. Here the *Aдab* anthologists picked out from the mass of Muhammadan Hadith those sayings that best illustrated their own agenda. Muhammad is recast in the robes of the prototypical *Aдib*, dispensing wise advice on conduct, etiquette, and decorum. The immediately following, as well as later citations, are examples of Muhammad's *Aдab* drawn from diverse anthologies of the ninth to the eleventh centuries:[6]

{He who gives people to drink should be the last to drink himself.}

{It is a good custom *[дunna]* for a host to escort his guest to the door of his house.}

{If a person sits down in your company do not get up before you ask his permission.}

{Test people by finding out whom they befriend.}

{He who has no manners *[aдab]* has no reason.}

{The person walking must be the first to greet a seated person; the mounted person must be the first to greet the walking; the younger must be the first to greet the older; the one descending must be the first to greet the one ascending} [reassurance is intended].

{Both friendship and enmity are inherited.}

{From among His servants God hates the foul-mouthed, the vulgar tongued, the person who asks for favoritism and the persistent.}

{Do not let the smallness of a favor stop you from doing it.}

{Make your visits infrequent and affection for you will increase.}

{God hates a sixty-year-old masquerading as a twenty-year-old.}

{Travel and you will gain wealth; if you do not gain wealth, you will at least improve your mind.}

{Do not show pleasure at a brother's misfortune. Perhaps
God will relieve him and inflict the misfortune upon
you.}

{Show respect to those from whom you learn and to those
whom you teach.}

{Most hateful among you to me are chatterers, people
who pretend to knowledge and people who speak with
affectation.}

{If you love your brother, let him know that you love
him.}

{Gabriel asked me so insistently to be kind to neighbors
that I thought he would decree that a neighbor is to be
counted as a legal heir.}

Although many of these sayings will also be found here and
there in the canonical Hadith collections, the *Adab* anthologies
highlighted them in one place in order to show that Muhammad
was not only a legislator and prophet but also a paragon of good
manners. Tracing parallels to such sayings in ancient Near Eastern
lore would not be a difficult undertaking since the *Adib*, as argued
above, descended from a long line of intellectual ancestors. Thus,
to dress Muhammad as an *Adib* was also to dress him as heir to the
best of ancient or perennial wisdom. {I was granted perfection of
speech} was a saying of Muhammad much quoted in works of *Adab*
to justify the elaboration of this particular image of the Prophet.
His was the last divine revelation but his own words too were a
kind of summa of the best and most elegant of human speech. As
the wisdom literature of ancient Persia and Greece became widely
known, it was not uncommon for *Adibs* to quote from that literature but to point out how much more succinctly the Prophet had
phrased the same thoughts.

Another prominent theme of *Adab* is the humility and modesty

of the believer, qualities now highlighted as characteristic of the
Aðib. Muhammad points the way in such sayings as the following:

{The lord of a people is their servant.}

{Modesty is a component of faith.}

{A cloak which drags behind is bound for hell-fire.}

{Relax. I am just the son of a woman of Quraysh who
used to eat dried meat [said to a man terrified when
seeing him for the first time].}

{Do not elevate me above my rank and say about me
what the Christians say about Christ. God took me for a
servant before He took me for a prophet.}

{God created no animal more honorable than the ewe [its
pudenda are covered].}

{The Prophet would be invited to a meal of barley bread
and lard beginning to smell and would accept.}

Such sentiments carried, in addition to a personal ideal, a political message to the rulers of an empire, Umayyad first then
Abbasid, rapidly assuming the trappings of imperial authority and
ceremony, and were meant to convey a counterimage of the essential simplicity of the ideal Muslim lord, as taught by the words and
example of the Prophet.

Another salient theme, given the general orientation of *Aðab*, is
wisdom and scholarship, the attainment of which is a central preoccupation of the *Aðib*. The respect in which Muhammad held
these attainments is reflected in such sayings as:

{Take wisdom even from the tongues of polytheists.}

{Mankind are of two sorts: scholars and students. The
rest are rabble.}

{A person is a scholar so long as he seeks knowledge. If

he thinks he has attained knowledge, he is in fact
  ignorant.}
{Have pity on three kinds of people: a noble man fallen on
  evil days, a rich man who has become impoverished and
  a scholar living among ignorant people.}
{The son of Adam has acquired nothing more valuable
  than a mind which leads him to right guidance and
  holds him back from death.}
{He who knows a piece of knowledge and hides it from
  others will be punished by God by having a bridle of
  fire tied around him on the Day of Resurrection.}
{Knowledge is a cupboard whose key is a question.}
{One should not kiss another's hand unless it is the hand
  of a member of my family or the hand of a scholar.}

In these sayings knowledge appears as an unceasing and open-ended quest, undertaken by scholars whose noble and elevated station in society is exalted by the Prophet himself. The human mind is portrayed as the highest of human gifts, saving a person from spiritual or moral "death." The human mind passes beyond the confines of religion to reach out even to the wisdom of the "polytheists," otherwise bound for hell. To be noted too is the emphasis on the public character and dissemination of knowledge and the implicit warning against all arcane or restricted teaching or learning.

The last in this series of *Adab* themes is the question of poverty and riches. How does Muhammad in his guise as the prototypical *Adib* address this issue? The message, as carried in the following sayings, is not entirely one-sided:

{In conducting your business affairs, be discreet. A
  prosperous person is always an object of envy.}
{Among the signs of the Last Hour is an overflow of

wealth, a proliferation of writing and pervasiveness of
commerce.}

{The best of gifts is the one offered by one poor person to
another.}

{What is scarce but sufficient is better than what is
plentiful but distracting.}

{Whoever is granted a bounty by God, its traces should
show on him.}

{Poverty could almost be the equivalent of [or "be
regarded as being as terrible as"; or "turn into"]
unbelief.}

{The poor of my community will enter paradise 500 years
before the rich.}

{He to whom God's favors are unending will have many
people needing him. Whoever cannot bear this burden
risks being deprived of God's bounties.}

{God likes to see the traces of His bounty upon His
servants and hates those who despair and those who
pretend to be in despair.}

{O God, neither wealth that overwhelms faith nor poverty
that makes one forget faith.}

We encounter in these sayings two contrasting models of a
Muslim lifestyle. Poverty is extolled as the final winner at the end
of days. But wealth cannot be anything other than a bounty from
God, which, though burdensome, should be gratefully embraced,
even advertised. One compromise solution, as per the last saying,
seems to be a sort of mean between these two lifestyles.[7]

Undergirding these themes from *Adab* is Muhammad's natural
eloquence. The literary taste of *Adab* put a very high value on the
succinct and pithy epigram, a piece of wisdom, a sharp portrayal,
captured in the fewest possible words. Any profound idea or image gained in profundity when phrased concisely and without

affectation: less is more. This or something similar was often how eloquence was defined according to *Adab*. To illustrate Muhammad's gift of the "perfection of speech," the following are often cited as examples of his innate, uninstructed eloquence:

{When summoned to a crisis, your numbers swell; where greed is involved, your numbers shrink [said to the Ansar].}

{War is trickery.}

{Support your brother, transgressing or transgressed. If transgressed, support his cause. If transgressing, warn him.}

{Had you known each other's secret thoughts, you would not have attended each other's funerals.}

{My community will continue to live in righteousness so long as it does not regard booty as gain and almsgiving as loss.}

{Debt demeans the noble.}

{A believer is not stung twice from the same hole.}

{Envy consumes good deeds as fire consumes wood.}

{Souls are like massed troops. Those who recognize their like become allies. Those who do not, do battle.}

{He who conquers his whims is truly powerful.}

{He who sows evil reaps regret.}

{Intimate conversations presuppose confidentiality.}

{Your worst enemy is yourself.}

Most of the sayings quoted here have floated very widely in literate Muslim circles across the ages and can still be heard today, sometimes as anonymous proverbs. Almost all of them are far shorter in their original Arabic than in their translations here; thus they were attractive as pithy maxims to the *Adibs* who collected or quoted them. In many *Adab* anthologies these or similar sayings of

Muhammad will be found right at the beginning of the chapters devoted to wise or eloquent speech, as if to set the standard against which all other wisdom is to be measured.

As canons of literary taste began to develop into "schools" of criticism, beginning in the ninth century, distinguishing the various figures of speech became one prominent focus of literary criticism. Examples of such tropes were sought in the Qur'an and the hadith of Muhammad in order to defend and justify this literary activity. Of particular interest in this field is a work entitled *Prophetic Metaphors (al-Majazat al-Nabawiyya)* by the celebrated Shiite poet al-Sharif al-Radiyy (d. 1015), who selected 375 hadiths of Muhammad and, devoting a few paragraphs to each, sought to show how the Prophet's speech best illustrated the uses of metaphor. Thus:

> The Prophet said: {Beware of sins which close the eyes.} This is a metaphor. By this phrase is meant grave sins committed by a person knowingly, as if he is closing his eyes to them out of deliberate blindness though he sees them, and purposely ignores them though he recognizes them. Similar to this is a line of verse which describes a she-camel: "Closing its eyes sends it forth even if no one drives it on." In other words, a she-camel, when approaching a pool of water from which she is being driven off, is led by extreme thirst to break in upon the pool. She closes her eyes, disobeys whoever is preventing it from reaching the water and moves on to reach it regardless.[8]

In the output of *Adab*, there was almost as much poetry as prose. When the *Adibs* of the ninth century first began the search for the criteria of literary excellence, it was poetry rather than prose that supplied them with examples of such things as the various figures of speech and how such figures were used to best, or worst, effect by poets. In other words, the emergent canons of literary criticism, from Ibn al-Mu'tazz in the ninth century to 'Abd al-Qahir al-Jurjani in the eleventh, were largely preoccupied with the criteria of poetic excellence. It was here that *Adab* had to deal head-on with the problem of Muhammad *and* poetry, referred to above.[9] What exactly was that problem?

Beginning in the Qur'an and continuing with Muhammadan Hadith, there is much faultfinding, at least outwardly, in poetry and poets. The Qur'an speaks of poets as empty boasters who are accompanied by "demons" or "tempters" *(al-ghawun)*, wandering aimlessly in every valley. Where Muhammad is concerned, God proclaims at Q. 36:69: {We did not teach him poetry, nor does poetry befit him.} Additionally, we have seen already how the charge of being a poet was one that was vigorously denied by God on Muhammad's behalf, and how important it was for Muhammad's message and self-identity to distinguish divine revelation from poetry.

If we examine the Hadith collection of Muslim, which devotes a couple of pages to this topic, the overall image is far less distinct.[10] Muhammad delivers some severe verdicts on poets: {It were better for a man's innards to be filled with pus than to be filled with poetry.} When the great *Jahili* poet Imru'l Qays, a poet who enjoyed a Homeric status on the Arabian poetic platform, was mentioned in his presence, Muhammad dismissed him as follows: {He is a man celebrated and held to be noble in this world but is a complete nonentity in the world to come. When the Day of Resurrection arrives, he will be the standard-bearer of the poets and will lead them into the fire of hell.} Some poets, we are told, felt the heat of the new faith around them and lamented the consequent loss of freedom to express whatever sentiments happened to capture their fancy. Thus a libertine poet and contemporary of

Muhammad, having embraced Islam, recites the following lament to his former beloved:

> *O Umm Malik, this is no tribal covenant;*
> *Rather, chains encircle necks.*
> *A young man has become like an old man, speaking*
> *Only the truth. Those who once found fault with me can now relax.*[11]

But much of this antipoetic severity is tempered by contrary hadiths that indicate a more tolerant attitude. Thus, having listened to the verses of Umayya ibn Abi al-Salt, Muhammad reportedly said of this pre-Islamic poet: {The fellow could almost be a Muslim.} We find him also quoting the verse of another great pre-Islamic poet, Labid ("In truth, everything apart from God is illusion") and pronouncing it {The most truthful line of poetry ever uttered}. Complicating the issue is the fact that Muhammad, as we have seen above in discussing the *Sira*, retained his own poets whom he would occasionally call upon to respond in verse to poetical defamations of Muslims or to deliver eulogies when prominent Muslims fell in battle. But his disdain for poetry is underlined by the instances in the *Sira* where he misquotes a line of verse, at which point Abu Bakr corrects him and then quotes the Qur'an about God not teaching him poetry and poetry not befitting him.[12]

It was *Adab* that led the way toward the complete rehabilitation of poetry in Arabic/Islamic culture. Poetry was quite simply the bread and butter of *Adab*. It was in *Adab* circles that the famous maxim "Poetry is the archive of the Arabs" *(al-Shi'r diwan al-'Arab)* circulated most widely, thus establishing poetry as the historical memory of the Arabs and as the record of their accomplishments. It is a bold assertion, seeking a status for poetry almost as imperishable as the Qur'an itself. In fact, one can still hear some Muslim *Adibs* today proclaiming their belief that poetry is second only to the Qur'an as a repository of wisdom. In *Adab* of the eighth to the twelfth centuries, the various antipoetical statements in the Qur'an and in Muhammadan Hadith are tackled with vigor, beginning with the early critic Abu Zayd al-Qurashi (d. ca. 787):

> The Prophet, upon whom blessings and peace, was ever *(lam yazal)* an admirer of poetry, and was lauded by poets whom he invariably rewarded. He would say: {Poetry is the archive of the Arabs.} In proof thereof, I was told . . . that the Prophet said {Some poetry is wisdom; some eloquence is magic.}[13]

Abu Zayd and later critics would affirm that anyone who aspires to a true knowledge of Qur'an and Hadith has need of ancient poetry as testimony for linguistic usage. Without poetry, they argued, much of the language of the Qur'an would be obscure. As for Qur'anic strictures on poetry, a critic such as Ibn Rashiq (d. 1064) deals with them as follows:

> Some who seek to disparage poetry argue that the Qur'an, the speech of God, is in prose, and that Muhammad is not a poet, quoting the Qur'an {We did not teach him poetry, nor does poetry befit him.} They imagine their argument is irrefutable, but it can in fact be turned against them. God sent His Prophet as an illiterate person, and not as a poet, to a people who knew this about him, and at a time when eloquence had reached the height of excellence, thus providing a miraculous sign of his prophecy and a proof against mankind. God revealed His speech in prose in order to provide a more manifest proof of its superiority to poetry, for poets are usually capable of expressing any idea they like. Hence God's speech threw down a challenge to all people, poets as well as others. Just as the Qur'an rendered poets incapable of imitating it while itself not being poetry, so also it rendered orators incapable of imitating it while itself not being

oratory. With the poets the case is even more compelling. Do you not see how his enemies counted him as a poet when they were defeated and seen to be impotent? It was then that they called Muhammad a poet, because of the awe and magnificence which poetry inspired in their hearts. The words of God are thus meant to establish a manifest proof against them. As regards the Qur'anic verse about poets being accompanied by demons, those addressed in this verse are the poets of the polytheists who defamed the Prophet in their verse. The believers among poets have no truck whatsoever with this verse.[14]

It was one thing for *Aδab* to defend poetry against its enemies, these being certain conservative circles who were more impressed by the literal strictures of the Qur'an than by its liberal interpretations in *Aδab*. It was quite another thing for *Aδab* to accord the poetry in praise of Muhammad much literary value. The great early anthologies of poetry such as *al-Mufaδδaliyyat* of al-Mufaddal al-Dabbi (d. 794) and *al-Aδma 'tyyat* of al-Asma'i (d. 828) contain no verse inspired by Muhammad or even by Islamic ideals. In spirit, these anthologies are largely pagan, pre-Islamic, and epic, even though they were collected a hundred and fifty years or more after the death of the Prophet. What is the reason for this critical neglect of poetry praising Muhammad or his revelations? One clue may lie in the early judgment, which I have alluded to above, that much of this poetry is spurious and fabricated to please the pious. Another clue is even more revealing of early critical taste. Here, for example, is the verdict of the celebrated critic al-Asma'i:

If you were to lead poetry into the path of virtue, you would enfeeble it. Do you not see how Hassan ibn Thabit attained eminence in pre-Islamic as well as Islamic times but when his poetry followed the path of virtue, as in the elegies he composed on the Prophet, on Hamza, Ja'far and others, his verse became feeble [*lana*]? The path of poetry is the path of "studs" [*fuhul*], of poets like Imru'l Qays, Zuhayr and al-Nabigha, who sing of encampments and departures, defamation and panegyric, flirtation with women, the wild ass and the horse, war and glory.[15]

There is little doubt that such views did not go unnoticed or unchallenged in pietist circles, since they represented poetry, almost defiantly, as best when celebrating precisely those "virtues" least palatable to the ethos of the Qur'an and Hadith. And yet if the Qur'an was understood as attacking poetry tout court, *Adab* left its readers in little doubt that poetry was a fundamental Arabic cultural achievement. But a compromise of sorts needed to be arrived at. This compromise took the form of sayings ascribed to Muhammad in his last days, suggesting that if poetry had an ethical purpose, it could do no harm: {There is no harm in poetry for one who seeks to put right an injustice, ward off poverty or give thanks to a favor done.}[16] If other poets had "demons" to inspire or follow them, Muslim poets such as Hassan are, according to Muhammad, aided by the Holy Spirit.[17]

Because of this uneasy coexistence between two contrasting views of the function of poetry, this was a cultural arena where the "tastes" of the Qur'an and of Muhammad did not win a clear victory. Poetry, whether ribald, libertine, boastful, or downright salacious, was here to stay. And no later poem in praise of Muhammad ever acquired in *Adab* circles the renown of "Banat Su'adu."[18] Nevertheless, one could speak of certain images of Muhammad in early Islamic poetry, images that were further elaborated in the mystical or ascetic poetry of later days. Let us turn first to images of Muhammad in Umayyad poetry.[19]

Traditionally it is the great poet Jarir (d. ca. 732) who is commonly described as the most pious of the lot, and this despite both his extravagant praise of certain Umayyad rulers as well as his obscene defamation of rivals. In lauding an heir to the throne, Jarir describes him as having been foretold in sacred scripture, an honor normally reserved for Muhammad. He boasts of the "Prophet of God" as if he were an ancestral tribal hero, yet another feather in Jarir's tribal cap. Praising the great Umayyad governor of the east al-Hajjaj, he lauds him, but very much inter alia, for having restored to Mecca, after a vicious civil war, the "covenant of the Prophet." Attacking the Christians, he accuses them of worshipping the Cross and defaming "Muhammad, Gabriel and Michael." Vilifying his great poetic rival al-Farazdaq (d. ca. 728), he calls upon people to stone him if he ever enters Medina, and to keep him away from "the tomb of the Prophet."[20]

Keeping these images in mind, one cannot escape the feeling that the vast majority of verse referring to Muhammad in Umayyad poetry is perfunctory, contrived, very limited in range, and shallow in sentiment. Muhammad is a figure of speech rather than a figure of destiny. From 'Umar ibn Abi Rabi'a (d. 711), admittedly a poet of love and dalliance, but important for his nearness to the age of Muhammad, come two basic figures of speech. First, there can be no boasting higher or more elevated than boasting of the Prophet, and, second, the Prophet as an oath, "By the tomb of Muhammad!" or else "By Him who sent Muhammad with the light!"[21]

Farazdaq, a poet far more attuned to the politics of his age than the love-besotted 'Umar, is nonetheless no more fertile in poetic invention where Muhammad is concerned. There is, to begin with, the stock tribal boasting of Muhammad, "of our number is the Prophet," but sometimes in the same breath there is the boasting of pre-Islamic heroes or military exploits. The poet will sometimes boast of scattering his enemies "with a sword the like of which Muhammad met his enemies at Badr." Another image is Muhammad's excellence used as a moral standard as in "You are the best of mankind except for Muhammad" or else "None is his equal except for Muhammad," usually addressed to a caliph or royal prince. A caliph will be praised for "following the *sunna* of Muhammad" or for "judging in accordance with the religion of Muhammad," or a grandee is lauded for having had as an ancestor a close companion of Muhammad. But the panegyric can occasionally turn exceedingly fulsome, almost grotesque, as in "Had Jesus not announced Muhammad, you would have been the prophet of light," or "Had there been another prophet after Muhammad, you would have been such."[22]

Thus a grand total of five or six stereotyped descriptions of Muhammad circulated among Umayyad poets, a group otherwise judged by both ancient and modern critics as among the most gifted and imaginative in Arabic literary history. There is no Umayyad ode devoted to Muhammad, no poem that celebrates his life or his message, no epic poetry that extols his military exploits. Even the Kharijites, the famous theocratic rebels of that period, among whom were a number of outstanding poets, were strangely silent about Muhammad. It was God who summoned them to a life of martyrdom, and not His Prophet, of whom there is barely any mention in their poetry.

This will not be the end of my remarks on poetry. Other ages displayed other poetic sensibilities. But a word or two by way of conclusion to this section is obviously needed. Could this silence about Muhammad's achievement be the result solely of the poetic taste of the age, namely, that virtue corrupts poetry? Why is Muhammad perceived largely as a distant model of excellence rather than as an intimate historical personality? Could it be that a century or more after his death, the basic structure of Muhammad's life had still not constituted a literary corpus sufficiently inspiring to a poetry of the most vivid and imaginative kind? There are no obvious answers to any of these questions. One must simply register the fact that although Umayyad poetry contains extremely valuable historical information on the society and politics of its age, there is hardly any information in it that can shed light on Muhammad's *Sira*. The Prophet of Islam is statuesque, frozen in the immortality of the there and then, a distant paragon. Apart from his victory at Badr, there are very few significant references to the major turning points of his life, his praxis, or the high drama of his achievements. That Umayyad poets would dare to extol the caliphs as second only to Muhammad in virtue, or even as Muhammad might-have-beens, suggests that they were portraying an essentially heroic rather than a prophetic founder figure.

It is reported that when the famous jurist 'Abdullah ibn 'Umar (d. 693) heard the following line of verse: "When you come to him, your sight is dimmed by the light of his fire / There you will find the best of fires, and nearby the best of fire lighters," he exclaimed, "Ah, that man must be the Prophet!" The critic adds: " 'Abdullah said this out of admiration for this verse, meaning that such praise can only be deserved by the Prophet."[23] It is almost as if the scholars of the new religion in its first century of existence were looking in vain for praise of Muhammad among poets. In any case, these images of the Prophet in Umayyad poetry must be regarded as among the very earliest to develop inside the Muslim community.

The Light of the World

MUHAMMAD IN SHIITE BIOGRAPHIES

Shiite biographies of Muhammad were fashioned by a certain sensibility, mood, and interpretation of Islam that broadly speaking may be called Shiite to distinguish it from Sunni sensibility, mood, and interpretation. Whatever the complex reasons that incline religions in general to fissure, in the case of Islam one important element that led to the emergence of its two major wings, Sunnism and Shiism, was disagreement over the historical significance of certain episodes in the life of Muhammad and of his earliest successors. In fact and up to the present day, the differences between the two groups' perceptions of ʿAli and his two sons are an example of what a recent writer has called "the persistence, indeed the perils, of memory."[1]

From this disagreement sprang further disagreement concerning the role and function of political leadership in the Muslim community. If pressed to suggest a quick and readymade distinction between these two attitudes to leadership, one might argue that whereas the Sunni mood emphasized the unity *(jamaʿa)* of the community as the highest political value, the Shiite mood emphasized the integrity of the ruler as the sole guarantor of good government.[2] This integrity was the foundation of the Shiite theory of the imamate. But this is not the place to discuss at any length the genesis and evolution of Islam's great schism; let us be content to assert that the nexus of Shiite sensibility was a widespread devotion to 'Ali, cousin and son-in-law of Muhammad, that was further deepened by the tragic death of several of his descendants. This devotion found its earliest expression in grief-stricken poetry wherein devotion shaded into adoration.[3] I will turn to this poetry later, but we begin with a sketch of the early building blocks of Shiite biography.

One central point of departure of the Shiite biographical tradition was undoubtedly the Qur'anic verse Qur'an 33:33—there were others—that down the ages served as a theological foundation for the Shiite mood: {God merely wishes to ward off abomination from you, O members of the house *[Ahl al-Bayt]* and purify you, purify you completely.} The Qur'anic context is, at least in some interpretations, an address to the wives of the Prophet. But the phrase *Ahl al-Bayt* was taken by early Shiite speculative thought to mean the immediate family of Muhammad, and especially his daughter Fatima, her husband 'Ali, and their children, al-Hasan and al-Husayn, and their direct descendants. The verse was further interpreted to mean that this family was divinely endowed with sinlessness *['isma]* as a result of God's desire to "purify" them "completely." A semidivine halo was rapidly drawn around various figures of this "Holy Family," a phrase nearest in meaning to *Ahl al-Bayt* in Shiite sensibility. But a semidivine halo will often need to partake of eternity if it is to serve as a cosmological principle and a historical consciousness. This transformation from private devotion to cosmic/historical justification was energized by the concept of "Muhammadan Light" *[Nur Muhammadi]*, which goes back to a symbolic reading of Qur'an 24:35, the context here being an extended parable of the light of God. This concept is crystallized in the tenth century in the celebrated Shiite historian al-Mas'udi (d. 956):

[From 'Ali:] When God was about to create the world, he set up the images of all humanity like fine dust, before He had leveled out the earth or raised the heavens . . . He caused a light to issue from His light and to be concentrated amidst these images which then formed as the image of Muhammad. To him God said, {You are the chosen, the elect . . . for your sake I will level the earth and raise heaven . . . I will set up your family as guides and grant them of My knowledge, making them My proofs to creation.} God then received [from mankind] the confession of divinity . . . Then He mixed in with the reason of mankind the election [intikhab] of Muhammad and his progeny and showed them that guidance and light are with him and the imamate is with his family . . . Muhammad's prophecy was first proclaimed in heaven. This light continued hidden until made manifest by Muhammad . . . then the light shone in our Guides [imams]. We are the lights of heaven and earth. Through us comes salvation and true knowledge. Our *Mahdi* [a messianic figure] is the savior of the community and the ultimate object of the light.[4]

Here then, in capsule, is a divine history of the world according to which God cast His light from eternity upon Muhammad and his descendants, making them both the cause and the salvation of creation itself. The Shiite historian adduces this report directly from 'Ali, without recourse to a chain of transmitters [*isnad*]. It is thus meant to be understood as much as a meta-historical credo as a historical report. It sets the stage for an eternal pedigree spanning the course of human history, and within which the life of Muhammad is to be understood.

Given this divine pedigree of light, it was out of the question for the Shiite biographical tradition as a whole to admit any moral stain, not only among Muhammad's family past, present, and future, but among all earlier prophets as well.[5] Accordingly, Shiite biographies of Muhammad had by the tenth century at the latest their own historical consciousness, their own parameters of biographical interpretation, their own sites of memory. The ambiguities we have seen above among the Sunni founding fathers of the *Sira* regarding such issues as Muhammad's faith before his mission or his "lapses" simply do not exist in Shiite biography or else are contemptuously denied. Muhammad, his ancestors, and his descendants are all by theological necessity immaculate.

I shall now narrow the discussion by turning to two biographies of Muhammad embedded in the general histories of two prominent Shiite historians, al-Ya'qubi (d. ca. 897) and al-Mas'udi. They are both pivotal historical sources for early Islam, and one place in which their Shiism can be glimpsed is in their narration of Muhammad's life. In the days of al-Ya'qubi, one prominent wing of Shiism, later called Imami or Twelver Shiism, was about to take shape. Imami Shiism gradually focused its devotion and its salvation upon twelve imams or divinely appointed guides: 'Ali, his two sons al-Hasan and al-Husayn, followed by nine others, making a total of twelve. Both historians were Imami Shi'ites, with well-conceived strategies of interpretation.

Al-Ya'qubi takes the sixth imam in the Twelver line, Ja'far al-Sadiq (d. 765), as his authority on the essential facts and dates of Muhammad's life, for example, the marriage of his parents, his date of birth, the death of his father, the date of his earliest revelations, and so forth. It will be recalled that other biographers gave conflicting dates for several of these notable events. But al-Ya'qubi tolerates no ambiguity in such matters: how can it be otherwise if the story is outlined by God? So when al-Ya'qubi comes to narrate the lives of Muhammad's grandfather, uncle, and father, their sinless natures and purity of faith are in full view. For example, the grandfather, 'Abd al-Muttalib, is an undoubted monotheist, indeed a precursor of the Qur'an in some of the laws and regulations he instituted:

> He rejected the worship of idols and embraced the unity of God . . . He fulfilled his vows and established laws and customs most of which were later revealed by the Qur'an. The Quraysh would say, " 'Abd al-Muttalib is the second Abraham."[6]

All his progeny enjoyed honor, prestige, and glory. He would pray for rain and his prayers would be answered. Muhammad eventually pronounced him to be a glorified figure on the Day of Resurrection:

> {God shall resurrect my grandfather 'Abd al-Muttalib as a single religious community by himself, decked out in the shape of prophets and the robes of kings.}[7]

Not a hint remains here of the uncertainty surrounding 'Abd al-Muttalib's ultimate fate in the biographies of the founding fathers or in Sunni Hadith. When al-Ya'qubi comes to the other central male figure in the family, Muhammad's uncle Abu Talib, the first of his qualities is his worldly prestige:

> [From 'Ali:] My father was a lord [of Quraysh] though poor, and no poor man before him was ever a lord.[8]

Abu Talib's wife Fatima, mother of 'Ali, about whom we hear little or nothing from the founding fathers, is portrayed as a virtuous Muslim woman who brought up the orphan Muhammad and was a surrogate mother for him.[9] In al-Ya'qubi's biography Abu Talib himself is far more cognizant of the merits of Muhammad's religion than he is in other biographical traditions. Why is this cognizance not made public? It may be recalled that in non-Shiite bi-ographies, several explanations are offered as to why Abu Talib re-fused to embrace the faith of his nephew. In al-Ya'qubi the answer is unambiguous: Abu Talib recognizes Muhammad's prophetic calling from the very beginning but wishes this fact to remain hid-den because of the enmity of the unbelievers. To dispel all doubt regarding Abu Talib's ultimate fate, al-Ya'qubi quotes a hadith from Muhammad that four people were to be saved from Hell as per a promise from God Himself:

{God promised me [salvation] for four people: My father, my mother, my uncle [Abu Talib] and a close friend I had in the *Jahiliyya.*}[10]

'Ali's role in the *Sira* is, as to be expected, pivotal. He is beyond doubt the first male believer. He is divinely elected and aided to protect Muhammad on the night of his *Hijra* to Medina. His mar-riage to Fatima, daughter of Muhammad, is ordained by God. In the military expeditions *[Maghazi]* of Muhammad, the spotlight is on 'Ali's heroism and his steadfastness. He repeatedly wards off danger from Muhammad at crucial battles such as Uhud, Hunayn, and Khaibar. At Hunayn, only 'Ali and nine other Hashimites stand fast, all other Muslims having fled the field. This last incident is meant to cover with glory both 'Ali and the other descendants of Abu Talib (the Talibids).[11] The Holy Family is thus at the very heart of the military drama as they had been at the heart of the di-vine message itself.

Finally, at the death of Muhammad, a voice was heard pro-claiming the following message:

"Peace be upon you, members of the house . . . {God merely wishes to ward off abomination from you, oh members of the house, and purify you, purify you completely} . . . You shall be severely tested in your property and persons and shall hear much harmful talk from those who possessed the Book before you and from the polytheists. It is more resolute for you to be patient and pious. God is the best consolation for anyone who dies or is afflicted." I [narrator] asked Ja'far al-Sadiq, "Who did you take that voice to be?" He answered, "Gabriel."[12]

This is a projection into the future of the trials and tribulations of the family of Muhammad and what they were destined to suffer at the hands of believers and nonbelievers alike. These lives of sorrow are an axial element in all Shiite historiography of Muhammad and his descendants, and of course of all Shiite sensibility, recalling in this instance the phrase of Virgil: "There are tears in the nature of things" *(Sunt lacrimae rerum)*. From a Shiite perspective, the *Sira* is haunted by the specter of the tears to come, and to read the *Sira* with true understanding is to bewail the ingratitude and indifference of other non-Shiite Muslims toward Muhammad's progeny. Here is the Shiite poet Di'bil (d. 860) mourning the martyrdom of al-Husayn (d. 680):

> *The head of the son of the daughter of Muhammad and of his heir*
> (wasiyy)
> *—O men, listen!—is raised upon a spear.*
> *And the Muslims see and hear,*
> *Filled neither with anguish nor with pious fear.*[13]

Crucial to the Shiite case, political as well as religious, is the incident at Ghadir Khumm, a station on the road from Mecca to Medina. At Ghadir Khumm, Muhammad, while making his way back to Medina after completing his last, or "Farewell" pilgrimage, is said to have made a public statement delegating his authority to 'Ali. In al-Ya'qubi, the incident is reported as follows:

The Prophet set off at night for Medina, and reached a place near al-Juhfa called Ghadir Khumm. This incident took place on the 18th of the month of Dhu al-Hijja. He stood up to speak in public, took 'Ali's hand in his own and said {Am I not closer *[alastu awla]* to the Muslims than they are to themselves?} Indeed, O Prophet of God, they replied. He continued, {Whoso among you considers me as his lord *[mawla]* 'Ali is his lord. O God, befriend whoever takes him as his friend and show enmity to whoever shows him enmity.}[14]

The Prophet adds that he will appraise his community on the Last Day by how well they put the Qur'an into practice and how well they treated his family.

A lot of ink (and blood) has been spilt over this incident in Muslim historiography and intra-polemical scholarship. Did Muhammad mean by this declaration an explicit delegation of political authority to 'Ali (the Shiite view) or was it a mere expression of esteem and amity toward him (the Sunnite view)? The founding fathers, it should be noted, say not a word about this incident, although it was widely known in their times. Thus the celebrated essayist al-Jahiz (d. 868), a staunch anti-Shiite, alludes to this incident and argues roughly as follows: If true, how is it that 'Ali himself never cited this incident as an argument against his innumerable opponents?[15] But perhaps I am drawing the line too sharply between the two interpretations of Ghadir Khumm. Thus, the great Sunni Hadith master Ibn Hanbal (d. 855), not exactly a friend of the Shiites, nevertheless includes the incident in his Hadith collection, but without comment, as do a few other Sunnite traditionalists. But where the founding fathers are concerned, the fact that they ignored the whole incident may stem, inter alia, from thinking that it was without substance, or else from their desire to avoid arousing the passions of sectarianism.

Let us now turn to the other celebrated Shiite historian, al-Mas'udi, for his treatment of the Prophet's life in his two surviving works of history.[16] We have already encountered al-Mas'udi and his account of the creation and of the "Light of Muhammad." Given this account of the genesis and evolution of human history, it was first of all necessary to rearrange the whole history of prophecy in order to substantiate the relationship between Muhammad and 'Ali. If 'Ali was Muhammad's heir and delegate *(wasiyy)* through an explicit delegation *(nass)*, the case for this would be greatly strengthened if it could be shown that all previous prophets also had their own explicitly designated delegates. This interest in the history of prophecy, common among Sunni historians, was intense and more theological in Shiite historiography of all hues. Al-Mas'udi was one of the earliest Shiite historians to pay sustained attention to this dual, Prophet/Delegate, manifestation of the prophetic phenomenon. He tells us that this interpretation of prophetic history was in fact a bone of contention among Muslims:

> This is a point of contention among the people of our religion between those who argue for explicit delegation *(nass)* and others who argue for choice. Those who argue for an explicit delegation are the party of the Imamate from among the followers of 'Ali and the pure among his progeny. They argue that God *did not leave any age free from the presence of a figure who calls for God in truth, whether he be a prophet or a delegate,* whose names and exact identities are explicitly designated by God and His Messenger. (Italics mine)[17]

Down the ages prophets are shadowed by "delegates" who at times accompany major prophets as the truest interpreters of their messages and at other times act as divine guides (imams) who ensure God's continuing concern and benevolence for His creation.[18]

The prime example of the interpretative role played by these "delegates" is the relationship between Moses and Aaron, or between Jesus and Peter, where Aaron and Peter act as the truest guides to the prophet's mission. It is finally and most illuminatingly exemplified in the relationship between Muhammad and 'Ali. The prime example of the second role of these delegates is the line of imams issuing from Muhammad through the line of 'Ali and Muhammad's daughter, Fatima. The "Light of Muhammad" shines constantly upon the foreheads of this processional of prophets, delegates, and imams.

This religious history of the world is one wherein the divine truth is accessible but where its full dimensions are not always visible. But as Muhammad's time draws near, God's plan becomes clearer. In pre-Islamic Arabia, destined to be the final home of revelation, religious perception is more acute than anywhere on earth. A quickening in the process of revelation through prophets is discernible as the divine plan unfolds toward its final disclosure. Naturally, many of the eleventh-hour prophets are Arabian. They await Muhammad's coming and sing his praises.

But when we come at last to al-Mas'udi's biographical treatment of Muhammad, its form and presentation are seen to be nearer to the catalog style than to a polished literary narrative. Arranged chronologically are the bare facts of the Prophet's birth, mission, expeditions, and so forth, without further elaboration, although the dates he accepts are always those "current among the family of Muhammad and their party (Shi'a)."[19] Immediately afterward, he tells us that he purposely chose to present Muhammad's life in the form of an epitome (jawami') to make it user-friendly to scholars and students. This was not an uncommon form for other biographies of Muhammad to take, before and after al-Mas'udi's time.

But the most significant theological issue in the career of Muhammad is clearly his relationship to 'Ali. 'Ali stalks Muhammad like no other Companion. Such questions as 'Ali's "sinlessness" (*'isma*), that is, whether he was an unbeliever before his conversion or followed Muhammad at all stages of his religious development, are salient issues of the biography. Then again, whether 'Ali was the first male Muslim, and how old he was when he converted are questions that seem to have deeper theological connotations for Muhammad's mission itself. Only Shiite views are given credibility. 'Ali was emphatically sinless, emphatically the first male Muslim, and definitely a discerning young lad rather than a gullible child at the time of his conversion, as suggested by many Sunni *Siras*.

It should be added here that al-Mas'udi's Shiism was not narrow-minded or imitative.[20] He set out to portray a world order in which the elevation of a certain family to the status of recipients of divine inspiration, the 'Alid imams, was a necessary, indeed rational component. That God was not solely a Creator-Judge but also a constant Guardian of His universe was to al-Mas'udi self-evident. Muhammad's revelations consummated divine revelations in a prophetic sense but introduced divine guidance in a messianic sense. Mankind, always in need of political and religious guidance, could not change its nature even after the advent of Muhammad, the "Seal" of Prophecy. It was an important aspect of the justice of God that mankind would always stand in need of a just ruler or guide, and it was precisely the absence of such a ruler or guide that signaled the onset of social chaos and political disorder.

By and large, Shiite scholars did not enter the field of prophetic *Sira* in any substantial manner, preferring to concentrate their biographical attention on 'Ali and his progeny.[21] But there were a few notable exceptions. One of them was the famous Shiite Qur'an commentator al-Tabrisi (d. 1154), whose work *I'lam al-Wara bi*

A'lam al-Hu∂a (Acquainting Mankind with the Great Figures of Right Guidance), devoted mainly to the biographies of the twelve imams of Shiism, begins with a Muhammadan *Sira*. This is a *Sira* that, on the face of it, contains a large number of biographical items in common with the work of the founding fathers. Read with care, however, the *Sira* of Muhammad as told here is not complete and self-sufficient but constantly looks forward to the story of 'Ali and his progeny who, in an esoteric or gnostic fashion, complete or complement or fulfill or make fully clear the message of Muhammad.

In explanation of the two terms "esoteric" and "gnostic" let us recall once again the "Light of Muhammad" passage cited above.[22] This light that God cast from the beginning of creation upon Muhammad *an∂* his progeny was seen by Shiite scholars of the ninth century—or perhaps earlier—as the light of a special, God-given knowledge, by reason of which the Prophet's progeny, the 'Alid imams, could act as divinely inspired guides to the community. For a Shiite biographer, it was important to show that this divinely selected line of imams had been referred to in earlier scriptures or revelations. In other words the imams needed to be reinscribed in prophetic history as firmly as Muhammad himself. In a typical passage, a quote in Hebrew attributed to "Moses in the Torah" is translated as follows:

"I [God] have accepted the prayer of Isma'il, I have blessed him, made him grow in strength, and multiplied his number through a descendant of his called Muhammad, whose number is 92. *I shall cause twelve imams, kings, to issue from his progeny and grant him a nation of great multitude.*" (Italics mine)[23]

This special knowledge was communicated *in secret*; it is a privileged and supernatural knowledge that undergirds the prophetic message, making the imams masters of all the sciences of creation, including all earlier revelations and all the languages of the world.[24] It follows that the Muhammadan message has two aspects, one exoteric and the other esoteric. The first is the message in its outward or literal dimension.[25] But the Prophet also taught a more secret or esoteric message, to which only the privileged have access through contact with its purveyors, the Shiite imams. The process of handing over this supernatural knowledge from the Prophet to ʿAli took place when Muhammad was on his deathbed:

> As the Prophet lay on his death-bed, he said, {Summon my brother and companion} and was then overcome with weakness. [Abu Bakr and ʿUmar were summoned in succession but the Prophet turned his face away from them.] Umm Salama [wife of the Prophet] said, "Summon ʿAli. He wants no one else." When ʿAli was called, he drew near until his face was close to the Prophet's. The Prophet spoke in private to him for a long time. ʿAli then rose and sat to the side until the Prophet became unconscious. He then left. People said to him, "O Abu'l Hasan, what did the Prophet intimate to you?" ʿAli replied, "The Prophet taught me a thousand chapters [gates] of knowledge, each chapter opening a further thousand. He bequeathed to me knowledge of what I shall do, God willing."[26]

This scene sets the stage for the transmission of the testament (waṣiyya) from the Prophet to ʿAli and his line. But we do not need to wait for the deathbed scene to detect this divinely instituted bond between the Prophet and his Waṣiyy, the heir and guardian of the message. Throughout the Sira of Tabrisi, ʿAli enjoys total and unchallenged prominence. He is by the Prophet's side at every single major event of his life. Even when the Prophet emigrated from Mecca to Medina (Hijra), which most other accounts agree he did with only Abu Bakr and two others for companions, the event is narrated in such a way that Muhammad waits outside

Medina for fifteen days until 'Ali can join him for the triumphal entry into the city:

> The Prophet of God waited [outside Medina] for fifteen days.
> Abu Bakr came to him and said, "Prophet of God, I wish you
> would enter the city for its people are most anxious to receive
> you among them." The Prophet answered {I shall not move
> from this spot until my brother 'Ali joins me.} The Prophet had
> sent 'Ali a message to join him with his family. Abu Bakr said,
> "I doubt whether 'Ali will join you soon." The Prophet replied
> {Indeed he will. He will speed here, God willing.} After fifteen
> days, 'Ali arrived with his family.[27]

When the mosque of Medina was being built, the Prophet laid out plots of land for himself and his companions round about where they could build their chambers and where their doors abutted onto the mosque. But God willed otherwise:

> The angel Gabriel descended upon the Prophet and said to him,
> "God commands you to order all those whose doors abut onto
> the mosque to close them. No door will abut onto the mosque
> except your door and that of 'Ali, and 'Ali can use it the same
> way you do." His companions were angered as was Hamza who
> said, "I am his [Muhammad's] uncle and he orders me to close
> my door but leaves open my nephew's door, who is younger
> than me?!" The Prophet came to him and said {O uncle, do not
> be angry because of the closure of your door while 'Ali's door
> remains open. I swear to God, it was not me who issued the or-
> der but God. It was God who commanded your door closed and
> leaving open the door of 'Ali.}[28]

This image of 'Ali as a "gate" to knowledge and true religious devotions echoes a well-known Shiite hadith of Muhammad: {I am the city of knowledge and 'Ali is its gate.} This "keeper of the gate" image confers upon 'Ali a position of ultimate authority on all matters Islamic: he is literally the key to understanding the message of Muhammad.

In conformity with the gnostic role assigned to 'Ali and his line, there occurs what one might describe as a rearrangement of the salience of the chief characters of the *Sira*. Towering figures such as Abu Bakr, 'Umar, and 'A'isha recede into the background, becoming either minor actors of no great significance or else characters whose motives, deeds, and words are shrouded in obscurity and no small measure of bad faith. To appreciate the full extent of this Shiite rearrangement of roles, one might recall that in an influential Sunni *Sira* like that of al-Baladhuri, for instance, Abu Bakr and 'Umar are everywhere, advising, supporting, and faithfully following their Prophet. When al-Baladhuri reaches the end of his *Sira*, he reproduces Muhammad's verdicts on these two figures: (1) A woman came to the Prophet to ask him for something. He said to her {Come back later.} She said, "Suppose I do not find you when I return?"—alluding to the possibility of his death. He replied {If you return and do not find me, go and see Abu Bakr.} (2) The Prophet said {I do not know how long I shall remain with you. Emulate those who come after me}—and he pointed to Abu Bakr and 'Umar.[29]

Further Sunni hadiths of Muhammad specifically designate Abu Bakr as the successor of the Prophet, as in the following report from 'A'isha:

When the Prophet was in his last illness, he said to me {Summon your father and brother so that I may write a document *(kitaban)* in favor of Abu Bakr for I fear the loose talk and ambitions of some people, but God and the believers will accept none other than Abu Bakr.}[30]

In Shiite *Siras*, on the other hand, the animus against these two figures appears, if anything, to have increased with the passage of time as between al-Mas'udi and al-Tabrisi. Abu Bakr and 'Umar are not only consumed with jealousy of 'Ali but are even made to witness the delegation of authority made at Ghadir Khumm and to renege on their oath of fealty to 'Ali when the Prophet passed away. There are strong hints of their treachery, or at least hypocrisy, in this regard:

> Among those who praised him highly on that occasion [at Ghadir Khumm] was 'Umar ibn al-Khattab who said to him, "Bravo, 'Ali! You have become my master *[mawla]* and the master of every believer, male and female."[31]

In the Shiite *Siras* 'A'isha, daughter of Abu Bakr, and Hafsa, daughter of 'Umar, both being preeminent wives of Muhammad in the Sunni tradition, are castigated by the Prophet in his last hours and compared by him to the ladies who attempted to seduce Joseph in the Qur'an:

> When the Prophet was in his last illness, Bilal came at the time of morning prayers and announced, "It is prayer time, God's mercy upon you." The Prophet said {Let someone lead the prayers.} 'A'isha said, "Let Abu Bakr lead the prayers," while Hafsa said, "Let 'Umar do so." The Prophet said {Desist. You are like the lady friends of Joseph} [who tried to seduce him in Qur'an 12:33ff].[32]

In the Shiite version of these crucial events there exists what might be described as an atmosphere of conspiracy with the aim of deliberately excluding 'Ali from succession despite the clear mandate issued by the Prophet, and so to retell the story as to cast suspicion on the motives of those who denied 'Ali's right to rule or attempted to thwart his succession. In the *Sira* of Tabrisi, however, this is done with care, innuendo being more common than outright condemnation. Thus, an incident like the *Ifk*, wherein 'A'isha's virtue was impugned and later vindicated by revelation, and during which 'Ali in the Sunni tradition advised the Prophet to divorce her, is passed over in almost complete silence by Tabrisi. In other words, there was a limit to the lengths that Shiite *Siras* could go in redrawing the portraits of the central figures of Muhammad's life, that limit being the explicit censure of the venerable figures who surrounded Muhammad. Yes, one could get away with downgrading them, with pulling them down a peg or two or three on the ladder of esteem while upgrading Muhammad's immediate family, for example, his daughter Fatima, a somewhat distant figure in Sunni *Siras*, and of course 'Ali and his progeny.[33] The Shiite *Sira* writer would on the whole resort to allusion and innuendo in this regard in an attempt to win the argument of history but would exercise care not to inflame communal passions. In this respect, the Shiite scholar was not very different in strategy from someone like the great Sunni historian al-Tabari (d. 923), who tells his readers on a number of occasions that he refrained from narrating the full details of certain controversial incidents in early Islam because of their "repugnant nature."[34] The *Sira* was a battlefield but the battle had its rules and the "weapons" needed to be deployed with care. The potential cost of inciting communal strife was enormous. Given the horror inspired in the hearts and minds of scholars, both Sunni and Shiite, by the specter of civil unrest *(fitna)*, it was important wherever possible to avoid inflammatory opinions and to put the spin on the message with subtlety and caution.

Shiism of all varieties produced a great deal of poetry in its first four or five centuries, and modern scholarship has not paid any sustained attention to it as a historical, biographical, or theological source.[35] I attempt a survey here of a few Shiite poets in order to round out the various Shiite images of Muhammad sketched above. The poets range from about the seventh to about the thirteenth centuries and although they do not by any means exhaust the poetic corpus, they have always been highly regarded by Arabic/Islamic literary critics. It is by and large a poetry of passionate veneration of Muhammad as a luminous figure who passed on his legacy to an equally luminous line of descendants and is thus quite distinct in sentiment from the poetry, already examined, which celebrates him as a glorified Arabian hero.

If the poetry attributed to him is genuine, Abu'l Aswad al-Du'ali (d. 688) would clearly be one of the earliest poets to proclaim the love of 'Ali and his family as essential to faith and salvation:

I love Muhammad with a passionate love
as I do 'Abbas, Hamza and the *Waṣiyy*.
I love them through love of God so that
I present myself, when resurrected, impeccable.
A love I was bequeathed ever since
the windmills of Islam turned, a love unequalled.
The sarcastic men of the tribe of Qushayr say to me
"Do not ever forget 'Ali!!"
Sons of the Prophet's uncle and his kin
these are of all mankind my greatest loves.
If love of them is rational, I hit the mark,
if irrational, I do not thereby sin.[36]

If genuine, these verses, while extolling 'Ali, also seem to include in the poet's circle of love a wider love for Muhammad's pa-

ternal uncles. This is not untypical of some very early Shiite sentiments, although one cannot use these sentiments to argue for the
authenticity of the verse. Notable here is a common Shiite creed
that love of the Holy Family is a prerequisite for salvation.

Far better authenticated is the verse of Kuthayyir 'Azza (d.
723), an Umayyad poet often favorably compared by critics to the
most illustrious poets of the Umayyad age. Kuthayyir's Shiism is
said to have been fanatical, his loyalty being apparently directed
at Muhammad ibn al-Hanafiyya (d. ca. 700), a son of 'Ali by a
woman other than Fatima, the daughter of Muhammad. It seems
that Kuthayyir believed that Ibn al-Hanafiyya was not dead, only
invisible, and that he would reappear as a conquering hero:

> *Truly the* imams *from Quraysh*
> *the just rulers, are fully four in number.*
> *'Ali and three of his sons*
> *these are the grandsons, no hiding the fact.*
> *One grandson is a grandson of faith and virtue*
> *and one grandson was buried at Karbala.*
> *One grandson the eye sees not until*
> *he leads the chargers, the pennant at their head.*
> *He is concealed, invisible to them awhile*
> *at Mount Radwa, feeding on honey and water.*[37]

The legend of the "Sleeping Hero," well known in many cultures, serves in this instance to comfort the sorrowing faithful that
a "grandson" of Muhammad will reappear to put mat-
ters right and avenge the ghastly persecutions of the Holy Family.
That Ibn al-Hanafiyya was not a grandson of Muhammad but only
a stepbrother of the two who were (al-Hasan and al-Husayn), suggests that in the eyes of some devotees membership in the Holy
Family extended laterally to cousins of Muhammad and their is-

sue. In other verses praising Ibn al-Hanafiyya, Kuthayyir describes him thus:

> He bears the name of the Chosen [Muhammad] and is his cousin
> ever unlocking fetters, ever relieving those in debt.
> Great of spirit, does not barter falsehood for right guidance,
> in his devotion to God cares not for any reprimand.
> We, God be thanked, recite his book
> here in Khayf, Khayf of sacred spaces,
> Where pigeons are free from danger, at peace,
> where an enemy is like an ally and friend.[38]

Ibn al-Hanafiyya is the Prophet redivivus, who reestablished the sanctuary, revived the moral order and received revelations. This is confirmed in stories related of Kuthayyir that he would pass by children of the 'Alid family and exclaim, "By my father, these are the little prophets!"

Kuthayyir's contemporary al-Kumayt (d. 743) ranged more widely in his celebrations of Muhammad's family. The Holy Family now springs from the seed of Hashim, great-grandfather of Muhammad, greatly extending its scope. The amatory prelude, common in the poetry of the age and directed at some beloved, named or unnamed, is scorned in favor of the true love of the poet, the members of the house of Hashim. It is they who "entrench the foundations of Islam," who are the champions of justice, who protect the weak, and whose knowledge is a gift from God. The poet writes:

> They are the family of the man of true speech
> Abu'l Qasim [Muhammad], the branch of the highest of lords.
> He who was best among the living and among the dead
> of Adam's brood, leaders or led.

When buried he was best among the dead
ever to have been laid in a tomb.
Best of infants, of sucklings, of babes in cradles
best of infants weaned.
Best of lads, then of young men, then of adult men
best lad, best young man, best adult.
God saved our skins from the precipice of hell
through him, a bounty from the Bountiful.
Not tempted by this world, his name is truth
his glory abiding while rocks last.[39]

The ode goes on to praise other Hashimites such as Muhammad's paternal cousin Ja'far, and his uncles Hamza and al-'Abbas but reserves special love for 'Ali and his two sons, heroic in victory, tragic in defeat.

In what is probably the most famous ode of the poetic corpus, commonly referred to as the *Hashimiyyat* (poems in praise of the Hashimites), al-Kumayt begins by abjuring all love except the love of the "Family of Muhammad," expresses the view that many verses of the Qur'an point to the family's right to rule, and then tackles the question of the Prophet's inheritance. Who are his heirs? The ruling Umayyads claimed Muhammad died without heirs:

They [the Umayyads] say: "We inherited it
[the caliphate] from fathers and mothers"
but no father or mother ever made you inherit it.
They claim they have rights and duties due from people
Nonsense! The rights of the Hashimites are more binding.
It is through the legacies of the son of Amina [Muhammad]
that men of east and west obey you.
They say he [Muhammad] left no heirs.
But were it not for his inheritance
his heirs would be the tribes of Bakil and Arhab,

'Ikk, Lakhm, Sakun and Himyar
Kinda, Bakr and Taghlib.[40]

The poet's argument is that if indeed Muhammad died leaving no heirs, no single Arab tribe has a better right to rule than any other. Roughly the same gallery of Hashimite figures is paraded and praised, and the poem ends with a description of the poet, mounted on his camel, roaming the lands in search of them.

The figure of Muhammad is captured in a number of images: he is a "shining lantern," "purest in descent from Eve to Amina," "transmigrating from age to age," "the love of his kin is true faith," "glorious in this life and the next, like two water buckets ever full for those who drink from them." 'Ali on the other hand is "chosen" by Muhammad, indeed by God, at Ghadir Khumm. To restore the true order of politics and nature, a Hashimite will arise who will usher in a "new spring" and cleanse the land of its ills.

A half century later, Shiism produced yet another outstanding poet, al-Sayyid al-Himyari (d. ca. 793), who alleged that he received his poetic calling in a dream, and from no less a person than the Prophet himself. From then on, al-Sayyid takes his mission to be to praise the 'Alids and defame their enemies, in verse that was much admired but also much feared, and sometimes even selectively excised, for its "extremism." There is great audacity in al-Sayyid's verse, to the point that in one ode he appropriates the voice of the Prophet:

Has it not reached you, and news does spread
what Muhammad said, as related,
To the possessor of his knowledge, the rightly guided 'Ali
as Khawla, a little girl, pranced in the house?
"Do you not see that Khawla will give birth to one
whose fire will blaze, pure of character, dauntless?
He shall bear my kunya [patronymic] and my name for

I bestowed them on him and on the Mahdi, after me.
He shall be made invisible to them until they say
'A tomb enfolds him in Tiba' [Medina].
For years and months he shall be seen in Radwa
in a mountain pass, with leopards and lions,
Living among gazelles, oryx
and young ostrich, going and coming as friends.
The wild beasts protect them and from them
they meet with no harm.
Through him they are secure from death
grazing in peace at meadow or spring."[41]

The man in the mountain is of course the same Ibn al-Hanafiyya we have encountered above. Khawla is his mother, the wife of 'Ali. This image of his living in perfected nature is drawn by the Prophet himself, and in most of al-Sayyid's verse the Prophet is really little more than the holy ancestor who guarantees the holiness of the family. More telling are the verses celebrating an early Shiite hadith, but found also in some Sunni hadith, which relates how al-Hasan and al-Husayn as young children would climb upon their grandfather's back, now taken to hold symbolic meaning:

The Prophet came upon Hasan and Husayn
sitting and playing in a corner.
He said, "I offer my life for you!" and then greeted them
for they were very dear to him.
So they sprang up, his shoulders beneath them:
how glorious the mount and its two riders!
Two boys, their mother being virtuous
made chaste for the chaste man.
Their sire is Ibn Abi Talib ['Ali]:
how glorious the children and their parents![42]

This is fairly typical of the way al-Sayyid builds his verse: Muhammad is introduced at the very beginning of an ode only to yield pride of place to the Holy Family whose excellence and right guidance is thereafter celebrated or defended. In his polemics with other Muslim groups al-Sayyid was frequently intemperate, going so far as to pronounce 'Ali a "prophet." This, when combined with some pronouncements by Kuthayyir, would suggest that in certain early Shiite circles, the Qur'anic description of Muhammad as the "Seal of Prophets" was not understood to mean that prophecy ended with him.

There is much in the poetry of al-Sayyid that throws considerable light on early Shiite belief and practice. But this does not concern us directly here except as it relates to the images of Muhammad. In al-Sayyid's verse, Muhammad is almost always mentioned in conjunction with his family: it is *Al Muhammad* who are at center stage. It is *their* sufferings and *their* promise of salvation that grieve but eventually comfort the true believers.

One other early Shiite poet deserves consideration in order to round out our discussion of this particular poetic corpus: Di'bil ibn 'Ali al-Khuza'i (d. 860). We have met him above, bewailing the martyrdom of Husayn and the apathy of the Muslims. But in Di'bil's time much had changed since the days when al-Sayyid and Kuthayyir mourned their absent hero, living amidst perfected nature and waiting to descend in final victory. The Shiites, for reasons too numerous to go into here, were in the mid-ninth century in the process of focusing their devotions upon one particular line of the 'Alids, soon to become known as Imami or Twelver Shiism. Imam number eight of this line, 'Ali al-Rida (d. 818), had won this particular family line enormous public prestige through being nominated by the caliph al-Ma'mun (d. 833) as his successor.[43] It looked for a brief while as if the Holy Family was finally coming into its own, but these hopes were soon dashed, putting what proved to be a final end to the political ambitions of this particular Shiite line. Thereafter, pacifism was to become entrenched in their theology of pious expectation, and Di'bil was a product of this new age of quietism, of long-suffering piety. Gone from his verse is any hope of *speedy* liberation from woe, although hope of eventual triumph is not gone. In the forefront is a poetry of deepest love for the Holy Family and deepest sorrow for the fate of its members and for the indifference of the Muslims. Di'bil's verse frequently captures in a poetic tableau certain incidents in the life of Muhammad, turned almost always to 'Ali's advantage:

> *'Ali mounted upon the shoulders of the Prophet Muhammad:*
> *Has any but 'Ali ever broken idols?*[44]

Another such incident concerns the hadith that has Muhammad enfolding in his cloak 'Ali, Fatima, and his two grandchildren, thereafter referred to as "The People of the Cloak":

> *By my father and mother! Five have I loved*
> *for the sake of God, not of some gift received.*
> *By my father! The Prophet Muhammad and his Wasiyy*
> *the two pure beings, his daughter and her two sons.*[45]

The incident at Ghadir Khumm is poeticized as follows, the verse functioning as drama:

> *He ['Ali] is assuredly pure, chaste, purified*
> *quick to virtuous and blessed deeds.*
> *As a young man and as an adult, best of both,*
> *most generous in times of distress.*
> *Bravest in heart, truest of brothers*
> *greatest in glory and kinship.*

Brother of the Chosen One [Muhammad], nay son in law and Wasiyy
from among all mankind, ever drawing a veil over sin.
Like Aaron to Moses, and this I assert in defiance of a group
of despicable hypocrites, wrinkled of skin.
He [Muhammad] said: "Verily, of whosoever among you I am master
this man here is master after my death.
He is my brother, my Wasiyy, *my cousin, my heir*
he shall settle my debts with all my enemies."[46]

Di'bil's most famous ode is an elegy on the disasters that befell the Holy Family, from which the following is a selection.[47] After beginning with a scene of desolation, quiet weeping, and memories recollected in sorrow, the poet continues:

Do you not see the days, and what evil they brought
upon people, what ruin, what long exile!
How, then, and from where can one seek closeness
to God, following prayer and fasting,
Save through love for the sons of the Prophet and his companions
and hatred of Umayyad matriarchs?
It was their brood that renounced the Qur'an's covenant and its law
shrouding its clear verses in falsehood and doubt.
The men of the Saqifa *gained rule*
not through claiming inheritance, but through spite.[48]
Had they offered the reins to the designated heir
matters would have been entrusted to one free of misdeeds,
Brother of the Seal of Prophets, purified of blemish
conqueror of heroes in battle.
If they deny his right, the Ghadir is his proof
as also Badr and Uhud, lofty of peaks.
O you who have inherited the knowledge of the Prophet, you his family
upon you peace, ever its breezes blowing!

He proceeds with a song of lamentation, contrasting the fate of the women of the Holy Family with that of the women of their tormentors:

> *The daughters of Yazid*[49] *in palaces, secluded in luxury*
> *while the Family of the Prophet of God roam the deserts?*
> *The Family of the Prophet of God with bloodied mounts*
> *while the family of Ziyad are safe on their camels?*
> *The women of the family of the Prophet of God*
> *are driven into captivity while the women of the family of Ziyad are*
> *decked out in wedding bowers?*
> *The family of the Prophet of God are emaciated in body*
> *while the family of Ziyad are thick in the neck?*

None who claim to love Muhammad can possibly fail to love his kin, and none who seek paradise can attain it save through love of that kin. Di'bil finds it extraordinary that Jews and Christians enjoy safety and security through loving their own prophets, false as this belief may be, while those who love the family of Muhammad are persecuted.

Here then is a sample of the ways in which Shiite poetry adds to the tapestry of Muhammad's images. A sanctity attaches to him in this poetry, a radiance that emanates from him and encircles his family. But the tragedies of his descendants are also *his* tragedy, and if in other biographies he is a victorious prophet, in Shiite sensibility he is a prophet disowned and disinherited by his ungrateful community. Hence his memory could not be recollected in tranquility but would be forever suffused with the tears of his true devotees.

VI

The Model Mystic

MUHAMMAD IN SUFI LITERATURE

The Sufi, or mystical, tradition in Islam continues to attract a great deal of both scholarly and popular attention from non-Muslim circles. On the scholarly level a large body of Sufi literature now exists in competent translations into European languages, while on the popular level many contemporary converts to Islam continue to come to the religion through exposure to Sufism. By way of contrast, the twentieth century witnessed a steady erosion in the popularity of Sufism and Sufi orders throughout the Muslim world, even though many celebrated modernist Muslim poets owe their inspiration to Sufi imagery or diction. Present-day Islamic activists view Sufism with suspicion and perceive it as pacifist and marginal, a judgment that is not entirely accurate given the long history of Sufi activism up to and including that of the nineteenth century.

In pursuing the images of Muhammad, my readers should keep in mind that my concern here is with Sufi texts and not with Sufi popular devotions and hymns of praise for the Prophet, of which there is a sizable corpus.[1] The Sufi texts on the other hand will often seem to readers familiar with, say, equivalent Jewish or

Christian texts, to emanate from the same mystical origin or pool of imagery. Consider as an example a well-known Sufi work, *Al-Isharat al-Ilahiyya* (Divine Allusions), by the celebrated *Adib* and Sufi Abu Hayyan al-Tawhidi (d. ca. 1023). From beginning to end, the work could easily belong to the canon of any monotheist mysticism one cares to name. Containing almost no allusions to Muhammad, and pruned of its Qur'anic citations, its Islamic provenance is practically hidden beneath its eloquent supplications to God and celebration of His love and mystery, of which the following passage is typical:

> Our God, How wondrous are Your secrets in us! Or rather how wondrous are Your signs upon us! Or rather how wondrous is our whole in our parts! Or rather how wondrous are our parts in our whole! You enjoin us to know You but You veil us from the essence of Your reality. You make us long for You, but then you block our path to You. By Your truth, may we neither move away nor be distracted, neither be quiet nor be still, until we reach You, and stand in Your presence . . . and hear Your sublime words: "My friends, I only wearied you so that you might find rest, and made you wretched so that you might find happiness. My secret within you is a mystery, and My way with you is wondrous. Be of good cheer. Peace."[2]

Such passages, usually referred to in Sufi texts as *munajat,* or intimate colloquies with God, account for the bulk of Abu Hayyan's work. But the point to remember is that this sort of discourse annuls the space between the Sufi "friend" and his God, leaving little room for a go-between, the Prophet or anyone else.

To counter the impression of indifference to Muhammad, Sufi texts that prioritize the Prophet will often adopt a defensive or apologetic tone, as if they were under scrutiny or on probation from the legalist community. This defensiveness has been justified since at many points in its history Sufism, again like mystical traditions of other religions, suffered repeatedly from accusations of antilegalism and worse that have been directed against it by scholars who thought that Sufism had strayed far beyond the fold of orthodoxy. The attack on Sufism reached one high point of intensity in Ibn al-Jawzi's (d. 1200) *Talbis Iblis* (The Confusions of Satan), where he attacks the Sufis' ignorance and lack of concern for the sacred law and, in consequence, what he characterizes as their gluttony, greed, and exhibitionism.[3]

A few words are in order regarding the history of Sufism.[4] It appears likely that Sufism arose as a result of two parallel developments: an increasing concern among certain groups with the ascetic life and practices, and an increasing concern to investigate the deeper meaning of certain Qur'anic revelations. The concern with asceticism is displayed in the very name "Sufi," which comes from Arabic *suf*, "coarse wool," worn by certain individuals and groups as a badge of protest against the sudden and dramatic wealth of the new Islamic empire, which generated visible habits of luxury among the elite.[5] Other factors were no doubt relevant too, for instance, the deeply embedded traditions of ascetic mysticism in earlier cultures of the Middle East to which Islam was heir, especially the Syriac and Iranian ascetic traditions.[6]

The concern with Qur'anic revelations manifested itself in meditation upon certain passages of the sacred text that the Sufis saw as having a special or symbolic meaning for them. Typical of such passages are Qur'an, suras 73 and 74, as well as Qur'an 24:34–40, which the Sufis prized for their imagery of God as an immediate and immanent reality. In describing the Sufi encounter with God and the life of solitude, the great theorist of Sufism Abu Hamid al-Ghazali (d. 1111) has this to say on the deeper significance of suras 73 and 74:

> As for the life of solitude, its value lies in avoiding worldly distractions and curbing the hearing and the vision, for these two are the corridors of the heart. The heart is like a pool into which flow turgid, evil-smelling and dirty waters from the rivers of the senses. The object of spiritual exercise *[riyada]* is to empty that pool from these waters . . . so that the spring at the bottom of the pool can burst forth, and pure and clean water can flow. Otherwise, how can a person clean out that pool while these filthy rivers flow into it, constantly replenishing what is lost? Hence one must curb the senses except as absolutely necessary and this can only be done through solitude in a darkened house. If a person cannot find such a house, let him cover his head with his sleeve or else veil himself with a blanket or shawl. In that case he will hear the call of truth and see the majesty of the divine presence. Do you not see how the call to truth came to the Prophet while he was in this condition? For it was said to him: O you folded in garments! O you shrouded in your mantle![7]

In the history of Sufism, two broad periods can be distinguished. There is an earlier period of individual Sufi masters or saints who were often itinerant preachers traveling from place to place and preaching the virtues of asceticism and the need to forsake the things of the world, as well as a piety based on direct and intimate experience of God, of God as an internal rather than external reality. The first period fell roughly between the eighth and tenth centuries. In the early part of this period the Sufi masters wrote down little or nothing. But the popular success of Sufism accompanied by the rising suspicions of legalist scholars induced some Sufis in the latter part of that period to collect the sayings of predecessors or write defensively in explication of their beliefs and way of life.

The second period, which for our present purposes stretched from the eleventh to the sixteenth centuries, was one in which Sufism became organized and institutional, arraying itself in religious orders *(tariqa)* each with its own saintly founder and rules, and with some interesting parallels to the medieval European Christian friars. They had their own houses, called *zawiya*, *khaniqah*, or *ribat*, where the spiritual life was well regulated.[8] There is little doubt that this evolution into religious orders was encouraged by the rise of powerful military-style Turkic dynasties in the central Islamic lands beginning in the eleventh century. These dynasties, the Seljuks and their successor states, patronized the new Sufi orders on a large scale, regarding them as valuable spiritual and military allies against external enemies. But most important, there was now a curriculum that the Sufi initiate needed to follow in order to attain Sufi gnosis, called *ma'rifa*, and Sufi revelation, called *kashf*. In tandem, we begin to see the appearance of texts that one might call theoretical, in other words texts in which Sufi beliefs and ethics are explained and defended.

The early Sufi "heroes" and masters, such as Ibrahim ibn Adham (d. 778), Da'ud al-Ta'i (d. 781), al-Fudayl ibn 'Iyad (d. 803), Ma'ruf al-Karkhi (d. 815), Bishr al-Hafi (d. 841), Dhu'l Nun al-Misri (d. 861), al-Sariyy al-Saqati (d. 865), and Abu Yazid al-Bistami (d. ca. 877), seem to have been so taken up by their encounter with God that one would be hard put to find, in the ecstatic pronouncements ascribed to them in later writings, much reference to Muhammad's role in their spiritual journey to God.[9] It was left up to later generations of Sufi writers to remedy this situation and develop to the full the image of Muhammad as the prototype of the Sufi "saint" *[waliyy]* and the exemplary teacher of Sufi ethics.

The Sufis, therefore, like other Muslim groups discussed above such as the *Adibs* and the Shiites, had their own take on Muhammad. In other words, they highlighted those aspects of Muhammad's life and practice that best suited their own teachings and agenda. Like the Shiites, some Sufis advocated the total sinlessness *('isma)* of prophets, and many adopted 'Ali as a prototypical Sufi saint on a level almost as exalted as Muhammad.[10] In a discussion of the relationship between prophets and saints, the celebrated Sufi author al-Qushayri (d. 1072) phrased the question as follows:

> If one asks, "Is the saint sinless?" I answer: "If you mean sinless by necessity, as is the case with prophets, the answer is no. However, the saint may be safeguarded by God from reverting to sin if he commits minor sins or transgressions."[11]

One central preoccupation of the Sufis, early and late, was to recapture the certainty of faith that they believed was possessed by prophets, that is, the unshakable faith that comes from direct experiential knowledge of God rather than from mental conviction on the one hand or simple imitation of parents and society on the other. In general, prophets are born with such certainty and with the perfect character that goes with it. A human being, on the other hand, needs, in the later Sufi view, to undertake a long and rigorous spiritual regime *(riyadat al-nafs; mujahada)* in order to arrive at certainty of faith and perfection of character. This is where the example of Muhammad was to become directly relevant to Sufi devotions. At every "station," to use a Sufi term, on this long journey to "friendship with God" or sainthood, as set forth for instance in Abu Talib al-Makki's (d. 996) *Qut al-Qulub* or al-Ghazali's (d. 1111) *Ihya' 'Ulum al-Din,* these two being among the most magisterial of Sufi texts, Muhammad's hadith and exemplary *sunna* are there to lead the seeker after truth *(murid)*. Abu Talib speaks of the love of the Prophet as the guiding principle:

> It is part of loving the Prophet to prefer his *Sunna* over indi-
> vidual opinion and rationality . . . while the true mark of his
> love is to follow him outwardly and inwardly. By following him
> outwardly is meant to perform all religious duties, to shun the
> illicit, to emulate his character and manners, to be on the look-
> out for reports of him, to have an ascetic attitude to the world,
> to avoid human company, to steer clear of ignorance and
> caprice, to shun all wealth and earthly glory, to draw near to the
> afterlife, to love the poor and keep their company, preferring
> them above all others . . . By following the Prophet inwardly is
> meant the stations of certainty and the visions of the sciences of
> faith like pious fear, contentment, thankfulness, modesty, sub-
> mission to God's will, trust in God, longing for God, a heart
> empty of all but God, and tranquility induced by the frequent
> mention of God.[12]

Given the co-optation of Muhammad by the Sufis as a model, it was not surprising that many Sufi writers would go on to claim that the Sufis were in fact the closest of Muslims to Muhammad, as asserted confidently by the great master al-Suhrawardi (d. 1234): "The Sufis are of all people those most fit to emulate the Prophet, most worthy to revive his example and adopt his moral conduct."[13]

So often is this idea reiterated that one might conclude that al-Suhrawardi's main purpose in writing his seminal work on Sufi ethics was to illustrate the nearness of the Sufis to the Prophet. Accordingly, certain incidents in Muhammad's life, for instance the cleansing of his heart as a child, acquire special meaning for the Sufis:

God having cleansed His prophet from the portion belonging to Satan, there remained his pure and prophetic soul, similar in form to human souls and appearing to possess certain moral traits of character which were retained as a mercy to mankind, for such traits were also to be found among his community; to be sure, more murky among his community because of the distance separating him from his community. But some of these character traits retained by Muhammad were progressively disciplined by divine revelations, since God desired to refine his character as a mercy to him especially, but also to his community . . . So the Prophetic heart grew ever more patient and calm after some turmoil . . . This indeed is how some defined Sufism: "To be well-mannered towards humanity and utterly sincere with the truth."[14]

In the view of al-Suhrawardi, Muhammad's life and the evolution of his character consisted of a series of tests, and as each test was successfully endured "his character was the Qur'an," as 'A'isha once described it. The parallel with the trials and tribulations of the Sufis is clear, since their journey too is a series of tests on the way to truth. Hence the revelations of the Qur'an with their moral commandments to Muhammad and, through him, to his community, act as successive ethical teachings that endow Muhammad and by extension his community with what is needed to refine and ennoble character.

Muhammad was thus internalized and made to be a living and active reality for the Sufi "traveler" on the path to God. For al-Shushtari (d. 1269), for instance:

Sufi saints must of necessity suffer the trials and tribulations of prophets, being their heirs . . . As for their frequent travels and their leaving their native lands, this is to conform with

Muhammad's injunction {Be in this world like a stranger or a passer-by.}[15]

In detailing the ethics of the Sufis, al-Suhrawardi lists them as follows:

Humility; patience in adversity; preferring others to self; forgiveness and self-restraint; cheerfulness; simplicity of manner; generosity; contentment; gentleness; conviviality; giving thanks.[16]

In all these virtues, the exemplar is Muhammad, whose sayings and actions are cited for every one of these virtues as models to be emulated. It is the Sufis who have reflected most deeply upon the inward significance of the Prophet's conduct and teachings. Consequently, it is the heart *(qalb)* rather than the mind *('aql)* that is the vital spiritual organ in Sufi devotions, and it is the heart that is the seat of spirituality. Al-Ghazali has this to say on emulating Muhammad and on the role of the heart in penetrating the "secrets" of his mission:

In general, most of mankind leans towards what is easiest and most comfortable for their nature. For the truth is bitter, and getting to know it is a most arduous task, especially the knowledge of the attributes of the heart and how to cleanse it from disreputable traits . . . That which is most precious and valued befits only the chosen few *(ahl al-khusus)*. Therefore the Sufi must rely in what he knows of the religious sciences on his inner vision *(basira)* and the consciousness of a pure heart, not upon written tomes nor emulation of what he hears from others . . . When emulating Muhammad and fully accepting his words and deeds, he must be careful to fathom their symbolic

meanings *(asrar)* . . . He must be ever prepared to search dili-
gently for these symbols, for if he is satisfied with mere memo-
rizing, he is nothing but a vessel of knowledge, and not truly a
knower. He whose heart has been unveiled and is illumined by
divine guidance becomes himself worthy of being emulated and
must not emulate others.[17]

But Sufism did have its dangers. One of the most symbolic
events in the life of Muhammad from the Sufi perspective was his
famous Night Journey *(Isra')* from Mecca to Jerusalem, and from
thence his ascent to God *(Mi'raj)*, alluded to in Qur'an 17:1, and
thereafter greatly amplified and embellished in pious literature.
The Sufis saw in this Muhammadan journey a paradigm for their
own path to the Divinity and, in imitation of that flight, we possess
some accounts of similar journeys undertaken by Sufis to the
Divine Presence and of encounters with the Divine.[18] In Sufi accounts the various heavens that Muhammad traversed and his
encounters with prophets and angels become symbols of the "stations" *(mawaqif)* at which God reveals to the Sufi the secrets of
such principles as truth, knowledge, love, and so forth. The language is often allusive and cryptic, almost para-Qur'anic, as befits
a "friend of God" who has become almost the equal of Muhammad
in illumination. A dangerous paradox now appears, for the closer
they came to God, the less need—or perhaps time—the Sufis
had to abide by the Islamic cult and the commandments of
Muhammad. This is precisely the accusation that al-Qushayri (d.
1072) and other defenders of Sufism were intent upon heading off
and denying.

Despite the best efforts of its defenders, Sufism was regarded
during its early centuries with deep suspicion by Muslim lawyers
and theologians as tending not simply to antinomian conduct but
also to antisocial behavior and the abandonment of societal responsibilities. Partly to counteract this impression, Sufi devotions,

hymns, and litanies would grow and develop, particularly inside
Sufi brotherhoods, combined with love poetry whose object was
the Prophet himself. These hymns in praise of Muhammad, alluded to above, came to be known as *mada'ih nabawiyya*, and were
developed into a high art by some brotherhoods. They were most
often sung on Muhammad's birthday, celebrated on 12 Rabi' al-
Awwal of the Muslim calendar. But even such celebrations of
Muhammad were not by any means universally approved by conservative lawyers, and thus they generated among other things a
lengthy debate on the legal permissibility of music.

Another area where the Sufis demonstrated their devotion to
Muhammad was the private prayer called *wird* (plural, *awrad*) that
the pious believer performed in addition to the five prescribed
times of prayer daily. Seven times of the day were specified for
these prayers by al-Ghazali. These prayers were, according to him,
meant to turn the attention of the faithful to God as completely as
possible since the temptations of the world will often overcome
even the most pious of believers.[19] These special prayers are ones
that Muhammad instituted or else were related by him to "saints"
who were taught these prayers in dreams.

In Sufi texts, dreams both of the Prophet and of Sufi saints are
frequent, often confirming the spiritual powers of a particular saint
or his ultimate destiny. According to a widely accepted hadith, if
one saw the Prophet in a dream, the dream was true since Satan
could not impersonate him. The following, typical of its kind, is
said to have been a dream of the towering Sufi master al-Junayd
(d. 910):

It is said that al-Sariyy [his uncle and mentor] would urge
him to address people in public. Al-Junayd said: "In my heart
was a modesty which prevented me from addressing a public
audience for I regarded my soul as unworthy of this. One
Friday night I saw the Prophet in a dream and he said to me

{Go forth and address people in public.} I woke up at once and came to the door of al-Sariyy and knocked upon it while he was still asleep. He said: "You did not believe me until you were told to do so?" So al-Junayd sat to preach in the mosque and the news spread that al-Junayd was preaching in public. A Christian youth, disguising his identity, came up to him and said: "O Master, explain to me the meaning of the following *ha-dith* of the Prophet: {Beware the perspicacity *[firasa]* of the believer for the believer sees with the light of Almighty God.}" Al-Junayd bowed his head in reflection then raised it and said: "Embrace Islam. The time for it has come." The youth embraced Islam.[20]

Images of Muhammad in Sufi literature are thus unusually mixed. At one end of the spectrum Muhammad is made absolutely central to Sufi devotions; at the other end a considerable body of Sufi literature makes God so exclusively its quest that Muhammad retreats to the background, as we have seen above for instance with Abu Hayyan's *Divine Allusions*. In broad terms, it was the theorists and defenders of Sufism, such as al-Qushayri, al-Suhrawardi, and al-Ghazali, who enshrined Muhammad as the first Sufi whereas the early Sufi saints, with their strange and ecstatic pronouncements, seemed more intent on following the path of direct and unmediated preoccupation with the majesty *(jalal)* and beauty *(jamal)* of God.

In what one might call the rehabilitation of Sufism, al-Qushayri's *Epistle on Sufism* occupies an important place. His task was formidable: he was struggling against a fairly lengthy tradition of enmity and suspicion between the Sufis and the lawyers. That this tension lasted at least two centuries beyond al-Qushayri (and remains with us in some sense today) is exemplified by a remark made by the great Andalusian/Egyptian Sufi saint Abu al-'Abbas al-Mursi (d. 1287), who complained: "We [Sufis] have partaken of the knowledge of jurists but they have not partaken of ours."[21] The celebrated Sufi theorist Abu Nasr al-Sarraj (d. 988) had already formulated the contrast between jurisprudence *(fiqh)* and Sufism even more pointedly as follows:

> Know that the uncovering by the Sufis of the inner truths *[mus-tanbatat]* and of the meaning of these religious sciences, as also their intimate knowledge of their details, is necessarily greater in extent than what the lawyers do in uncovering the meaning of outward regulations of the law. This is because the Sufi type of knowledge is endless, for it is made up of divine allusions, visions, inspirations and free gifts which its true possessors imbibe from the sea of divine gifts, whereas all other sciences have a definite limit and end. All sciences culminate in Sufism . . . for the object of the quest [God] is limitless. Sufism is thus the science of God's revelations . . . and God multiplies His revelations without end.[22]

In view of this polarization, al-Qushayri's program is announced at the very outset of his work: he hopes his *Epistle* will help to restore Sufism to its true law-respecting origins and path. He acknowledges and laments that the Sufism of his age has deteriorated to the point where Sufis no longer respect the *shari'ah* of God and His Prophet, imagining themselves to be above all ritual and regulations and no longer concerned with the commandments of the faith. He thus wishes to protect the reputation of Sufism from those who would give it a bad name, describing them as follows:

> The sanctity of the *shari'ah* departed from their hearts. Indifference to religion they regard as the best attitude to adopt.

They deny all difference between licit and illicit . . . they make light of performing acts of worship, they hold prayer and fasting to be of little worth . . . they allude to the highest of truths and states of contemplation *[ahwal]* and claim they are free from the slavery of chains . . . they allege they have been granted the secrets of unicity and are no longer subject to human regulations.[23]

The first task for al-Qushayri was to review the biographies of distinguished Sufis from the beginning down to his own days and to show how in each case the Prophet's example was the guiding principle. To al-Junayd is attributed the remark that "all paths are blocked before mankind except the path of him who emulates the example of Muhammad."[24] The point is reiterated: they were all as one in respecting the religious law.

The bulk of the *Epistle* is made up of chapters each of which is devoted to a principal ethical concern of Sufism such as fear of God, hope, hunger, silence, repentance, asceticism, and so forth. Each chapter, as is appropriate in a work of rehabilitation, begins with a Qur'anic verse and/or a hadith from Muhammad, followed by pronouncements made by Sufis in relation to the topic. One might call it an anthology with an agenda whose purpose is to show how Muhammad led the way for genuine Sufism and was the ideal teacher of Sufi ethics. Of the many hadiths that depict Muhammad as the first Sufi, one in particular is significant in showing Muhammad's constant nearness to God. Nothing distracted him from God. Alone among prophets, Muhammad could remain perpetually in the presence of God *and* attend to the earthly affairs of his community:

We said, "Prophet of God, whenever we see you, our hearts grow soft and we become like the people of the Hereafter. When we leave your company, this world becomes attractive to us and we embrace women and children." The Prophet said {If you were to remain at all times in the condition *[hal]* in which you were when you were with me, the angels would shake your hands with their very own, and visit you in your houses.}[25]

In discussing this passage, al-Qushayri would argue that this shows how Muhammad, like the Sufi saints who followed his example, was capable of rising and remaining close to the highest truths, unaffected by the contingencies and distractions of existence, while he was simultaneously able to deal with mundane reality and to perform what the law commands.

In al-Qushayri's and similar Sufi texts, the presence of *hadith qudsi,* or divine hadith, was dense. This category of Hadith, as we have seen earlier, was related by Muhammad as coming from God but was not part of the Qur'an even though it was divine speech. Halfway between Hadith and Qur'an, this type of hadith was particularly meaningful to the Sufis as bridging the gap between God and the human condition and signaling the myriad ways in which the truly pious can approach the divine. But the path to God must always pass, according to al-Qushayri, through the *shari'ah,* as in the following divine hadith:

{Those who seek to draw near to Me shall not do so in any manner other than by performing My commandments. The worshipper will strive constantly to draw near to Me by performing supererogatory acts *[nawafil]* to the point where he loves Me and I love him. Once I love him, I become his ears and his eyes. Through Me he sees, through Me he hears.}

But although Sufi practice has always been and must always remain anchored in Muhammadan example, this did not mean that certain commandments of the *shari'ah* could not be interpreted in ways that differed from their normal juristic import. Perhaps the

most striking of these commandments (and the one with most resonance for us today) is jihad, commonly understood to mean fighting in the cause of God. The following hadith is quoted and then
elaborated by al-Qushayri:

> The Prophet was asked about the best kind of *jihad*. He replied
> {It is a just word in the presence of an unjust ruler.}[26]

Jihad in al-Qushayri is subsumed under a chapter entitled
Mujahada, which turns out to mean curbing the desires of the soul,
and is equated among other things with moral courage and a willingness to speak the truth even at the cost of personal harm.
Accordingly, jihad in Sufi terminology is internalized and comes to
refer to the "battle" between the Sufi and the base desires of his
soul, the tendency to seek ease, safety, and comfort. It is a salient
example of the manner in which Sufis dealt with the inner or spiritual meaning of some major Islamic commandments or Prophetic
hadiths. Thus al-Sarraj devoted a whole chapter of his work on
Sufism to the manner in which the Sufi masters "uncovered the inner meaning" of some sayings of Muhammad of which the following is typical:

> Sahl al-Tustari [d. ca. 886] was asked about the following
> hadith of Muhammad {The believer is one who is overjoyed by
> his good deed and mortified by his sin} and replied: "His good
> deed is the bounty of God. His sin is his soul if he puts his trust
> in it."[27]

The last section of the *Epistle* deals with the controversial issue
of *karamat,* usually translated as the "charisms" of Sufi saints.[28]
These charisms may be defined as God-given powers, spiritual or
physical, granted to certain Sufis in order to confirm their sanctity.
These mini-miracles of the saints appeared to the theologians of the

community to be suspect, not least because they seemed to compete with or to extend the miracles *(mu'jizat)* of the prophets, whose function was to establish the truthfulness of a particular prophecy. Some theologians argued that since prophecy itself had ended with Muhammad, miracles were no longer possible. The Mu'tazilite theologians in particular rejected Sufi *karamat* as denigrating the miracles of prophets and argued that God would not ceaselessly violate custom and the laws of nature in favor of an endless line of holy men. They further argued that if Muslims were to accept *karamat*, this would turn them into Christians, for these latter were constantly searching for miracles among their saints. This debate is the context for the following passage from al-Qushayri:

> If someone says: "How is it permissible to reveal these *karamat*, some of which are greater in significance than the miracles of prophets? Is it permissible to prefer saints to prophets?" We [al-Qushayri] answer, "These *karamat* are in fact an appendage to the miracles of our Prophet. In the case of any prophet whose charisms were revealed to a member of his community, these charisms are counted as belonging to the totality of his miracles. Had the prophet in question not been truthful, the charism would not have been revealed at the hands of one of his followers. But the rank of a saint does not attain to the rank of a prophet, as per general consensus. When Abu Yazid al-Bistami [a celebrated early Sufi master] was asked about this question he said, 'One may compare the case of the prophets to a skin containing honey from which one drop oozes out. That drop is similar to all that saints can perform by way of *karamat* whereas what the skin contains is similar to what our Prophet can do.' "[29]

Al-Qushayri insists on the reality of *karamat*, which are generically of the same kind as miracles. Like miracles, *karamat* are violations of the natural order involving a saint and a sign of a saint's sanctity. However, prophetic miracles are public acts that God commands His prophets to proclaim before people whereas a true saint must hide his *karama*. Muhammad therefore made no secret of his miracles, many of which reduced his opponents to silence or confirmed the faith of his followers, but a true saint will not advertise his *karama* nor use it to silence opponents, since a saint's *karama* could well be the result of demonic deception or self-delusion.

Connected with the controversial *karamat* of the Sufis were their occasionally startling pronouncements, which their enemies labeled *shatahat,* or dangerous religious aberrations. These would often be defended by reference to similar Prophetic hadiths and the need to understand the inner meaning of what were characterized as offensive sayings. For example,

> It is related of al-Shibli [Sufi saint; d. 945] that he said in one of his sessions: "God has worshippers who, if they were to spit on Hell, would extinguish its fires." This was found hard to take by some who attended that session. But the Prophet also said: {On the Day of Resurrection, Hell will say to the believer "Pass on, O believer, for your light has extinguished my flame".}[30]

Thus the charisms of the Sufis are extensions and confirmations of Muhammadan miracles, while their occasional "aberrations" are esoteric expressions of certain truths first expressed by the Prophet and then taken to heart by his most devoted and most spiritual disciples.

In any discussion of images of Muhammad in Sufi literature, there is no escaping the "Great Shaykh" Muhyiddin Ibn al-'Arabi (d. 1240), a much traveled, immensely productive, and highly contro-

versial figure in his own days and beyond. Ibn al-'Arabi's intellectual system and its influence can only be compared to al-Ghazali's
for its sweep and originality. But while Ghazali's system seems relatively amenable to analysis, that of Ibn al-'Arabi is so complex
that any attempt at summarizing it would run the risk of distorting
it. The reason is that Ibn al-'Arabi saw the cosmos as an intercon-
nected and animate whole suffused by the light of God. The language he used necessarily reflected that wholeness, while beyond
language lay a realm of visions, dreams, and spiritual experiences
intended to illuminate and reflect, mirrorlike, the complex edifice
of an overlapping reality.

Neither Ibn al-'Arabi nor Ghazali can be considered main-
stream Sufis: they were far too interested in the sciences of their
age, and far more engrossed in system building than were the "av-
erage" Sufis. Hence the following remarks on Ibn al-'Arabi can
barely hope to touch the periphery of his uncommonly difficult
structure of thought, but may be found of some use in investigat-
ing the images of Muhammad within Ibn al-'Arabi's writing.

His magnum opus is undoubtedly his *Al-Futuhat al-Makkiyya*
[Meccan Revelations], a large work that one could read as a tour
of the spiritual world in the form of a running commentary on certain passages of the Qur'an and on a number of Muhammadan hadiths. It is a prose work but frequently breaks into verse to express
the more esoteric layers of meaning. It speaks to the reader in the
voice of someone revealing inner truths; at one point Ibn al-'Arabi
swears that every single letter of his book was written from "divine
dictation."[31] The work has a haunting quality derived not so much
from reflection but from living and "tasting" the sacred text; the
commentary records the experience of that immersion. Alternately
straightforward and impossibly dense, it flows like a stream of consciousness, taking no account whatever of the where or when of
revelations. Thus, as a Qur'anic commentary, it differs radically
from all other commentaries in its complete disregard of the histor-

ical context *(asbab al-nuzul)* of Qur'anic revelations, placing and treating the Qur'anic text on the same eternal level of analysis. Accordingly, immense figurative importance is attached to every Qur'anic word quoted, as well as to word order and numerical qualities. As Ibn al-'Arabi unfolds these deeply hidden meanings, the Qur'anic text itself is transformed into a living and throbbing reality that he calls "Universal Man" *(Al-Insan al-Kulli).*[32]

Our point of departure is the cosmos *(kawn)* as an animate entity:

> The whole cosmos is a body and a soul through both of which existence had its origin. The world is to Truth *[al-Haqq*, i.e., God] as the body is to the soul . . . The world is Truth condensed, man is the world condensed and the Truth is the purity of the condensed, i.e., Perfect Man.[33]

The cosmos is, as it were, ensouled by God and encapsulated in Man:

> Just as nothing exists in the world which does not glorify Him [God] so also nothing exists in this world but is found in its inward reality and meaning in Man, as revealed by its true form.[34]

The reason for the existence of this cosmos is Perfect Man *(Al-Insan al-Kamil),* a figure with origins in Middle Eastern religious cultures but pivotal in late Sufism.[35] Who or what is Perfect Man? In trying to answer this question we will, I believe, draw pretty close to Ibn al-'Arabi's image of Muhammad, for the two images are intertwined.

At one level of existence—and levels of existence are paramount in Ibn al-'Arabi—Perfect Man is Adam.[36] Taught "all names" by God, Adam was master of the secrets of the cosmos and thus superior to all other beings. At another level, Perfect Man is a status attainable by all who come to knowledge of God through knowledge of self: "Whoso knows himself knows his God" is a hadith repeatedly cited throughout the *Futuhat*, almost like a mantra. It follows that Perfect Man does have "heirs and descendants," otherwise unnamed but almost certainly the "saints" *(awliya')*, who are described as those "capable of deducing" *(yastakhrij)* the "treasures of God's knowledge" from contemplation of self.[37] Even more startling is the assertion: "Turn Perfect Man inside out and you will find God."[38] Here, Perfect Man stands for the perfection of creation, which is a mirror image of its Creator, the mirror being yet another favorite Ibn al-'Arabi metaphor.

So, then, is Perfect Man Adam? Is he a spiritual status? Is he perfected creation? Or is he all three together? I will not pursue Perfect Man further except where the concept leads into and illuminates the images of Muhammad, as in the passage that follows. Given the eternal dimensions of Ibn al-'Arabi's edifice of meanings, it will come as no surprise to find that Muhammad in this edifice is at least as much a cosmic principle as he is a historical figure. To begin with, Muhammad is identified with the Rational Soul *(Al-Nafs al-Natiqa)* and the World Soul *(Nafs al-'Alam)*, both categories familiar to Islamic philosophy but applied now to Muhammad for what appears to be the first time in the Islamic tradition.[39] In Islamic philosophy these categories are immaterial principles, emanating from the One. In Ibn al-'Arabi, they are embodied in Muhammad:

> Since Muhammad was granted this status while Adam was still between water and clay, we conclude that he is the sustainer who nurtures *(yamudd)* every Perfect Man described in divine or rational law. The first of the line was Adam when God made him a deputy and heir *(khalifa)* of Muhammad. God granted him knowledge of all names, this being derived from the station of perfection of speech *(jawami al-kalim)* granted to

Muhammad. Deputies followed one another until the time came for the coming into being of the form of Muhammad's body in order to manifest the rule of his status through the joining of his two origins. When he appeared, he was like the sun: every light was incorporated in his light. He approved of some laws instituted by his deputies and abrogated others, and his concern for his community *(umma)* was shown through his presence among them, thereby turning them into {the best Umma ever to have been created among mankind}.[40]

Of significance in this passage is the reference to the "two origins" *(nash'atayn)* of Muhammad, which is an important clue to Ibn al-'Arabi's conception of Muhammad as a figure both above history and within it, a supernatural being divinely and uniquely endowed with endless knowledge.

As Perfect Man is an emanation of Muhammad, so also are all prophets, whom he likewise "sustains, nurtures and inspires."[41] He is described as "the first and the last," as "God's clearest proof," as "preserver of the world," and as one "in whom are gathered the truths of the world."[42] Muhammad is reported to have said that the world came into existence because "I was an unknown treasure, and I wanted to be known"; he enshrined love as the movement that created the world and incidentally explained Muhammad's partiality for women as a "longing of the all for its parts."[43] At least as startling in this galaxy of epithets is the view that, proceeding from 'A'isha's famous definition of Muhammad's *character* as the Qur'an, goes beyond this to assert the *identification* of the one with the other:

He who wishes to see Muhammad from among those in his community who did not live in his time should regard the Qur'an. If he does so, no difference will be found between regarding it and regarding Muhammad. It is as if the Qur'an has assumed *(intaòha'a)* a bodily form called Muhammad ibn 'Abdullah ibn 'Abd al-Muttalib. The Qur'an is the speech of God and His epithet *(òifa)* while Muhammad is the epithet of God Almighty in his totality. So Muhammad cannot be considered as absent from this present world for he is the form *(òura)* of the Qur'an.⁴⁴

Shadowing this processional of divine emanations is the concept of "sainthood" *(wilaya)*, a status so wide in "circumference" that prophecy itself is subsumed under it.⁴⁵ But whereas the prophetic line ended with Muhammad, the saintly status has no end.⁴⁶ It is clear that the great Sufi masters in Ibn al-'Arabi's view were among those "saints" who continue to be nourished by divine knowledge:

> The saint may be called an heir *(warith)*. Heirdom is a divine epithet as in [Qur'an 21:89] {God is the best of inheritors}. The saint does not receive prophecy from prophets until the Truth [God] inherits it from them then delivers it to the saint, this being more worthy of what he deserves, so that the saint pertains to God and to no one else. Some saints inherited knowledge from the Prophet, these being his Companions, but the scholars of law take it from one another, so the line of descent grows far too long. The saints however receive knowledge from God. Abu Yazid al-Bistami said: "You have taken your knowledge from one dead man after another but we have taken our knowledge from the One who is Living and Deathless."⁴⁷

We live in a cosmos in which every created being, animate or seemingly inanimate, throbs with the praise of God. Muhammad, with his diverse cosmic epithets, is the reason for the world's existence and nourishes its spirituality. It is precisely his timeless status and perfection that make it possible for divine illumination to continue to shine upon those who recognize the "Muhammadan truth" that lies concealed *(batin)* within the human soul or else is manifest *(zahir)* in the Qur'an.

Clearly, there is very little here that bears much resemblance to the images of Muhammad encountered thus far. Are we to seek the origin of these images in Christian conceptions of the Logos? Or is Muhammad as Perfect Man a Neoplatonic adaptation? Or is the Shiite concept of *Nur Muhammadi* of some relevance? Ibn al-'Arabi's system is doubtless an amalgam of gnostic, theosophical, and philosophical ideas but they are all suffused with the man's own passionate and relentless disclosures of the Unseen *(ghayb),* through knowledge "inherited" from God but made possible by "Muhammadan Truth." No purely historical understanding of Muhammad will do, and no amount of legal or rational knowledge can reveal the full truth about him, unless and until one internalizes him as the ultimate revealer of the secrets of God's cosmos. Only then does one become a true follower of Muhammad.

VII

The Prophet Canonized

MUHAMMAD'S *SIRA* IN A NEW CANONICAL AGE

Readers might recall a scheme of periodization of the *Sira* suggested at the beginning of this work, where the early *Sira* works of the four founding fathers were called a *Sira* of "primitive devotion." It was a *Sira* so much in awe of its subject that it gathered in its net almost all the reports that fell into it, paying little attention to their consistency. The guiding principle was inclusion rather than exclusion. If any stories were found that some Muslims thought offensive or that contradicted other stories in the same narrative, it was thought better to include them rather than exclude them in the name of any pretension to piety. This is not to say that the founding fathers did not put a spin on their narrative: there can be no image without a spin. Being Sunni, the founding fathers were clearly not sympathetic, for example, to Shiite counter-narratives. But by and large the Sunni *Sira* preserved a great deal of historical material in a raw, unprocessed state, with little or no attempt made at establishing consistency or harmonization.

I shall now argue that at a certain point in history the development of the *Sira* entered on a new age, one that might broadly be described as canonizing, moralizing, exclusivist, rationalizing, and uniform. The explicit intention of this new age of *Sira* writers was to impose some kind of order on the medley of narrative materials, to fit them for service in the cause of a party or a system of ethics. We have already encountered certain signs of this new age in Shiite and Sufi biographies of Muhammad, where the agenda is intrusive and the spin is visible. In the Shiite images, Muhammad's life is a preparation for the coming of the "Holy Family"; in Sufi images Muhammad is the patron of Sufi "saints" and a cosmic principle who provides a key to the symbolic interpretation of reality. More typical of that new age, however, are a series of works that explicitly address the contradictions, or what I earlier called the "antibodies," of the *Sira*, where these "antibodies" are detected, brought out, reviewed, and, as it were, ironed out.

The question now arises: What is it in Islamic culture and history that moved the *Sira* from the age of "primitive devotion" to an age of canonization and consistency? What motives or factors drove this second age of *Sira* writers to reexamine and then reconstruct Muhammad's image? And can one suggest a time frame for this transformation? If we deal with the last question first, we might propose the eleventh and twelfth centuries as the period during which the new type of *Sira* developed. By that time, Islamic culture had fully sharpened its polemical and theological tools in struggles against both internal and external enemies. On the internal front, Islam had now definitely split into many legal camps and two great wings, Sunnism and Shiism. Threatening from the sidelines were skeptics, "heretics," and philosophers of various hues, many of whom were hostile to the idea of prophecy in general or indifferent to the role of the prophet in human history. On the external front, Muslim thinkers, following centuries of debate with non-Muslims, were now fully conversant on a number of serious charges laid against certain aspects of Muhammad's life by, for example, Christian theologians. All these factors had an impact on the *Sira* and helped to move it into new directions. But before we come to the new age we need to examine in some detail the intellectual background that made that new age possible.

Two thinkers, I will argue, played a role of considerable importance in moving the *Sira* into a more critical and canonical direction: the great *Aδib* and Hadith expert Ibn Qutayba (d. 889) and the even more celebrated *Aδib* and Mu'tazilite theologian al-Jahiz (d. 868). Ibn Qutayba was much disturbed by the manner in which various factions of the community used divergent Muhammadan hadiths to justify their own peculiar or fractious understanding of faith and practice, and much concerned also to ward off the attacks of skeptics who questioned the rationality of certain reports in the *Sira*. A work he entitled *Ta'wil Mukhtalif al-Haδith* (Interpreting Divergent Hadith) was aimed principally at showing that contradictions in the Hadith and the *Sira* were apparent and not real. As urgent a task for Ibn Qutayba was pruning the Hadith of the fantastic or fanciful, these being favorite targets of rationalists and others who often treated the Hadith as little more than a bag of superstitions. In standing up for the Hadith and defending its integrity, Ibn Qutayba regarded himself as something of a champion because

> *Haδith* scholars have had no one to defend them or interpret divergences, to the point where they are content to suffer calumny in silence. In their reluctance to offer any defense, they appear as if they accept the charges leveled against them.[1]

Having reviewed and then refuted the opponents of the Hadith among rationalist theologians and Shiites and having exposed their *own* ignorance and contradictions, he proceeds to defend the scholars who collect both authentic and inauthentic Hadith by claiming that they do so not because they *believe* all the hadith they collect, but because they wish to distinguish and single out the acceptable from the unacceptable.[2] The bulk of the work is then devoted to a kind of dialectic of objections and answers: such and such a hadith is contradicted by reason *(nazar)*, such and such hadiths are antithetical, such and such a report in the *Sira* makes no sense given its historical circumstances. Ibn Qutayba addresses each objection fully, refuting the charge of contradiction on linguistic, rational, commonsensical, or contextual grounds. The following exchange is typical:

> They say: here are two contradictory reports. You [Hadith scholars] relate that Muhammad said {No prophet ever disbelieved in God.} Yet you relate that as a child God sent two angels who extracted a black spot from his heart and washed it and returned it to its place. You then say that for forty years Muhammad followed the religion of his people and that he married his two daughters to unbelievers. Quite apart from denigrating the Prophet, the divergence and contradiction here is quite obvious.[3]

Not so, answers Ibn Qutayba. The Arabs of Muhammad's day believed in certain remnants of the religion of Abraham, including the belief in resurrection and in angels. Muhammad did indeed follow some remnants of that Abrahamic religion. Thus he clearly shunned idols but he was not yet apprised of the laws and regulations of Islam. Marrying his daughters off to unbelievers may be regarded as the act of one not yet made aware of God's prohibition against such marriages. Where no divine law existed as yet, one cannot speak of transgression.

And so it goes. Ibn Qutayba was not averse to quoting the Old and New Testaments nor even some of the "natural" explanations of phenomena that were current in medical or philosophical circles in order to bolster his arguments for the authenticity or rationality of some of Muhammad's sayings or actions. It is clear, however, from his extended defense of the Hadith and the *Sira* that these texts were by the ninth century subject to a vigorous and systematic attack mounted largely by rationalist theologians who found them soft targets. It is equally clear that the Mu'tazilite theologians were in the forefront of that campaign to apply analytic criteria to studying the Hadith and the *Sira* and to prune the texts of what they regarded as superstitious accretions.

It is probable that Ibn Qutayba had in mind al-Jahiz and the Mu'tazilite theologians when he pointed out that the objections to certain reports in the *Sira* were coming from people he called the "rationalists" *(ahl al-nazar)*.[4] If we turn to al-Jahiz we find a thinker of far broader horizons, one whose ideas were to haunt his younger contemporary Ibn Qutayba. Al-Jahiz, a towering figure of premodern Arabic/Islamic culture, held to a theory of knowledge that distinguished between innate rational capacity *(al-'aql al-mawlud)*, which he thought limited, and the experiential mind *('aql al-tajarib)*, which he held to be limitless. Nature, on the one hand, and history, on the other, are the two most important realms to be investigated by the experiential mind. Leaving nature aside for the moment, history for al-Jahiz was precisely where God interacted with His creation and thus the study of history was of critical importance for the understanding of religion. Man, however, delights in reports of the bizarre and the unusual, leading to a vast accretion of religious superstition. He held the Hadith scholars responsible for this and frequently coupled them with the despised "commoners" *('awamm)* as purveyors of laughable but eventually harmful legends. A true understanding of Muhammad's prophecy must be accompanied, according to al-Jahiz, by an understanding of the *phenomenon* of prophecy in a broad historical perspective: Why did God send prophets? How are prophets related to one another? How are they empowered by God?

So the problems of the *Sira* raise more fundamental questions, ones that transcend the knowledge to be gained by attempts at harmonizing reports as practiced by his contemporary Ibn Qutayba. First we need to know the truth conditions of historical reports. Second, we need to investigate the nature of prophecy itself. If, for instance, consensus of opinions *(ijma')* on a particular report is taken as a truth condition by Hadith scholars, for al-Jahiz it is imperative to investigate how and when consensus itself can be a truth condition. How, for example, do we deal with the consensus of Christians that Jesus is God? Al-Jahiz holds that it is the primary task of theology to investigate the theoretical issues that underlie the assumptions of the religious community and to put them on a firmer rational footing:

> What subject can be greater in import than one which, had it not existed, there would be no firm basis to prove the divinity of God, nor any proof for any prophet, nor would it have been possible to distinguish between a real proof and a false one? Through this science [theology] one can distinguish between the true community and the sect, between orthodoxy and heresy, between the peculiar historical report or article of faith and the generally accepted report or article of faith.[5]

As for prophecy, which concerns us more directly here, we find in his writings the early beginnings of what was to become a thriving genre of Islamic religious history: the genre commonly referred to as the "signs" *(dala'il; a'lam)* or "proofs" *(hujaj)* of prophecy.[6] Here al-Jahiz begins with the basics: in the first place, why is prophecy necessary? Because God's universe is a very diverse place, seen most visibly in the diversity of human beings. Given their very different regional habitats, professions, and mental endowments, aggression among them is endemic. To repress human aggression, and to institute the laws that bring order into human relations, God sends prophets, who reveal a succession of these divine regulations. Prophecy is hence the answer to the ever-present evil of social chaos *(fitna)*, the nightmare scenario of Islamic political thought.

Why does God send so many prophets? Because according to al-Jahiz,

> A historical report may in its origin be weak and then become strong, and may be strong in origin but grow weak, depending on the circumstances and accidents of time which accompany its first appearance and its spread until it reaches its ultimate limit, significance and interest. Since this is an alarming matter, and the more ancient reports are prone to be lost, God instituted for us at the beginning of every period of time a landmark, meant to restore and strengthen historical reports, and to renew what is about to vanish. God did this through prophets and messengers. Thus, it was Noah who renewed the history elapsing from Adam to his own age and thereby prevented it from becoming flawed. When history again grew feeble, God sent Muhammad to renew the narratives of Adam and Noah, Moses and Aaron, Jesus and John. Muhammad, being himself truthful, and endowed with truthful signs, informed us that the Last Hour shall come and that the line of prophecy ends with him.[7]

Given that most of humanity is not privileged to have witnessed at first hand the miraculous achievements of prophets, prophecy for al-Jahiz acts as a reawakening of history, and Muhammadan prophecy in particular is the final and most truthful rewriting of all earlier history.[8] This, then, is one such "proof" of Muhammad's message: his history is better attested to than any other. Other "proofs" include such things as his own extraordinary gifts of character, the immense devotion of his followers, the "miraculous" agreement regarding the basic facts of his life and achievements among people who otherwise agree on nothing, and the challenge he threw down before his proud and eloquent society to answer his moral reprimands or match the eloquence of the revelations he brought them, a challenge to which his society could not respond.[9] This last "proof" leads al-Jahiz to propound, perhaps for the first time in a systematic shape, the theory of prophetic excellence, according to which prophets are said to have gained their elevated status from surpassing their own societies in an art or science in which these societies excelled. Thus, Moses excelled in magic in an age known for its high magical arts; the resurrection of the dead by Jesus rendered him more excellent than any physician in an age distinguished for its medical art; Muhammad's eloquence excelled in an age celebrated for its eloquence.

Two things may be said about these arguments for the truth of Muhammad's prophecy. First there is the humanist tenor of the argument; that is, these "proofs" are derived largely from the accurate manner in which the facts of his life and character were preserved and came down to us. This in itself is a "proof" no less miraculous than the miracle of any other prophet. Second, al-Jahiz deliberately chose not to cite as proof any of the miracles of Muhammad widely circulating in his day, nor any citations from the Old and New Testaments purportedly announcing Muhammad's coming. This is not entirely surprising given the difficulties that rationalist theologians, especially the Mu'tazilites, encountered in digesting the miracles of Muhammad, and their fear that these miracles were an easy target for the enemies of Islam to question and refute.

So from al-Jahiz and Ibn Qutayba there descended a rich intellectual tradition of defending and canonizing Muhammad's prophetic career with "proofs" drawn from a wide spectrum of sources. Ibn Qutayba pioneered the method of meticulous examination of the Old and New Testaments with the object of identifying allusions to Muhammad in these earlier Scriptures, and the argument for prophetic excellence, first systematically formulated by al-Jahiz, was elaborated by later generations.[10] In their very different ways, namely, Ibn Qutayba's concern with internal harmonization and al-Jahiz's concern with the establishment of external rational criteria of proof, both writers were intent on protecting the integrity of the *Sira,* on placing its narratives on sounder foundations of harmony and accurate history. Many of their arguments, one might add, continue to be employed in contemporary Muslim biographies of the Prophet.

Herewith begins a chapter in the examination of Muhammad's life during which, among other things, *Sira* writers sought to place that life in a wider context of the history and phenomenon of prophecy. From Ibn Qutayba descended a tradition of identifying the "proofs" of Muhammad largely with his miracles. These latter were now projected on a wide screen to include both the Annunciations of his coming as well as the allusions to him in earlier Scriptures. From al-Jahiz descended a tradition that concentrated on a more "rationalist" explanation of prophecy, prophets, and miracles. The "school" of Ibn Qutayba was of course prevalent among the Hadith masters while the "school" of al-Jahiz influenced theologians and philosophers of various hues. How did these ideas infiltrate the cultural climates of the two or three centuries that followed?

An early work in the Hadith mode is Abu Bakr al-Firyabi's (d. 913) *Dala'il al-Nubuwwa* (Signs of Prophecy), which consists largely of a listing of food and water miracles, with a small number of conversion miracles. There is nothing to distinguish this work from a typical work of Hadith of its age except for its concentration on a single subject. The purpose appears to have been didactic: to gather together in one place for the benefit of students all the miracles of Muhammad's prophetic career. Much more ambitious in scope is another work of *Dala'il,* and although it is cast in the mode of Hadith, its author is far more aware of the need to expand, defend, or justify its miraculous stories: it is the *Dala'il al-Nubuwwa* of Abu Nu'aym al-Isbahani (d. 1038). A consummate Hadith expert but with deep interests in both Sufism and theology, Abu Nu'aym provided his work with an introduction in which he argued that all prophets are endowed by God with four "gifts": There is first of all excellence in kind; thus no prophet has ever suffered from bodily infirmity, mental confusion, a base genealogy, or moral defect. Second, there is excellence in endowment. When kings, for example, send forth an ambassador they endow him with special graces and additional honors that enable him to perform his mission with greater ease. When the merciful God entrusts a prophet with a mission, He supplies him with additional gifts to strengthen his heart, sharpen his intellect, and to enable him to acquire virtue and to persevere with determination. Third is the provision of right guidance. When God honors someone with a mission, His wisdom decrees that he be granted the ability to preach right guidance. The fourth gift is that God instructs the prophet if he is in error. When God turns with kindness toward His creatures, He ensures that His chosen messenger, in order to bear the brunt of prophecy, does not lack divine instruction. These four gifts cannot be acquired through hard work. They are divine gifts manifested only in places and times of greatest need, when the great mass of humanity is about to fall into error.[11]

He asserts that the theologians of his day have answered adequately the objections to prophecy advanced by "atheists and philosophers," so he will not replicate their efforts. Instead he intends to pursue the more humble task of collecting, from all "wells" of knowledge, the more trustworthy and better known of Muhammad's "proofs." But this is no ordinary or silent anthology of miraculous Hadith. The Annunciation section is very large and contains stories of wonders not found anywhere else. The author then comments on this section as follows:

> What this section contains of Muhammad's life circumstances, from the time that his mother Amina married until she became pregnant with him, his delivery, his life with his foster-mother Halima, until he reached the age of twenty-five, with all its accompanying wonders, constitutes proof of his prophecy, being so much out of what is commonly accepted and customary.[12]

This last phrase is of course a nod in the direction of theologians and "naturalists" who were intent on defining custom *(ʿada)* and the ways in which it could be said to be broken. We shall come to them later, but Abu Nuʿaym takes it for granted that his "proofs" are all in one sense or another manifest breaches of custom. To bolster this claim, he devotes an entire section to the miracles of other prophets and to showing how Muhammad's miracles are more wondrous, telling, and numerous than all of those miracles put together:

> If it is said that Abraham was singled out as the intimate companion of God, Muhammad was the intimate companion and beloved of God. If it is said that Abraham broke in anger the idols of his people, Muhammad broke 360 idols in the Kaʿba by merely pointing at them, whereupon they fell. If it is said that Moses turned the staff into a serpent, Muhammad was granted more wondrous signs: the longing of the tree stump for him and the trees that came crawling to him at his bidding.[13]

And so it proceeds. Page after page of prophets' miracles and wonders of speech and conduct are outdone, outshone by Muhammad's. The largest category is the miracles of Jesus, but here too Muhammad outperforms Jesus in every department. The work ends with a detailed description of Muhammad's physical characteristics accompanied by a few attempts at a physiognomy.

With Abu Nu'aym we arrive at a summa, a work that best captures the Hadith tradition on the proofs of prophecy as first systematized by Ibn Qutayba. The work lacks Ibn Qutayba's polemical defense of the integrity and coherence of Muhammadan hadiths, but it is far larger in scope and richer in miraculous narratives. It is also more relaxed and confident in tone, taking for granted that the objections to Muhammad's miracles have been decisively answered, but developing to the full the idea of Muhammad's superiority in miracle working, clearly to counter an important set of objections issuing probably from Christian circles.

What now of the al-Jahiz "school"? A motley crowd meets us here, not all of whom by any means were directly influenced by al-Jahiz, but most of whom grappled with the kinds of subjects that he had so succinctly broached. On either side of al-Jahiz stood two important and original thinkers on the subject of prophecy, general and Muhammadan. These were the Christian convert 'Ali ibn Rabban al-Tabari (d. ca. 861) and the Zaydi Shiite Ahmad ibn al-Husayn al-Haruni (d. 1030).

'Ali ibn Rabban writes with the passion of the convert in order to justify his conversion to his former coreligionists:

Among the Prophet's miracles is this Qur'an. It is a miracle for reasons I have not seen discussed fully by any author in this genre, but merely in broad and general terms or claims. While still a Christian I would argue about the Qur'an and an uncle of mine, a learned and eloquent Christian scholar, would argue back that ornaments of rhetoric do not constitute proofs of prophecy since these are common among all nations. But when I rejected imitation and force of custom and upbringing, and carefully considered the themes of the Qur'an, I found the matter to be as asserted by Muslims. For I have not found any book, whether written by Arab, Persian, Indian or Byzantine, that joins the unicity of God and His praise and thanks, to firm belief in prophets, the urging to virtue, command of good and forbidding of evil, and exhortation to Paradise and censure of Hell—like this Qur'an, since the world began. He who brought us such a book, with such a place in the hearts by reason of both its majesty and sweetness, and endowed with such good fortune and triumph, while the person bringing it was an illiterate who could neither write nor have had any knowledge of rhetoric— such a book must beyond any doubt constitute proof of his prophecy.[14]

In further establishing the proofs of Muhammadan prophecy, he uses his considerable knowledge of the Bible and other scriptures to "reveal" how Muhammad's name had been subjected to distortion *(tahrif)* or concealment *(kitman)* by earlier religious communities. Like al-Jahiz, 'Ali ibn Rabban is much concerned with the nature and veracity of historical reports, because the doubts expressed about the historicity of Muhammad's *Sira* are among the principal objections to Islam advanced by non-Muslims.[15] In his work a detailed discussion ensues on the various kinds of consensus that are used as the basis of historical reports, which in turn leads to comments on other criteria of historical truth as well as the internal contradictions in historical reports of non-Muslim religions. The proofs for Muhammad are summarized under ten headings:

1. His call to the One God, in which he was at one with all prophets.

2. His ascetic, chaste, and truthful manner of life and his praiseworthy *Sunna.*

3. His miracles, which only true prophets can produce.

4. His foretelling of certain events, all of which took place in his lifetime.

5. His foretelling of great events, all of which took place after his death.

6. The Book he brought, which is necessarily and indisputably a prophetic miracle.

7. His triumph over all nations, which is necessarily and indisputably a prophetic miracle.

8. His followers who transmitted his history, who were the most virtuous of people, from whom no deceit can be thought possible.

9. His status as the Seal of Prophets: Had he not been sent, all previous prophecies regarding him among earlier prophets would need to be considered false.

10. Prophets long before his time had prophesied his coming, mission, home country, career, and the submission of all nations and kings to his rule.

It is in points nine and ten that 'Ali ibn Rabban truly shines as a defender of Muhammad. Combing the Old and New Testaments for allusions to Muhammad, he finds much to criticize in earlier scriptures. Thus he finds the Torah, while containing laudable laws, to be too narrowly focused on the Israelites and their history. The Gospels, containing wonderful wisdom and sermons, nevertheless contain few if any laws. The Psalms, too, despite their beauty, are lacking in laws. The revelations of the Old Testament prophets consist of little more than denunciations of the Israelites. The Qur'an, by contrast, contains all these qualities and more, and its appeal is universal. The Qur'an is in and of itself a miraculous proof, and emphatically so because its revealer was illiterate. 'Ali ibn Rabban concludes that had Muhammad *not* been sent, *all* earlier prophecy would necessarily have been in vain, since it all points to him.[16]

From 'Ali ibn Rabban and his age descend the fifty or so allusions to Muhammad detected in earlier scriptures that were to become the loci classici of many later biographies of the Prophet. One typical list of allusions and commentary occurs in a work of the *Dala'il* genre called *A'lam al-Nubuwwa* (The Proofs of Prophecy) by Abu Hatim al-Razi (d. ca. 933), an Isma'ili Shiite. I cite the passage at length because it may be of special interest to readers with a biblical background or expertise, and it illustrates the manner of argument employed:

In the Torah we find: God Almighty said to the Israelites: "I shall appoint a prophet from your brethren and shall put my speech upon his mouth" [cf. Deuteronomy 18:15]. The brethren of the Israelites are the Ishmaelites. The prophet who rose among the Ishmaelites is Muhammad. In the Torah too we find: "God came from Sinai. He shone from Seir and illuminated from the mountains of Paran" [cf. Deuteronomy 33:2]. The coming of God from Sinai is the coming of Moses, because God gave him the tablets on Mount Sinai. His shining from Seir is the appearance of Christ, because he was from Seir, from the land of Galilee and from a village called Nazareth. His illumination from the mountains of Paran is the appearance of Muhammad from Mecca, because Paran is Mecca. In the Torah also is found: "Ishmael learnt archery in the wilderness of Paran" [cf. Genesis 21:21–22]. It is an indubitable fact that Ishamael grew up in Mecca and learnt archery there. In the Gospel we find: "Jesus said, I shall go and the Paraclete, the spirit of truth which does not speak of itself, will teach you everything. He will witness to me as I witnessed to him and he shall be sent in my name" [cf. John 14:25–26; 16:13–15]. The phrase "shall be sent in my name" means that he will be a law-giver like him. No lawgiver appeared after him who was like him except Muhammad. He witnessed to Muhammad as Muhammad was to witness to him. In the Psalms we find the following, describing Muhammad: "He rescues the weak who has no supporter, he shows mercy to the wretched, prayers are said for him constantly and blessings are pronounced upon him every day. His mention shall last for ever and his kingdom shall stretch from sea to sea" [cf. Psalm 72:4–15]. This too is un-doubtedly a description of Muhammad because his law will last until the Day of Resurrection without abrogation, nor will there be another prophet after him. It is he whose mention will last for ever and he upon whom prayers and blessings are pronounced every day and at every moment. In the Book of Isaiah we find: "God said to me, Post a watchman and let him report what he sees. What the watchman saw and reported was: two riders have come, one on an ass and one on a camel. As I observed, one of the riders came up and said: Fallen, fallen is Babylon. All the rotting images of its gods are fallen to the ground. What I have heard from God the mighty lord of Israel I have told you" [cf. Isaiah 21:6–10]. By the rider on a donkey is meant Christ because he entered Jerusalem riding on an ass. By the rider of the camel is meant Muhammad because he entered Medinah riding on a camel. At Muhammad's hands Babylon was cap-tured and its images were destroyed. In Isaiah we also find: "My servant with whom I am well pleased is the praised one *[Ahmad al-mahmud]* through the praise of God; a new praise at which the wilderness and its inhabitants will rejoice" [cf. Isaiah 42:1, 11]. This is an explicit reference to his name. The wilderness means the desert because it is the home of the Arabs. In it lies the land of Hijaz from which Muhammad appeared. In Isaiah we also find: "Let the desert rejoice and let the wilderness and wastelands exult and let them bring forth light like the light of fenugreek *[ɹhanbaliǒ]* and let it be illuminated and bloom like the fan-palm because it shall through Ahmad give forth the glory of Lebanon" [cf. Isaiah 35:1–2]. In Isaiah also there occurs: "To us a child is born, to us a son is given and upon his shoulders is the sign of prophecy" [cf. Isaiah 9:5–6]. No prophet carried on his shoulders the sign of prophecy except Muhammad. In the Book of Habakkuk we find: "The heavens are unveiled from the majesty of Muhammad and the earth is filled with his praise" [cf. Habakkuk 3:3]. This, and much else besides, is mentioned in his book.

In the Book of Daniel we find the vision which he saw and interpreted and whose explanation he mentioned. In it, there occurs: "I saw the Ancient of Days sitting and a thousand thousand servants waited upon him, and scribes without number" [cf. Daniel 7:10]. He mentions many things already cited in this, our present work. He also says, "And I saw, coming on the clouds of heaven, one like a man. He came to the Ancient of Days and was led into his presence. On him they conferred kingship, sovereignty and glory, and all peoples, nations and languages would become his servants. His sovereignty will last for ever and his kingship will never pass away" [cf. Daniel 7:13–14]. We have already cited this vision and its interpretation, which saves us from repeating it here. In this book, also, and in interpreting the dream which the king saw, and toward the end of his speech, Daniel says: "The God of heaven will in those days set up a kingdom which will never change or pass away. It shall not leave kingdom or sovereignty to any other nation but it will shatter and annihilate all other kingdoms and itself shall last for ever and ever" [cf. Daniel 2:44]. This interpretation was given in explanation of the king's dream in which he saw a stone striking the statue made of iron, bronze and earthenware. This is a well-known incident in the Book of Daniel and Daniel's pronouncements, and has wide circulation among the public of our own days. In the Book of Jeremiah, we find: "I have made you a prophet to the nations to tear up and knock down, to destroy and overthrow, to build and to plant" [cf. Jeremiah 1:10]. In the Book of Hosea there occurs: "I am the Lord your God who pastured you among the nomads, in a land of desolation and waste" [cf. Hosea 13:5]. No prophet ever appeared from a wasteland except Muhammad, for he appeared from the desert.

These then are the signs of Muhammad in the books of prophets. The People of the Book read them and do not deny what we mentioned because they are written down in these books. But they are overcome with caprice and struck down with blighted hope and blindness in order that God may bring to pass what has been decreed. There is much else in these books of this kind but we have omitted most of these references because of the condition of brevity we imposed upon ourselves above, whereby we mention from every topic a little but avoid being all-inclusive. What we have cited above is therefore not something which can possibly be said to be the result of collusion, nor is it something transmitted by only one, two or three men. For these are prophecies uttered by prophets who lived at diverse periods, and long before Muhammad.[17]

Turning now to the other al-Jahizian figure, namely al-Haruni, and his *Ithbat Nubuwwat al-Nabiyy* (Proving the Prophecy of the Prophet [Muhammad]), we have the kind of work that issues directly and explicitly from al-Jahiz but develops his arguments in various directions. Here it is not so much what earlier prophets foretold that constitutes Muhammad's proof but rather Muhammad's own extraordinary career. Would a reasonable man seeking only power behave as Muhammad did and expose himself so willingly to enmity and envy? Would such a man gratuitously challenge his audience by claiming to foretell events that could easily turn out to be false and so undermine his credibility? How could such a proud people as the Arabs, never united under one king, have so humbly submitted to his rule? These and similar events in his life are the most irrefutable proofs of his truth. To these are added his glorious Companions and one other novel theme, the excellence and superiority of his nation's religious sciences: a triumphant, unanswerable theology and a celebrated and unsurpassable body of jurists.[18]

This then is how the authors of the *Dala'il* works strove in their various ways to instruct their readers regarding the truth of Muhammad. These authors had done their job competently, helping to build up a solid case for the sincerity and veneration of their Prophet. This case was based upon a wide gamut of arguments drawn from Muslim and non-Muslim scriptures to which were added others drawn from history and plain rationality. To defend Muhammad, his *Sira* was turned into an argument or even at times into a legal brief intended to silence his detractors. For this genre would have been unwarranted had it not been that prophecy in general and Muhammad in particular were under attack from many quarters: Muslim "heretics," non-Muslim theologians, skeptical philosophers. But the *Dala'il* works did not simply defend him; they also celebrated his achievements. In other words, they canonized his *Sira,* helping to enshrine the love of Muhammad among the members of his community. The *Dala'il,* a literary genre to which many different schools of thought contributed, even some widely considered schismatic, provided a common ground of agreement among Muslim scholars, helping them to close ranks, to rally to the flag of their Prophet. This development coincided with an era when their greatest political symbol, the institution of the caliphate, could neither unite Muslims nor be easily defended. It was Muhammad's historical record, duly re-interpreted, that was the final refuge.

To the crisis of political leadership one must add a Kulturkampf of intense proportions that erupted in Muslim cultural circles beginning in the ninth century. It is not my intention to examine this "cultural struggle" in any detail but simply to focus on one aspect of it: the great debate about prophecy and prophets that began when the cultural history of other civilized nations of antiquity first became widely known to Muslim scholarship. In essence, one might formulate the dilemma as follows: Why is it that so many otherwise admirable civilizations, for example, the Greeks and Indians, make no mention of prophets or repudiate them outright?

It was the historians, *Adibs*, natural scientists, theologians, and philosophers of Islam (and not, say, the Hadith scholars) who concerned themselves most intimately with foreign cultures and who first raised questions about the nature and function of prophecy. We have seen in the *Dala'il* works that defending Muhammad necessitated a defense of prophecy in general. Any attack on prophecy was by implication an attack on Muhammad. But other thinkers wrestled with more theoretical issues. Given that truths about God, virtue, the afterlife, and so forth can be attained through reason by the philosophers, what room is left for a prophet? If the universe necessarily obeys natural laws, how can miracles occur? What precisely is a prophet, why do we need him, and how does he acquire his knowledge?

Some of these questions, for example, about the truth or otherwise of a prophet, have already received answers of a sort above, in the *Dala'il* works. The more abstract issues relating to prophecy were left up to what may very loosely be called the "rationalists." I shall, rather rashly, give the following definition of them: thinkers who believed that unaided human reason could provide answers to questions relating to God, prophecy, existence, and ethics *independently from* or else *in conformity with* divine revelation.[19]

Two Muslim philosophers, al-Kindi (d. ca. 866) and al-Farabi (d. 950) may be taken as representing two contrasting views on the relationship between philosophy (unaided human reason) and prophecy (divine revelation). Kindi, the conformist, sees no necessary contradiction between the philosopher and the prophet. The prophet is what one might term an "instant" philosopher, someone who acquires his knowledge of reality directly and immediately from God, without having to suffer the long apprenticeship of the student of philosophy. Furthermore, a prophet is likely to answer theoretical questions far more clearly and concisely than a philosopher.[20] In subject matter, however, the philosopher and the prophet deal with the same grand themes: God and creation, the good life, human destiny, and so forth. One might therefore interpret Kindi as arguing that philosophical truth is merely a more abstract or even abstruse form of prophetic truth. Al-Farabi was more radical. Al-Farabi defined religion as "opinions and acts, decreed and limited by conditions set for the group by their first leader, whereby, in practicing these opinions and acts, he seeks to attain his own specific end in or through them." If the "first leader" is virtuous, he seeks for his group true happiness; if not, then he seeks some of those false ends considered pleasurable, for example, power, glory or victory.[21]

Given this definition of religion as "opinions and acts decreed and limited," it is then argued that these can only be reflections of more certain truths, of ultimate truths fortified by philosophical "demonstration" *(burban)*. The virtuous prophet in al-Farabi is not "an instant philosopher" but more like a popularizer of philosophy, a philosopher of the masses, whose "opinions and acts" are derived *from* philosophical theory, from metaphysics and ethics. Al-Farabi's discussions of prophecy are couched in terms so theoretical and so lacking in any allusions to Muhammad or Islam as to seem like what Aristotle might have said if he were brought back to life and asked to write on prophecy. The philosopher is a person whose wisdom comes from emanation from the Active Intellect *(al-'aql al-fa'al)*, through the medium of the Acquired Intellect *(al-'aql al-mustafad)*, and then to his own Imprinted Intellect *(al-'aql al-munfa'il)*. A prophet on the other hand, receiving his wisdom from the same sources, is one whose imaginative faculty *(quwwa mutakhayyila)*, rather than the imprinted intellect, is developed to the highest degree.[22]

The prophets' forte, their special skill, consists in transforming philosophical truths into opinions that are palatable to the masses. This is a major theme in a marvelous philosophical tale, the *Hayy ibn Yaqzan,* by the Andalusian philosopher Abu Bakr ibn Tufayl (d. 1185), known to the medieval Christian West as Abubacer. Briefly summarized, the tale tells of a child on a desert island who is raised and surrounded entirely by animals, who reaches through his own remarkable intellect to the highest truths of the universe, including the oneness of God and the basic rules of ethics. When he finally comes face to face with a fellow human, a monotheist man of religion and of a retiring and rational disposition, and learns his language quickly, the following exchange ensues:

> Asal [the man of religion] described to him [Hayy] all that the religious law *(shari'ah)* contains by way of description of the divine world, paradise and hell, the resurrection, the balance and the straight path. Hayy understood all this and found nothing therein to contradict what he himself had witnessed during his sublime meditations. He came to know that the person who described all this and transmitted it was indeed a truthful messenger from his Lord. So he believed in him and embraced his message. There were two things however which puzzled him: why did the truthful messenger strike parables for people re-

garding the divine world? Why did he not tell them the truth directly, which would have prevented wrong beliefs like God's corporeality? And why did the prophet permit the acquisition of wealth and thus divert people from seeking the truth?[23]

Hayy, insisting on leaving the island to return to Asal's city to preach the unadorned philosophical truth, discovers that most human intellects cannot handle theoretical truths whereas the figural or rhetorical truths of religion are the ones that are most appropriate to their minds. He then decides to return to his island with Asal, where they devote the rest of their lives to contemplation.

From the Muslim philosophers, prophecy had received various definitions, many concerned with the nature and mode of knowledge of the prophetic soul and how these definitions compare with the philosophical.[24] Prophecy as truth-made-palatable is perhaps a fair summary of the philosophical position as found in al-Farabi and Ibn Tufayl. Other philosophers such as Ibn Sina adopted a view closer to that of al-Kindi. One might therefore argue that there were broadly two different rationalizations of prophecy by the philosophers. The first saw prophecy as an ability to represent demonstrative truths in an imaginative guise, suitable for consumption by the people at large. The second saw prophecy as a capacity for reaching rational conclusions more quickly and with less effort than is the case with philosophers.

But other Muslim groups, notably the theologians, felt they needed to grapple with more immediate polemical tasks, as we have seen above with al-Jahiz. The enemies of prophecy were both inside and outside the gates, and more direct and specific answers were needed to problems raised by Muhammadan prophecy than what might be found in the theoretical speculations of the philosophers. Where the philosophers were primarily preoccupied with fitting prophecy into a rationalist worldview and accounting for it in general terms, the theologians were occupied in the more immediate task of justifying the claims of particular prophets, situating Muhammad in relation to them and defending their historical record. There was overlap, of course, concerning such issues as verifying the claims of prophets and sifting out false prophets from true.

Arguably the most influential adversary of prophecy and prophets in premodern Islamic culture is the celebrated philosopher and physician Abu Bakr Muhammad ibn Zakariyya al-Razi (d. 925), known to the medieval West as Rhazes. In a public debate preserved for posterity by his opponent, al-Razi is reported to have advanced three principal objections to prophecy. The first objection concerns the harm that prophets bring, which he formulates as follows:

Why do you hold it to be necessary that God singled out one particular people for prophecy rather than another, preferred them above all other peoples, made them to be guides for mankind and caused mankind to need them? Why do you hold it to be possible for the Wise One in His wisdom to have chosen this fate for them, setting some peoples against others, establishing enmities among them, and multiplying the causes of aggression, thus leading mankind to destruction? It would have been more worthy of the wisdom of the Wise One, more worthy also of the mercy of the Merciful, for Him to have inspired all His creatures with the knowledge of what is to their benefit as well as to their harm in this world and the next. He would not have privileged some over others and there would be no cause for quarrel and no dispute amongst them, leading to their destruction. This would have been more protective of them than to cause some to act as guides for others, with the result that each religious community comes to believe in their own leader and to declare all other leaders false. Thus, they draw the sword against one another, calamities are widespread and they perish through mutual aggression and strife. Many have perished in this manner, as is plain.[25]

This of course is an attack on the "chosen people" concept often taught by prophets and the aggression and harm that result from it. Al-Razi clearly implies that Muhammad, too, like his predecessors, privileged his own group over all others.

The second objection has to do with the anti-intellectual thrust of prophecy and its perceived fables and absurdities:

Those who adhere to religious laws received their religion from their leaders through imitation. They forbade rational investigation of religious principles and were very strict in this regard. They transmitted from their leaders traditions which oblige them to abandon rational inquiry as a matter of religious belief and others which brand all who challenge these traditions they relate as unbelievers. Among these traditions related from ancestors are the following: "Debating religious questions with affectation is unbelief"; "Whoever subjects his religious belief to analogical reasoning will remain forever confused"; "Do not reflect upon God but rather upon His creation"; "Predestination is a mystery of God: do not delve into that mystery"; "Beware of profound reflection for those who came before you perished through profound reflection."[26]

The third objection has to do with the flat contradictions that exist among prophets and their teachings:

Jesus claimed he was the son of God; Moses claimed that God had no son; Muhammad claimed he was a creature like all other humans; Mani and Zoroaster disagreed with Moses, Jesus and Muhammad concerning the Eternal One, the creation of the world and the origin of good and evil. Mani disagreed with Zoroaster regarding the two worlds and their causes. Muhammad claimed that Jesus was not crucified. The Jews and Christians deny this and claim that he was killed and crucified.[27]

These objections elicited lengthy refutations from al-Razi's opponent, which, despite their considerable interest, need not concern us here. It is enough to remember that al-Razi was not a lone "heretic" but belonged to a group called in a recent study the "free thinkers" of medieval Islam.[28] A thinker such as Ibn al-Rawandi (d. 860), for instance, would question the claim that the Qur'an constitutes a proof of Muhammad's prophecy by arguing thus:

You are mistaken and prejudice has clouded your intellects. If someone were to make the same claim in favor of an ancient philosopher that you make for the Qur'an, and argued that the proof of the truth of Ptolemy and Euclid in what they brought forth is that Euclid produced his work and claimed that humans are incapable of producing its like, would that constitute proof of his being a prophet?[29]

It would be wrong to think that "heretics" such as al-Razi and Ibn al-Rawandi were marginal to the intellectual life of their times. Their arguments against prophecy and prophets were widely known to contemporaries as well as later generations, who often reproduced them at length prior to refuting them. This debate about prophecy drew in a host of thinkers, many of whom, given the breadth of their interests, cannot easily be categorized as either pure theologians or pure philosophers or even pure mystics or jurists. From this rich mixture of diverse methodologies came diverse answers to questions on the definition of prophecy and how Muhammad in particular fulfilled its conditions in the best possible manner. In the process what we often encounter in this canonization of Muhammad is a defense of all preceding prophets, this being a precondition of establishing the truth of his own mission.

So from medicine comes the definition of a prophet as a "physician" of the soul, one who like Muhammad needed at times to apply "surgery" to cut off a diseased member of society or else one who "treats" the soul for the diseases of ignorance and savagery.[30] From the sciences comes the view that since some knowledge in the sciences clearly goes beyond the rational, its source must be the prophets, who alone have access to a realm beyond reason.[31] From jurisprudence comes a singular but fascinating discussion as to whether a prophet can be a woman—answered in the affirmative for a *nabiyy* (a prophet who brings no divine law) but not for a *rasul* (a prophet with a divine law).[32] From theology comes a rich debate as to whether prophets may sin before or after their mission, with particular attention paid to certain incidents in the life of Muhammad. The emerging (Sunni) consensus in this regard is that no major sins can possibly be ascribed to prophets, but moments of forgetfulness are possible, which in no way invalidate the truth of the prophets' mission.[33] From Arabian history comes the question as to how prophecy may be related to sorcery, and the answer is that both are spiritual powers granted from on high but with the difference that prophecy is a guide to intellect, a program of reform, and a teacher of ethics.[34] From intensive study of the *Sira* comes a dissection of the progress of Muhammadan revelations that singles out six chronological stages of revelations, starting with true visions in dreams, then purification, then glad tidings of prophecy brought by an angel, then the descent of Gabriel with the simple announcement of prophecy, then the private commandment to warn, and finally the commandment to proclaim the message in public and to all mankind.[35] Finally, from philosophy and Sufism comes a description of prophecy as a mode of apprehension that lies outside the realm of reason, a state that can sometimes be approximated in mystic devotions.[36]

There are two thinkers, however, who deserve separate treatment and fittingly summarize and develop many of the issues that have been raised above: the famous jurist Abu al-Hasan al-Mawardi (d. 1058) and the celebrated Mu'tazilite theologian Al-Qadi 'Abd al-Jabbar (d. 1024).[37] Both writers seek to reinterpret the *Sira* in order to protect it from heresy and superstition. Both men were well aware that the *Sira* was the Achilles heel of religious tradition, the softest part being the question of Muhammad's miracles: Are they credible? Were they accurately transmitted? Is belief in them necessary? How do they compare with miracles of earlier prophets? What is the definition of "miracle"? Al-Mawardi's *A 'lam al-Nubuwwah* (The Proofs of Prophecy) is juristic in spirit although with pronounced theological interests. It argues that the Qur'an was Muhammad's greatest miracle. Its unsurpassable and inimitable eloquence in an age celebrated for its eloquence constitutes Muhammad's greatest proof and by extension demonstrates the complete truthfulness of its revealer. It follows from Muhammad's truthfulness that the Prophet was a monotheist from his earliest years and never an idol worshipper. All reports that question this fact must be rejected as false. Muhammad's miracles are, in the best juristic manner, classified and distinguished by types, complete with explanation and commentary. Apart from the Qur'an, these miracles include his God-given immunity *('isma)* from harm by enemies intent on killing him, food and water miracles that surpass the miracles of other prophets, the curing of the sick, foretelling future events, his prayers being answered by God, wild animals and trees announcing his mission, his purity of origin, and his supremely virtuous traits of character. Al-Mawardi refutes objections by skeptics, whether these relate to the transmission of reports or to their intrinsic credibility. On miracles of prophets that were transmitted by single transmitters *(khabar al-wahid)*, a problematic issue for both jurists and theologians, al-Mawardi argues as follows:

> If someone says, "The miracles of prophets cannot be demonstrated through reports transmitted by single transmitters" two responses may be made. First, single transmitters ascribed these miracles to him [Muhammad] while surrounded by a numerous concourse of people who saw that transmitter, heard his report, believed him and did not call him a liar. It is impossible for a large number of people to refrain from refuting falsehood, as it is impossible for them to fabricate falsehood. And while it is possible for a large number to agree upon the truth, despite being separated in time and place, and impossible for them to all agree on a falsehood, this is because the motives which induce to truth are, in general, mutually corroborative whereas the motives inducing to falsehood are in particular contradictory. This is why the truth spoken by the most lying of people exceeds his lies, because he cannot but speak the truth whereas he is free to lie. Second, these reports were transmitted through many channels and under diverse circumstances. Hence it is impossible that they be lies in their totality, even if lying is possible in individual cases. Therefore, their totality constitutes multiple transmission *(tawatur)* even if they are single transmissions in each case and cannot, when considered singly, constitute proof.[38]

Spoken like a judge, one could add, but one with a deep interest in theology and one who has done a close reading of al-Jahiz on what constitutes rational proof.[39] The problem of the nature of transmission was of abiding concern to jurists and Hadith masters,

but al-Mawardi here extends the analysis to take in the psychological aspects of truth telling and deceit.

The second work of roughly the same period is an even more impressive and original analysis of the reports of the *Sira*, entitled
Tathbit Dala'il al-Nubuwwah (Establishing the Proofs of Prophecy) by
the great Mu'tazilite theologian 'Abd al-Jabbar (d. 1024). This work
was written against a backdrop of a vigorous campaign of Isma'ili
propaganda emanating from the Fatimid Empire of Egypt and Syria
(ca. 969–1171) and claiming among other things the arrival of a new
age of justice that would be miraculously different from any that preceded it, and brought about by a series of caliph-imams, supernatu-
rally inspired. This challenge necessitated a full discussion of
miracles in general, and of Muhammad's miracles in particular. The
debate over miracles had begun in earnest approximately two centuries before 'Abd al-Jabbar.[40] But his contributions to that debate
remain of major interest in setting its future parameters.

The variety of Mu'tazilite theology that 'Abd al-Jabbar embraced posited a universe of order and reason: man possessed free
will; God ruled creation in justice; the goodness of God implied
that all His acts toward creation were necessarily for His creatures' best interests *(al-aslah);* nature possessed regular laws that
could be broken only in exceptional and carefully defined circumstances; all ascriptions of attributes to God that smack of corporeality or question His utter unicity must be radically reinterpreted.
From these and other Mu'tazilite principles 'Abd al-Jabbar drew
his portrait of prophecy and miracle. He begins by arguing that

1. A religious law complements and details what human
   reason can only know in broad and general terms.
2. No true messenger *(rasul)* can come without a
   religious law *(shari'ah).*
3. God sends His messengers for the best interests
   (masalih) of His creatures.

4. The laws of prophets do not conflict with human
   reason *('aql)*.

5. There are two preconditions of true prophecy: rational
   apprehension that the prophet is sent by God and that
   he is a breaker of custom *(kharij 'an al-'ada)*.[41]

The miracles of Muhammad were one area where the Mu'tazilite theologians needed to tread with care. Anyone suggesting a
belief in a universe of regularity and order would always find it difficult to explain miraculous reversals of that order. The Qur'an, on
the other hand, was full of the "signs and wonders" of creation and
contained numerous reports of prophetic miracles. It was necessary therefore to lay down the rule for the occurrence of miracles
if one wanted to avoid a haphazard and unruly universe run by a
sort of sorcerer-God. 'Abd al-Jabbar advances the view that the
life of Muhammad was itself the real miracle, a process during
which he proceeded against all custom, all norms, from abject
weakness to great power.[42] All the prophecies he uttered concerning events after his death came true: he defeated the nations and
attained all his objectives. But how is custom *('ada)* to be interpreted? Many are the evidentiary signs *(ayat)* that violate custom,
as many as the instances where Muhammad, against all expectations, won through or achieved his aims. There are instances in
which to have said something other than what he did in fact utter
would "normally" have been far more prudent, or to have revealed
something from God and not be contradicted would have been impossible. There are instances in which his defiance of powerful enemies was an act no man of reason would commit were it not that
Muhammad placed absolute trust in God. There are cases in which
his followers would certainly have abandoned him had they enter-
tained the slightest doubts about his sincerity. Finally, there are instances in which the Qur'an heaps scorn on proud and powerful
adversaries and challenges them to debate, but where no answer

was ever received from a conceited and eloquent people. All these instances collectively must be considered breaches of the normal course of custom and thus miraculous.

The "breaking of custom" is defined as "an increase in the normal course of things" *(ziyada 'ala al-amr al-mu'tad)*. Such a phenomenon is, as it were, reality magnified, as in the following example from a Mu'tazilite theologian quoted approvingly by 'Abd al-Jabbar:

> We do not deny that before the start of Muhammad's prophetic mission there did occur something like a shower of stars. But we know from the evidence we presented that what occurred at the time of the Prophet's mission was something which violated custom, for the sky was filled with such showers. It is this increase in the normal course of things that constitutes proof [of prophecy]. This may be compared to the Flood. For the waters before Noah's time would often rise and increase in a normal, well-known manner. But when Noah came into the world, the waters increased in a manner that violated custom. That increase is itself the evidential sign or proof.[43]

Miracles in the Mu'tazilite view were essentially apologetic, that is, intended by God to demonstrate a prophet's truthful mission. As prophecy ended with Muhammad, so did miracles, which were now regarded as phenomena of the past. Equally to be doubted are all allusions to miraculous events that took place *before* the start of Muhammad's mission.[44] This view had the effect of drawing a large Mu'tazilite question mark across a substantial section of Muhammadan miracles to be found in the *Sira,* which I have been referring to as the Annunciation miracles. One way out of the difficulty was to view these miracles as miracles performed for *another* prophet living in Muhammad's pre-mission days.[45] For 'Abd al-Jabbar, these restrictions on the occurrence and function of miracles were necessary in order to maintain the integrity of Mu'tazilite principles regarding the physical universe, but also in order to avoid the path leading to superstitious belief in the persistence of miracles, as among Christians or "heretical" Muslims. The emphasis on Muhammad's miraculous life was at least as convincing as any single miracle he may have effected.

And so we come to the end of this discussion of the many ways in which Muhammad's *Sira* was being reformulated. A rich tradition of views, polemical, densely intertextual, mutually sustaining, created a climate through which the later medieval *Sira* was now set to travel. I have not attempted to describe in any detail the filiations of influence among these writers but preferred instead to treat them as a single tradition bearing many and echoing views. In broad terms, a reader of this tradition is struck by the manner in which the general phenomenon of prophecy overshadows almost every discussion of Muhammadan prophecy, creating not just new ways of seeing Muhammad but also a corpus of writings on prophecy of unusual interest in premodern culture.

VIII

The Universal Model

MUHAMMAD IN LATER MEDIEVAL BIOGRAPHY

We have seen in the previous chapter how the *Sira* was subjected to rational analysis with the purpose of defending it from attack or misrepresentation. The *Sira* could no longer be allowed to speak for itself; it had to be filtered through the voice of a commentary of one description or another. The "Proofs of Prophecy" genre, at its greatest flourishing between the ninth and eleventh centuries, had set the tone. Thereafter the traditional works of *Sira* would begin to reflect the rich corpus of commentary now available and increasingly to show how the *Sira should* be written.

By "the later medieval *Sira*" I mean the *Sira* that, with a few exceptions, was written under the Mamluk Empire and the early Ottoman periods (ca. the thirteenth century to ca. the eighteenth century), a period that I will sometimes call the "premodern." Scholarship in this period frequently assumed monumental or encyclopedic dimensions. It was an era of massive tomes, multivolume works that sought to recapitulate and reformulate the culture of the past. There is hardly any field of traditional scholarship that did not witness an immense enlargement in scope and treatment during this time. It is not easy to suggest reasons for this surge in productivity. But part of the answer must surely lie in a rapid expansion of the *'ulama'* class as a result of state patronage, an equivalent expansion of the reading public, and a greater concern, often encountered in the introductions of these works, with what authors referred to as the need for "completeness" *(tamam; kamal)* and accessibility *(sahl al-tanawul)* of knowledge.[1]

In this era of recapitulation, the *Sira* too began to bloat, to swallow and regurgitate its antecedents, and to lay down the groundwork for a *Sira* that was to last to the present day. In the process, this new premodern *Sira* went behind the four founding fathers to preserve for us sizable fragments from the very early layers of *Sira* writing, and then to organize the vast material accumulated in a manner often referred to as "comprehensive" *(jami')* or "well arrayed" *(madbut)*. The resulting image is of a Prophet who is, and should be, seen in a more supernatural light, but it also mines his every saying, act, or gesture to the last nugget for its legal or ethical value.

One candidate as a pacesetter in this new field of reconstituted *Sira,* the *Sira* as it *should* be written, is al-Qadi 'Iyad (d. 1149) and his *Al-Shifa bi Ta'rif Huquq al-Mustafa* (The Remedy Concerning the Determination of the Just Merits of the Chosen One [Muhammad]). The title itself merits pause.[2] The "remedy" suggests a preexisting malady or complaint, most probably a state of ignorance regarding what ought to be known or asserted about the "Chosen One" *(al-Mustafa)*. This latter term is significant as an epithet of Muhammad, suggesting an elevation of his status into the realm of the cosmic and the centrality of his role in God's plan for the universe. We have already encountered, especially in Shiite images but also elsewhere, the attempt to construct for Muhammad a pedigree stretching back to the very beginning of creation. The *Nur Muhammadi* theory of the procession of heavenly lights or else such hadiths as "I was a Prophet when Adam was still half-way between soul and body" had assigned Muhammad a status not much lower than that of the Qur'an as God's pre-eternal word. Among some Sufis, the epithet "Perfect Man" *(al-Insan al-Kamil)* had also been applied to him.

The Qadi 'Iyad now takes up these images and transforms them into a thematically arranged portrait of the eternal prophet, the purpose being defined as follows:

> This work is not composed in order to combat those who deny his prophecy or question his miracles . . . Rather, we have addressed it to the people of his community who have answered his call and believe in his prophecy, in order to fortify their love for him and act as a model for their actions.[3]

The work is therefore not so much a polemic as a tribute of love. Muhammad in the Qur'an, Muhammad's name all over paradise, his pre-eternity, and his miracles constitute the first half of the work, a celebration of a divinely chosen being who spans past, present, and future. He came to us from pre-eternity and he awaits us in paradise. While he was with us he was essentially the miracle worker, whose miracles are extolled as follows:

> The miracles of our Prophet are more evident than those of all other prophets. First, they are more numerous. No earlier prophet was granted any miracle that our Prophet did not equal or surpass . . . As regards their number, consider the Qur'an, the whole of which is a miracle . . . The Qur'an contains approximately 77,000 words. If *Sura* 108 is made up of ten words—the divine challenge being {to produce one *sura* like it}—and we divide the total number of words by the words of that *Sura,* i.e., ten, we end up with more than 7,000 sections of the Qur'an, each of which is a miracle . . . And yet one single *Sura* may contain a foretelling of future events, such that the

number of miracles is multiplied . . . The second aspect is the manifest character of his miracles. The miracles of other prophets were relative to the experiences and arts of their age [Moses sent in an age of magic; Jesus sent in an age of medicine]. God sent Muhammad when the sciences of the Arabs were four in number: eloquence, poetry, history and soothsaying. The Qur'an revealed to Muhammad surpassed all four of these sciences . . . Finally, the miracles of other prophets vanished with them and ceased to exist when the miracle ended, but the miracles of our Prophet do not end or cease; his signs are ever-renewed and do not decrease in significance.[4]

Readers may recognize in this passage echoes of earlier views, now more precisely and more cogently enunciated, and the last sentence is a clear rejection of the Mu'tazilite view of miracles.

In the second half of the work we move from the divinely chosen Muhammad to the Prophet as human paragon, and the tone, despite the author's introductory disclaimer, is more polemical. Here the emphasis falls on Muhammad's immunity from sin (*'isma*). Like all other prophets, he was totally sinless, immune from both major (*kaba'ir*) and minor (*sagha'ir*) sins, for if the latter are allowed, the former might also slip through the net and be admitted.[5] This immunity extends even to the period before his mission and is defined as follows:

You who look carefully into our work must by now be convinced about the truth regarding his immunity from sin [*'isma*], such as any ignorance of God and His attributes . . . or of any legal issue transmitted through revelation from God. Further we assert his immunity from lying, intentional or unintentional, from the moment that God sent him . . . as also his immunity from this before his mission and from all major [*kaba'ir*] and mi-

nor *[ṣagha'ir]* sins, and his immunity from continued forgetfulness . . . and in all his moods such as being pleased, angry, serious or joking.[6]

Could he occasionally be absentminded? Yes, but not forgetful.
Was he subject to magic spells? Yes, but this does not detract from
his immunity from sin. Did he joke? Yes, but only to lighten the
hearts of the believers. If his judgments regarding purely worldly
issues were occasionally faulty, for example, in the famous case of
the date season of Medina, this is because he needs to be a *human
model*.[7]

What did all this mean for his *Sira* in general, one so tightly
protective of its subject, so intent upon depicting him in monumental terms? It meant that Muhammad's immunity from sin completely precludes, among other things, an episode like the "Satanic
Verses," which was judged in this light to be implausible and
unacceptable. Not only is its chain of transmission defective;
Muhammad's immunity renders any Satanic inspiration, however
momentary, rationally and legally impossible. It is dismissed as follows:

> This is the kind of episode that appeals to historians and com-
> mentators who are overly fond of curiosities and oddities, who
> stretch forth to grab from books every report, both the authen-
> tic and the inauthentic.[8]

Again, an episode such as Muhammad's controversial marriage
to Zaynab bint Jahsh is explained as a marriage ordained by God
and not a match motivated by lust. Why should he lust for her?
She was his cousin, he had known her all his life, and he had married her off to his adopted son Zayd. Why then should he suddenly
be consumed with passion for her? It is the heretics and the weak-

minded who peddle such stories. As for 'A'isha's sarcasm, on this and other occasions, al-Qadi passes over it in silence.[9]

Here then is a *Sira* that conforms not to traditional narrative forms but rather to a set of criteria according to which the *Sira* *ought* to be written. Theology, reason, history, and the rules of Hadith transmission are all deployed to filter the *Sira,* to exclude from the record anything that detracts from the grandeur of the image. It is a *Sira* pruned of sensationalism, and yet it is also one that seeks to draw Muhammad closer to his community through love. In fact, al-Qadi 'Iyad's remarks on the love of Muhammad exceed any other such remarks to be found in any *Sira* hitherto. This is how al-Qadi defines love in general and the love of Muhammad in particular:

> Love in reality is an inclination towards what a human being finds agreeable *either* through delight in perception such as the love of beautiful images, tunes, food and so forth *or* through delight in mental apprehension involving such noble states as love of virtuous people, of scholars or of men of upright life and honorable deeds *or else* love of one who did one a favor or benefaction. Muhammad combines all the above three reasons that necessitate his love.[10]

The miraculous prophet, the moral paragon, the supreme object of love: these three images of Muhammad, at once sublime and endearing, coexist in al-Qadi's construction of the "Chosen One." But where does al-Qadi come from, as it were? Is he part of a larger "school" of *Sira* writing, and if so, can his intellectual affiliations be more precisely defined? My contention is that al-Qadi was a representative of an Andalusian group of authors who gave new shape and content to the *Sira.*[11] This group included the celebrated polymath Ibn Hazm (d. 1064), the critical biographer al-

Suhayli (d. 1185), and perhaps also the later Ibn Sayyid al-Nas (d. 1334). They all exhibit what the late Marshall Hodgson, speaking of Andalusian literature in general, called "a special provincial flavor, attractive for its relative freedom from established restraints."[12]

Where *Sira* is concerned, these authors are distinguished by a certain critical rigor that seeks to cut through the sloppiness of biographical reports, and so to turn the *Sira* into a more concise guide to conduct, ethics, and law. They all seem to believe that if one carefully reviews the historiography of the *Sira*, from its earliest layers upward, one will detect its inner logic as a divine plan, and so acquire a consistent method to assess its credibility.

Ibn Hazm's contribution to the *Sira* is no more than a short treatise, *Jawami' al-Sira al-Nabawiyya* (Epitomes of Prophetic *Sira*), but one that was to exert considerable influence on later biographies. The tone throughout is concise, almost snappy. The intention is to establish beyond any doubt the modicum of hard facts that can be known about the Prophet's life. The biographical material often resembles a list or roster of names and dates, almost everywhere accompanied by the phrase "this is the most accurate version" or else "this version is fanciful." His critical tools come either from the armory of Hadith criticism or from common sense and internal logic. The narrative section is made up largely of *Maghazi*, with lists of their participants, and to which a firm chronology is assigned with a curt authority that sometimes overrides consensus:

> Then followed the Battle of the Ditch in the month of Shawwal, Year Five of the Hijra. This is the version to be found among historians of the *Maghazi*. The plain fact is that it took place in Year Four, beyond any doubt. This is because of the following report from Ibn 'Umar [d. 693; celebrated early traditionist]: "I was passed in review before the Prophet of God on the day of

the Battle of Uhud, and I was then fourteen years old. But he rejected me. Later on, I was passed in review before him aged fifteen on the day of the Battle of the Ditch, and he allowed me to join the army." It has thus been proven that only one year separated the two battles and that the Battle of the Ditch took place without any doubt before the expedition to Dumat al-Jandal.[13]

But the intention in Ibn Hazm's work is not simply accurate history; it is also, and perhaps as urgently, a quest for a more reliable *sunna*, a genuine storehouse of prophetic conduct. Discussing various aspects of Muhammad's character such as his forbearance, courage, justice, generosity, simplicity, shyness, lack of malice, humility, love of the poor, and so forth, Ibn Hazm concludes:

In him God joined a virtuous manner of life to perfect governance, he being an illiterate person who could neither read nor write, who was born and bred in a land of ignorance and of deserts, a land of poverty and shepherds. God raised him surrounded by affection, an orphan with no mother or father, and taught him all the excellencies of virtue and of praiseworthy conduct. God inspired him with knowledge of past and future events, with the means to attain salvation and victory in the afterlife, happiness and honesty in this life, commitment to duty and the abandonment of idle curiosity. God grant that we may obey his commands and emulate him in all his acts.[14]

During that age of reabsorption of the *Sira*, the second member of the Andalusian "school," al-Suhayli, was an outstanding biographical critic. His major opus, *Al-Rawd al-Unuf fi Tafsir al-Sira al-Nabawiyya li Ibn Hisham* (Virgin Pastures: An Exegesis of the Prophetic *Sira* of Ibn Hisham), is a running commentary on the principal "founding father" of the *Sira*, Ibn Ishaq/Ibn Hisham. Al-

Suhayli subjects that *Sira* to the kind of exegetical examination normally found in Qur'anic *Tafsir*, the science of Qur'anic exegesis, an effort that denotes the immense growth in the prestige of the *Sira*. He defines his purpose in writing as follows:

> To clarify what is found in the *Sira* of Ibn Ishaq as amended by Ibn Hisham namely, an obscure phrase, an arcane point of grammar, perplexing language, a complex genealogy, a noteworthy point of law, or a deficient historical report which can be firmly decided.[15]

There follows a dazzling display of learning in practically all the relevant fields of *Adab* and the religious sciences. His critical method deliberately eschews philosophy, proceeding solely from the self-evident consistency between Qur'an and Hadith, and from the obvious wisdom of God as manifested in the *Sira*, which becomes a storehouse of that wisdom.[16] From his conception of consistency is derived the view that when historical reports are reviewed with care, they will be seen to reinforce one another.[17] The same holds true of Muhammad's miracles. Commenting, for example, on the truce of Hudaybiyya (628) during which, according to one version of events, Muhammad stretched forth and covered or erased from the document his epithet as Prophet of God, hence indicating his ability to read, al-Suhayli pronounces the following verdict:

> The report states that the Prophet erased his own name, writing "This is a truce entered into by Muhammad son of 'Abdullah." Some, including Bukhari, imagine that he wrote this with his own hand. But while admitting his illiteracy, they nevertheless claim that God guided his hand at that particular moment in time as a special dispensation, and imagine this to be a miracle.

To this line of argument one can respond as follows: It would indeed have been a miracle were it not that it would contradict another miracle namely, the fact that he was illiterate and could not write. It is upon his being illiterate in a nation of illiterates that his proof rests, and whereby any denier may be refuted and all doubt is dispelled. Why should God guide his hand and turn this into a miracle? The real miracle is that he could not write. It is impossible that miracles should contradict one another. Therefore, the true meaning of "he wrote" is "he ordered to be written."[18]

What we have here in al-Suhayli is a commentary grounded in the conviction that the *Sira* ran along a rational track predetermined by a divine plan. Therefore it must by necessity possess a rigor or uniformity that the student of the *Sira* can detect if its internal consistency is kept in mind. Among many other things the *Sira* demonstrates that Muhammad was just and fair *even* as a suckling infant, confining himself to one breast and leaving the other to his foster brother; that his status with God was so elevated that we should accept the report that his parents were resurrected in order to believe in him and then returned to the dead; that no greater proof of his truth can be found than that a son should be willing to kill his own beloved father for his sake.[19] In al-Suhayli too we glimpse an early endeavor to derive legal principles from the *Sira*, an endeavor that eventually resulted in works in which the law in the *Sira* was a primary concern. Since al-Suhayli's days, his commentary has been associated with the *Sira* of Ibn Ishaq/Ibn Hisham to the extent that the original *Sira* and al-Suhayli's commentary are frequently spoken of in the same breath.

The last and perhaps honorary member of that same Andalusian "school" is Ibn Sayyid al-Nas (d. 1333). With his *'Uyun al-Athar fi Funun al-Maghazi wa'l Shama'il wa'l Siyar* (Highlights of

Prophetic History in the Fields of *Maghazi*, the Prophet's Virtues and Biographical Reports), we return to *Sira* in the strictly narrative sense of the term. Here is a biography of Muhammad that a reader today might well regard as the most "modern" *Sira* to be found anywhere in the premodern age. Structured like a contemporary graduate dissertation, it opens with a critical examination of the primary sources, which includes a rehabilitation of Ibn Ishaq's credibility as a biographer. It proceeds by weaving together a composite *Sira* whose building blocks consist of the founding fathers, interspersed with more recent authorities and fortified with "fieldwork," that is, reports heard directly from contemporary scholars and specialists, mostly in Damascus. At the end of many chapters one finds a "footnote" section made up of linguistic, topographical, and other explanations. The work ends with a "Chronological Chart" of the prominent events of each year followed by what appear to be "Appendices" devoted to such topics as Muhammad's miracles, wives, servants, children, horses, and physical characteristics. The work terminates with a "Bibliography" wherein the author records the manner in which his sources were transmitted to him, and an "Epilogue to the Reader" asking for indulgence and for any errors found to be corrected.

Of all premodern *Siras*, this *Sira* of Ibn Sayyid al-Nas is unquestionably the easiest for someone with a modern sensibility to read, follow, and consult. Ibn Sayyid al-Nas spends little time arguing about the minutiae of historical facts, preferring to cut through to a synoptic version of events based on the best evidence, although weaker versions are curtly alluded to. The author scrupulously identifies his sources and often engages them in argument. His comments on the incident of the Satanic Verses are typical of his synthetic reconstruction. At issue is Muhammad's alleged prostration in prayer *(sajda)* following the "revelation" of the Satanic Verses, signifying his temporary acceptance of the goddesses of Mecca:

Al-Suhayli said: "This report about the *sajda* was cited by both Musa ibn 'Uqba [d. 758; a respected early biographer] and Ibn Ishaq, but the theologians use rational argument to reject that report. Some who accept its veracity advance diverse views, e.g., that Satan fabricated and spread the news about the *sajda*, but Muhammad himself did not utter these words. This would make sense were it not that these same people also accept the *hadith* that Gabriel said to Muhammad, "I never revealed these verses to you." Another view holds that Muhammad did utter these words, of his own free will, but was alluding to angels and the validity of their intercession. Yet another version holds that Muhammad said this with reference to the views of unbelievers, i.e., that it was *they* who uttered these words, and he cited the words in amazement at their unbelief. [al-Suhayli concludes:] "I imagine that the veracity of this report is not firmly established."

I [Ibn Sayyid al-Nas] say: "I was told that al-Hafiz al-Mundhiri rejected that report completely from the viewpoint of its transmitters. My teacher, al-Dimyati, disagreed with him. My own view concerning this report is that it is merely one among many such reports to be found in the *Sira*. The principle advocated by most scholars is to adopt a lenient attitude *(tarakhkhus)* towards reports of the *Sira* that teach compassion and asceticism *(raqa'iq)* and where no legal commandment is involved. Such reports, according to most scholars, are admitted more easily than strictly legal commands, because no legal injunction is at stake. As for this particular report about Muhammad's prostration, and given the above stricture, one simply ascribes it to its relevant sources unless its veracity is conclusively established, thus requiring interpretation. But it is unlikely that its veracity can be so established."[20]

As a group, these writers had between them set new standards for the study of the *Sira*. They were far less committed to earlier models of the *Sira,* and far more willing to remold the *Sira* in substance and structure. Turning the *Sira* inside out, they not only reengage with its earliest strata, a great boon to modern researchers, but also manage to reconstruct a biographical corpus that is more amenable for use as a guide to conduct. The combined impact of this group remains to this day of central importance for the study of the *Sira.* They must also be regarded as the immediate predecessors to the authors of the fourteenth-century renaissance of the *Sira* that was to unfold in Damascus.

How is one to define "the fourteenth-century renaissance" in Damascus? Was this "renaissance" in *Sira* works part of a larger literary revival? There is not, so far as I know, any study that examines in detail the literary contours of that age, so one must proceed with caution.[21] It is well established, however, that fourteenth-century Damascus had been attracting waves of refugees, first those fleeing from the Crusaders and then from the Mongols, who eventually would enrich the city with their diverse cultural traditions. Also relevant is the long peace that descended upon the Mamluk Empire during approximately the first half of the fourteenth century. During that long peace, there is evidence of an extensive program of construction of religious buildings by ruling elites and a consequent expansion in the patronage network of scholars.[22]

Be that as it may, and in the domain of *Sira,* there is a veritable burst of productivity to which the term fourteenth-century "renaissance" is in my view appropriate. The cluster of biographers of this time include such luminaries as al-Hafiz Mughultay (d. 1361), Shams al-Din al-Dhahabi (d. 1348), Ibn Shakir al-Kutubi (d. 1363), Ibn Kathir (d. 1373), and, perhaps the most impressive of them all, Ibn Qayyim al-Jawziyya (d. 1350). Among them they would expand the *Sira* in volume but also bring to a high point the critical apparatus with which the *Sira* needed to be assessed and employed. There were basically two ways in which the *Sira* was reconstituted: either in the manner of Ibn al-Athir (d. 1233)—not strictly speaking a Damascene nor a fourteenth-century figure but with strong Syrian connections—or in the manner of Ibn Kathir (d. 1373). The first hammered the *Sira* into continuous annalistic narrative while the second poured it forth in all its diversity of versions and then reordered it by indicating the most credible of its versions and the manner in which these versions could be harmonized.

Ibn al-Athir's *Al-Kamil fi'l Ta'rikh* (Universal History) was a world history that quickly gained enormous prestige. Its early sections contain a *Sira* that is free of *isnad*, compact, devoid of alternative versions of events, and focused on the thread of the story. In line with the work's "universal" coverage, Ibn al-Athir includes many chunks of history from outside Arabia that are contemporaneous with the *Sira;* he has a penchant for dialogue among participants and for the drama of events, and is distinctly less interested in miracles. It is possible that Ibn al-Athir's deep interests in *Adab* might explain the way in which well-known incidents of Muhammad's life are given a crisp, theatrical form as in, for instance, the famous encounter between the victorious Prophet and Hind, the vicious wife of his most determined enemy, Abu Sufyan:

When Muhammad had finished with the ceremony of homage from the men, he turned to homage from women. A number of Quraysh women came forward . . . Hind was veiled, fearing she would pay the penalty for what she had done to Hamza [the Prophet's uncle]. To them he said: {Will you pay me homage on condition you associate none with God?} Hind replied: You place on us conditions that you do not place on the men. And yet we agree. He said {and that you do not steal.} Hind said: By

God, I might have filched a little from Abu Sufyan! Abu Sufyan, present at that moment, said: You are excused past misdemeanors. The Prophet said: {Is that you, Hind?} Yes, Hind replied. Forgive the past, may God forgive you. The Prophet said {and you do not commit adultery.} Hind said: Does a free woman commit adultery? The Prophet said: {and that you do not kill your children.} Hind said: We brought them up when young and you killed them at Badr when they grew to manhood. You and they know best! At which point 'Umar laughed. The Prophet said {and you do not commit sin with hands or legs.} By God, responded Hind, the commission of sin is an ugly act but a little leniency is preferable. The Prophet said: {and you do not disobey me where a virtuous commandment is involved.} Hind replied: We would not have sat here in this assembly if we intended to disobey you.[23]

This is Ibn al-Athir at his most dramatic, recasting a well-known incident of the *Sira* and playing one character off against another, as in a play. There is no attempt to mitigate the arrogance and sarcasm of Hind's surrender to Islam, possibly to enhance the drama of the occasion.

To be noted also in his graphic historical treatment is the way in which Ibn al-Athir ties together the various elements of the story with frequent and reflective authorial interventions. Thus, Year 9 of the Hijra (630) is commonly referred to as the Year of Delegations, when tribal delegations from all over Arabia came to Medina to offer their submission to Muhammad. This event, left unexplained in most accounts of the *Sira,* is seen by Ibn al-Athir as Arabia's submission to Quraysh as much as it was Arabia's submission to Muhammad:

When the Prophet of God had conquered Mecca, and the tribe of Thaqif had embraced Islam, and he had concluded his expedition to Tabuk, tribal delegations from every corner of Arabia set out to meet him. The Arabs had in fact been waiting to see what Quraysh would do before embracing Islam. Quraysh were the leaders of the people, the possessors of the Sanctuary and the undoubted descendants of Ishmael son of Abraham, and all Arabs recognized these qualities. It was Quraysh which had declared total war against the Prophet. When Mecca was conquered and the Quraysh embraced Islam, the Arabs realized they could not war against him nor even remain hostile, so they entered the religion of Islam {in droves} as in the phrase of the Qur'an.[24]

This sober, realpolitik analysis of a major episode of the *Sira* is quite typical of Ibn al-Athir's limpid and tightly fastened narrative. It is also a forward-looking treatment, more concerned with the *Sira*'s relationship to later Islamic and world history than it is with isolating it as a unique, miraculous, or meta-historical era.

By contrast, the *Sira* of Ibn Kathir, also embedded in a chronicle of universal history, could not be more different in style and treatment. Where Ibn al-Athir is curt and dismissive, Ibn Kathir tells all, in a massive outpouring of *Sira* materials cast in Hadith form. His two exemplars are the *Sira* of Ibn Ishaq and the *Musnad* of Ahmad ibn Hanbal. Around these two basic texts Ibn Kathir weaves an extensive canvas of sources, ancient and contemporaneous. From Ibn Ishaq comes the basic, and by then authoritative, narrative structure; from Ibn Hanbal comes the plethora of hadiths, transmitted in their various versions according to their distinct individual transmitters. The result is a *Sira* of great richness and diversity but one wherein Ibn Kathir, donning the robes of the Hadith master, picks and chooses among these versions the accounts he finds the best attested to based on their chain of transmission and the best based on their inherent substance. *Sira* and Hadith are now a single tapestry, but one that needs to be stitched together and harmonized. Here is Ibn Kathir on Muhammad's "Farewell Pilgrimage":

The Farewell Pilgrimage in the Year 10: it is also called the "Pilgrimage of the Final Message" as well as the "Pilgrimage of Islam" and the "Farewell Pilgrimage." This is because the Prophet bade farewell to people and never went on pilgrimage thereafter. It is called "Pilgrimage of the Final Message" because he transmitted the law of God in word and deed and there remained no principle of Islam left unexplained. Having expounded to them the ritual of the pilgrimage in all its details, God revealed to him the verses {Today I have completed your religion for you and made good My grace upon you, and have chosen Islam as your religion.} My intention here is to clarify all aspects of that pilgrimage. Transmitters of historical reports have differed very widely indeed in their versions of that incident, in accordance with the degree of knowledge possessed by each. This was especially true in the era after the Companions. With God's help and favor, I shall cite what the masters mention of these accounts in their books and proceed to harmonize between them in a manner that would fully satisfy the minds of all who contemplate and closely examine them, combining the method of *Hadith* with an understanding of its true significance.[25]

What he states as his strategy here is roughly what he does elsewhere in his *Sira*. Laying the differing versions side by side, he includes versions that he designates as obscure in meaning *(gharib)* or even odd and singular *(munkar)*. Like other Hadith masters, Ibn Kathir holds that the juxtapositioning of weak hadiths alongside strong ones helps to highlight the inferiority of the former and to reinforce the authenticity of the latter. As a result, certain sections of the *Sira,* for example, the Annunciation stories, are very large, but the ordering hand of the historian is always visible, placing events in their proper chronological sequence and preferring some accounts to others. Thus, in narrating the incident when Muhammad and Abu Bakr took refuge in a cave while escaping their Meccan pursuers during their famous *Hijra* to Medina, Ibn Kathir unfurls the many versions of that celebrated episode and concludes one particular version as follows:

> [Abu Bakr said:] When we were in the cave, I said to the Prophet: If one of our pursuers looks down at his feet he will spot us. The Prophet said {O Abu Bakr, what think you of two people the third of whom is God?} Some writers of the *Sira* add that when Abu Bakr said what he did, the Prophet said {If they approach us from this end we will exit from that.} Abu Bakr looked, and there was the cave, with an opening on its other end to which was adjoined the sea and a boat tied nearby. Now this is not to be denied from the viewpoint of divine omnipotence but the story is not supported by any *isnad,* strong or weak. We do not authenticate any account simply with reference to our own authority, but adopt only well-connected *(sahih)* and well-attested *(hasan) isnads.*[26]

With Ibn Kathir we feel we are in the presence of an author who makes full and extensive use of all the major works of *Sira* and Hadith that were available to him. Over the centuries these works had multiplied beyond count and Ibn Kathir thought it necessary to spread them out and tackle their divergences head-on. Although he adopts the inclusive strategy of Ibn Hanbal who piles up his hadiths with hardly any commentary, Ibn Kathir is nevertheless far more in evidence as author, skillful arranger, critic, and harmonizer. If different versions of the same event do not disturb what he calls "the basic structure of the story" *(aṣl al-qiṣṣa)*, there is no reason to exclude them. Even Shiite versions of certain events are included, although they are roundly condemned as fabrication.

Here then are two contrasting visions of the *Sira,* the one strict in organization and narrative in form, the other far more expansive and transparent in laying bare and then critiquing its sources. Adopting an annalistic approach, Ibn Shakir al-Kutubi's *Sira* is in essence an epitome of Ibn al-Athir's. By way of contrast, and adopting a Hadith methodology like that of Ibn Kathir but without his expansiveness, are the *Siras* of al-Dhahabi and al-Hafiz Mughultay. The works of these latter authors were important landmarks in the *Sira* literature of the fourteenth century.[27]

Al-Dhahabi was a historian and Hadith scholar of renown whose *Sira,* like that of Ibn al-Athir, constituted the first part of his massive *History of Islam.* But the traditionist in him is on full display in his *Sira* where he is decisive in rejecting defective reports, detailed and explicit in discarding Shiite versions, contemptuous of "storytellers" *(quṣṣaṣ),* and forthright in tackling the "antibodies" of the *Sira.* Here, for example, is al-Dhahabi on 'A'isha's sharp tongue, a subject left to stand, sometimes ignored, and rarely addressed in *Sira:*

> 'A'isha said: Whenever Khadija's name was mentioned, the Prophet never tired of praising her and asking God's forgiveness for her. One day he mentioned her and my jealousy got the better of me so I said: God has compensated you fully for that old hag. He was extremely angry so that I became greatly troubled at heart and said to myself: O God, if You turn away Your prophet's anger from me, I will never speak ill of her again.[28]

This is 'A'isha in repentance mode, no longer allowed to get away with her tart remarks in a *Sira* grown more bowdlerized and pruned of "storytelling." There is no harm in leaving divergent versions side by side provided no matter of grave import is involved or else common sense can reconcile them. Were there one or two openings of Muhammad's breast? The answer of al-Dhahabi is that there were two openings, one when Muhammad was a young boy and one before his "Night Journey" *(Isra')*, since both reports are well attested. Was the nocturnal journey a separate incident from the ascent to God *(Mi'raj)?* The answer al-Dhahabi provides is typical of his determination to achieve concordance:

> How is one to reconcile the various versions that Muhammad met the other prophets in Jerusalem and that he also met them in heaven? The answer is that he saw images of them more than once. Thus he saw Moses while on his night journey standing up and praying in his tomb. He saw him again in Jerusalem and he saw him also in the Sixth Heaven, him as well as other prophets. They had been made to ascend to God like our Prophet. Prophets are alive with their Lord as are the martyrs. But their life is not like the life of people of this world or of the next. They enjoy a life of a different kind. Likewise, it is said regarding the life of martyrs that God places their souls in the bodies of green birds that fly about in Paradise and then nestle in lanterns hanging beneath the Throne. So they are alive with their Lord according to this line of reasoning while their bodies remain in their graves. These matters transcend the human mind and faith in them is necessary.[29]

Al-Dhahabi does indeed include a lot of miraculous stories that "transcend the human mind," thereby conforming to a trend in the writing of the *Sira* that was first detected in the Qadi 'Iyad, discussed above. I refer of course to the miraculousness of Muhammad, a vision of him that in the fourteenth century gained the upper hand over earlier visions of his humanity. But in order to protect that vision from degenerating into superstition and "storytelling," it is fortified in al-Dhahabi by a frequent rejection of accounts he judged as defective in transmission, internally implausible for chronological or rational reasons, or peddled by "heretics."

The *Sira* of al-Hafiz Mughultay, an epitome of a larger *Sira* and history of the caliphs still unedited, is nevertheless comprehensive in scope, including both a life and a *Maghazi* as well as concluding sections on the Prophet's virtues *(shama'il)* and miracles. This inclusiveness was characteristic of most *Siras* of the period, as the "proofs of prophecy," once a separate genre, became gradually incorporated in biography. The structure of the text is rigid; the version preferred for any incident comes first and is then followed by several "it is saids." Points of contention, even those on which there was a large tradition of commentary, are dealt with in summary fashion:

> There is dispute concerning the *Isra'* (the Night Journey) and *Mi'raj* [the Ascent to Heaven]: did they both take place in one night or not? Did both or either occur in a state of wakefulness or in a dream? Did the Ascent precede the Journey? The correct answer is that the Journey took place in a state of wakefulness and involved the Prophet's body, that it took place more than once, and that Muhammad saw his Lord with his very eyes.[30]

The same terse and authoritative style is evident in the chapter devoted to the virtues *(akhlaq)* of Muhammad:

> He was the most courageous of men . . . He was the most generous of men: he was never asked for something and said "No." He was the most self-restrained of men: asked to curse a group of unbelievers, he said {I was sent as a mercy, not as a torment.} When his front teeth were broken and his face was wounded [at the Battle of Uhud], he said {O God forgive my people for they

have no understanding.} He was more shy than a virgin in her bower and never stared at anyone . . . He never took revenge for personal reasons nor flew into a rage except when the sacred injunctions of God were violated . . . He never found fault with any food: if he liked it he ate it; if not he left it. He never ate while reclining . . . He liked sweets and honey . . . He left the world never having had his fill of barley bread . . . A month or more would pass when no cooking fire was lit in his house and when his food was simply dates and water. He mended his sandals, stitched his clothes and joined in the domestic chores of his family. He visited the sick, milked the ewe, answered every invitation from rich or poor . . . He rode on a mare, a camel, a she-mule and an ass and placed behind him his servant or someone else. A total of thirty people rode behind him . . . At the Battle of the Ditch, he was exhausted with hunger and tied a stone around his waist to assuage it even though he owned much earthly treasure brought him by the Almighty.[31]

Arguably the most impressive of the Damascenes is the great Hanbalite jurist and polymath Ibn Qayyim al-Jawziyya. His major study of the *Sira,* entitled *Zad al-Ma'ad fi Hadiy Khayr al-'Ibad* (Provisions for the Afterlife from the Guidance of the Best of Creatures) is not strictly speaking rendered in narrative mode but is more like a work of jurisprudence *(fiqh)* with the *Sira* functioning as the mine of examples. His strategy is one of recapitulation of early sources combined with a review of the opinions of various jurists on diverse points of contention. The arguments deployed are sometimes so technical that the reader feels they are addressed to *fiqh* specialists.

Typical of his method is the way he deals, for instance, with the

Battle of Uhud. Twelve pages are allotted to that famous Muslim setback followed by twenty pages of legal conclusions and opinions based on the narrative. Thus:

> The following are some of the legal injunctions and points of law which that Battle encompassed: that once *Jihad* is embarked upon, and a man puts on his armor, there can be no turning back until the enemy is encountered; that Muslims need not go out to meet an advancing enemy but may elect to remain in their houses from where they may fight if this proves a better strategy for victory; that the supreme commander [imam] may lead his army through lands owned by his subjects, even if the landowners are unwilling to allow it; that women may march out to battle with men, and that their help may be sought; that a martyr is neither washed for burial nor are prayers pronounced upon him nor is he to be enshrouded in anything other than the clothes he wore; that martyrs are buried where they fall; that two or three may be buried in the same grave; that if a Muslim accidentally kills another during *Jihad* mistaking him for an unbeliever, the supreme commander should pay his blood-money.[32]

Apart from points of law such as these, there are also ethical maxims to be derived from that military defeat, such as:

> To acquaint the Muslims with the consequences of disobedience, failure and internal strife . . . Once they experience the consequences of such actions, they would become more cautious and better prepared in future encounters; to emphasize the fact that the wisdom of God in relation to His Messengers and their followers is to send them victorious at one point and allow them to be defeated at another, but final victory will always be theirs. If they are always sent victorious, they would be joined

by both believers and others, and it would not be possible to distinguish the true believers from the others ... If God grants
them constant victories, the souls of the believers would grow
arrogant, for constant victory is like constant bounty from God.
Human beings can only be improved if good times are alter-
nated with bad ... The calamities that befall them are thus like
the foul tasting medications prescribed as cure by a physician.[33]

The work represents what is probably the most ambitious attempt made by a premodern author to reformulate the *Sira* in legal
and ethical terms. But there is much besides. A great deal of the
analysis derives from theology and psychology, such as the examination of the necessity of prophecy, the investigation of certain
states of the soul such as anger and merriment, as well as numerous asides on topics such as the Prophet's speech mannerisms or
his spiritual healing. The analysis is almost always referred back to
the wisdom *(hikma)* of God. Why, for example, did it take so long
for God to reveal the innocence of 'A'isha during the terrible *Ifk*
crisis, when she was falsely accused of adultery?

Among the reasons for the long pause in the descent of revelation is the fact that the whole issue had been thoroughly discussed and aired and totally predisposed the minds of the
believers towards God's revelations to His Prophet in this matter. So when the divine revelation descended, it came at a time
when the Prophet and his family were most in need of it, as also
Abu Bakr and the other believers. Therefore the revelation
came upon them most opportunely, causing them all the greatest happiness and peace of mind. Had God revealed the truth to
His Prophet from the very first instant, such examples of God's
infinite wisdom would have been pointless ... The Prophet did
of course possess proof of 'A'isha's innocence, more so than the
other believers. But in order to fortify his patience, steadfast-

ness, gentleness and trust in God, the revelation of her innocence came to him in such a way as to grant him contentment,
peace of mind, and elevation of status with God.[34]

Muhammad as healer had also become a widespread aspect of
his image by the Mamluk period. The so-called *al-Tibb al-Nabawi*
(Prophetic Medicine) was a body of medical traditions assembled
across time and purported to contain recipes and cures taught by
Muhammad.[35] Ibn al-Qayyim offers a unique interpretation of
Muhammadan medicine:

> His medicine is unlike that of the physicians for it is certain,
> positive and divine, issuing from inspiration, the niche of
> prophecy and perfection of mind, whereas ordinary medicine is
> mostly guessing, intuition and experience. One cannot deny
> that many sick people derive no benefit from prophetic medi-
> cine, for it can only benefit those who accept it inwardly and be-
> lieve in its curing potential through unwavering and obedient
> faith. Consider the Qur'an. That too is a spiritual cure. But if it
> is not similarly accepted into the heart, no soul can be cured of
> its disease. Hence Prophetic medicine suits only those with de-
> cent bodies. If people are averse to it, this is like their aversion
> to Qur'anic cure. No blame attaches to the medicine itself but
> the fault lies in an evil nature and a corrupt locus.[36]

But there is one passage in Ibn al-Qayyim that has special ethical interest because in it the author attempts to reconcile the often
contradictory examples set by Muhammad in the *Sira*. It is here
quoted at length because of its importance:

> Among those things that must be recognized is that God has
> placed His prophet in the very highest category of every trait of
> virtue, making him its most unique recipient. Thus, if one fac-

tion of the Muslim community were to claim in argument to possess these virtues to the exclusion of other factions or groups, another faction can appeal to the same set of virtues to make a similar claim.

If those who go on raids and *jihad* use his example to claim they are the best of the community, the scholars of religion can with equal right claim the same distinction.

If ascetics and others who abstain from worldly affairs claim his example as arguing for their superiority, so too can people who engage in the affairs of the world and exercise power and government over subjects in order to establish the religion of God and impose His commandments.

If the poor and patient man cites his example, so too can the rich and grateful man.

If the pious use his example to argue for the superiority of acts of worship, the scholars can use his example to argue for the superiority of knowledge.

If the humble and self-restrained cite his example, so too can the mighty and powerful who repress or punish evildoers.

If people of dignity, gravity and sobriety cite his example, so too can people of good temperament who engage in acceptable humor which does not transgress the bounds of truth and ease of company with family and friends.

If his example is cited by people who loudly proclaim the truth and speak it to other people's face as well as behind their back, so too can argue those who practice gentleness, shyness and respect, and so refrain from rudely telling a person off to his face.

If those who practice their piety with rigor use his example, so too can those who seek for ease and convenience in piety, and who emphasize the breadth and ease of religious law.

If his example is cited by one who devotes himself to the reform of his religion and his heart, so too can his example be cited by one who takes care to mend his body, his standard of living and his worldly affairs, since the Prophet was sent to reform both the world and religion.

If his example is used by one whose heart is not tied to, nor has faith in, human affections, so too can it be cited by one who cultivates his affections, placing them in their proper order and giving them due weight.

If his example is used by those who go hungry and are patient in their hunger, so too can his example be used by those who eat and give thanks to God for their being full. And if his example is cited by one who practices forgiveness, pardon and patience, so too can one who exacts revenge cite it when revenge is right and proper.

If one who gives for the sake of God and offers friendship for the sake of God can cite his example, so too can one who refrains from giving for the sake of God and makes enemies for the sake of God.

If one who saves nothing for the morrow uses his example, so too can one who saves a year's supply of food for his family.

If one who eats rough food such as barley bread and vinegar were to cite his example, so too can it be cited by one who eats delicious food like grilled meat, sweetmeats, fruits, melons and so forth.

If his example is used by one who fasts continually, so too can it be used by one who eats continually, for he used to fast to the point where it was said of him that he never broke his fast, and would break his fast to the point where it was said of him that he never fasted.

If his example is used by one who abstains from the delights and desires of this world, so too can it be used by one who loves the most delightful things that the world has to offer: women and perfume.

If his example is used by one who is kind and meek with his

womenfolk, so too can it be used by one who disciplines them, causes them pain, divorces them, abandons them or gives them the choice to stay or to leave.

If his example is used by one who abandons the attempt to seek his own means of livelihood, so too can it be used by one who takes the initiative himself and thus engages in renting or hiring, in buying or selling, in borrowing and lending and mortgaging.

If his example is cited by one who avoids intercourse with women in menstruation or during the fast, so too can it be used by one who embraces his menstruating wife but without intercourse or kisses his wife while fasting.

If his example is cited by one who shows mercy to sinners in due measure, so too can it be used by one who executes the commands of God, cutting off the thief's hand, stoning the adulterous and flogging the wine drinker.

If judges use his example to pass judgment in accordance with circumstantial evidence, so too can it be used by judges who pass just sentence in accordance with clear evidence, for the Prophet imprisoned and punished people on suspicion . . .

The intention in this chapter is to demonstrate that poor and patient people have no better claim to his example than the rich and grateful. Those who have the highest claim to him are the most knowledgeable about his life and example, and who follow that example most closely.[37]

The question arises: if the Prophet has attained the highest category of *every* virtue, how can he be described as both worldly and otherworldly, both humble and mighty, both rigorous and easy in religion, both abstaining from pleasures and indulgent, and so forth? Can these ethical opposites be reconciled? Can they *all* be virtues?

It is possible to argue that one detects behind Ibn al-Qayyim the hand of Aristotle and his school. In other words, while virtue for Aristotle is normally a mean between two extremes, it is sometimes closer to one extreme and sometimes closer to the other, depending on circumstances. Thus courage, a mean between rashness and cowardice, can sometimes be closer to rashness (e.g., jumping into a fire to save one's child) and sometimes closer to cowardice (e.g., refraining from jumping into the fire to save one's pet). In each case the action can be described as courageous although closer to rashness in the first instance and to cowardice in the second. Again, in times of plenty the generous thing to do is to be a spendthrift whereas in times of draught or famine, the generous thing to do is to be thrifty and miserly.

It is in this sense, I think, that one should understand Ibn al-Qayyim's remarks on the Prophet as being a model of opposite ends of an ethical polarity. For Aristotle, it is the person possessed of "practical wisdom" who knows when to be a spendthrift and when to be miserly, although he is at all times generous. For Ibn al-Qayyim that "practical wisdom" *(ta 'aqqul)* was precisely what distinguished Muhammad's prophetic career.

Before leaving Ibn al-Qayyim, mention should be made of a work of his devoted entirely to a refutation of Jewish and Christian views of Muhammad, and to a very detailed analysis of biblical texts said by Muslims to refer to Muhammad. The tone of this work, entitled *Hidayat al-Hayara* (Guide of the Perplexed), is polemical. Beginning with an attack on the absurdity of Jewish and Christian beliefs, he proceeds to show how, contrary to Jewish and Christian interpretations of certain biblical passages referring to a future prophet, such passages can only refer to Muhammad. In the process he displays an intimate knowledge of Christian and Jewish biblical exegesis. But there is one passage in particular that deserves attention. It is his own account of a debate he held in Cairo with a Jewish scholar on the subject of Muhammad:

In Cairo once, I debated a Jewish scholar, regarded by the Jews as outstanding in his knowledge and primacy. Addressing him, I said: "By calling the lie to Muhammad you have thereby insulted God most grievously." In astonishment, he said, "A person like yourself can say this?" I replied: "Let me prove it to you. If you assert that Muhammad was an unjust king who subjected people by the sword and was no prophet from God, and yet he remained for twenty-three years claiming to be God's prophet sent to the whole of mankind, and proclaiming, 'God ordered me to do this and that, and forbade me this and that'— all of it being false and worthless . . . while endeavoring to change the religion of other prophets and abrogating their laws, there can only be two conclusions. You can either say that God observed, witnessed and knew all this, or that the matter was hidden from Him and He knew it not. If you say He knew it not, you would be ascribing the worst sort of ignorance to Him . . . And if you say all this happened with God's full knowledge and witness, two conclusions would follow. He could either have been able to change this course of events and prevent him from proceeding with his mission, or not. If unable to do so, you would thereby ascribe impotence to God, and void His divinity. If He was able to do so, while all the while sustaining, supporting and exalting him, granting him victory over his enemies and answering his prayers, and granting him wonders and miracles exceeding a thousand in number, this would mean ascribing the worst sort of injustice and foolishness . . . to the Almighty. For how can it be otherwise, when God witnesses and supports him whereas this is regarded by you as false witness?" He said: "God forbid that God should do this to a liar. Rather he is a true prophet, and whoso follows him prospers." I said: "Why then do you not embrace his religion?" He said: "He was sent to unlettered nations who have no Scripture. We however possess a Scripture which we follow." I said: "You have lost

your argument. All people, high and low, know that he announced himself to be a prophet to the whole of mankind . . . If
his message is true, it must be followed." He fell silent.[38]

This is a version of the argument from divine benevolence: a
good and just God could not have tolerated such a long and triumphant career if the prophet concerned was a liar. Naturally,
these debates end with the victory of those who conducted and
then recorded them. But this debate in particular illustrates how
Muslim believers arguing about Muhammad with believers of
other religious communities had shifted their arguments from the
plane of history to that of theology. Muhammad was now a world-
historical figure, the truth of whose mission was demonstrable by
logic as well as by correct exegesis of biblical references.

We have seen at several points previously the increasing application of theology, psychology, ethics, and Hadith criticism to the reports of the *Sira*. We have also seen how many *Sira* writers strove
to introduce consistency into these reports. No work in this later
medieval period went further in the direction of establishing consistency than the *Sira* entitled *Insan al-'Uyun*, but more widely
known as *Al-Sira al-Halabiyya* (The Aleppine Sira) in reference to
its Aleppine author Abu'l Faraj Nur al-Din al-Halabi (d. 1631).
This work is in one important sense the end of the line of premodern *Sira*. It displays many of the features so far encountered in the
later medieval period: a very thorough use of sources from diverse
times, and an impressive command of theology, hadith, history,
theology, natural science, philosophy, biblical literature, and
Sufism, interspersed with personal memories and reflections. It is
for these reasons that this *Sira* attained "best seller" status from its

own days until the present and is possibly the one that is still most widely consulted today.

Uppermost in the mind of its author is the intention to reconcile conflicting or divergent versions of the same event. Consider the enigmatic figure known as the Christian monk Bahira whom one report identifies as a Jewish rabbi. So what was he? Well, says the author, he could have been a rabbi who later converted to Christianity. One report has him living not in Busra but in a village nearby. He may have lived in both places, dividing his time between the two. Or else consider the incident(s) in which Muhammad's breast was opened. One way to reconcile differing accounts is to regard some reports as having been abbreviated while others related details at length. Were there three angels present or two? There is no significant contradiction so long as we accept that one angel cut open Muhammad's breast. Was only the chest cut open or also the abdomen? The meanings are too close to matter much. Was the bowl in which Muhammad's heart was placed made of emerald or gold? There could have been two bowls, one of each kind.[39]

This act of harmonizing is called "collation" (jam'). The idea is to bring these reports into harmony by using diverse stratagems derived from a wide spectrum of disciplines. The intention is not to "shoehorn" every report into an artificial harmony with every other: some conflicting reports, for instance, are left unresolved, especially when no legal point is involved. But once we establish why and how historical narratives come to vary, we can more easily bring them into concord. Thus, apart from the abbreviation of some reports and the enlargement of others, some reports transmit the general import (ma'na) of an incident while others transmit it verbatim. Certain reports can be reconciled when we bear in mind the changing sense of a word across time. In more general terms, the author argues that not mentioning some incident does not mean that it did not occur. Finally, the principle of what "befits" *(al-la'iq)* Muhammad's sublime station is invoked in the acceptance or rejection of reports.[40]

Al-Sira al-Halabiyya is an immensely rich *Sira* that delves into the minutiae of Muhammad's life and prophetic career. Like other *Siras* of its period it displays an excessive interest in the supernatural and the miraculous to which both theological and scientific explanations are appended. It is as if the *Sira* of Muhammad has now joined the Qur'an as a fitting subject for the most extensive exegesis. Reports that barely take up a paragraph or two in the works of the founding fathers are expanded to fill many pages. Thus a mysterious figure of the *Sira* such as the Persian convert Salman al-Farisi is given a full biography, more detailed than anywhere hitherto. And a curious phrase such as the "tinkling of the bell" *(salsalat al-jaras)* said to have accompanied the earliest revelations to Muhammad is given three pages of commentary.[41]

We have come to the end of the later medieval *Sira*. Many of its distinguishing characteristics have been outlined in the preceding pages. At the risk of some repetition, let me take stock here and enumerate its principal features: its tendency toward the comprehensive but also its tendency to produce epitomes; its increasing tendency to glorify or sanctify Muhammad through his miracles but coupled with the attempt to streamline his laws and conduct; its use of a very wide spectrum of sciences to bring rational order and harmony into the *Sira*, most prominently Hadith criticism; its richness as a source for very early biographical materials; its tendency to ignore or else openly reject reports that place the Prophet in a bad light; and finally, its sensitivity toward the misinterpretation of certain episodes of the *Sira* by "heretics" or misguided theologians, principally the Shiites and the Mu'tazilites. This, or something similar, was the legacy left by the later medieval *Sira* to modern times.

IX

The Hero

The title "last of the premoderns" must surely belong to Muhammad Baqir al-Majlisi (d. 1698), whose massive work *Bihar al-Anwar* (Oceans of Lights) is probably the largest single-authored book in Arabic literature. Al-Majlisi was a prominent Iranian public figure as well as an outstanding Shiite religious scholar who roamed beyond his Shiite literary heritage to engage the Sunni heritage head-on, much as the Safavid Empire to which he belonged was engaging the Ottoman. Four volumes of his work are devoted to a Muhammadan *Sira* that in many ways consummates the premodern tradition of biography.

Al-Majlisi's *Sira* rests on a tripod of Qur'an exegesis, Hadith, and historical reports. Qur'anic passages provide the context, Hadith pins down the authoritative glosses, and the historical reports illustrate and amplify the *Sira*. The landscape of his *Sira* is floodlit from the start: Muhammad and his immediate family are all in existence as lights seven thousand years before the creation of the world. Muhammad is placed within a quintet that includes 'Ali, Fatima, al-Hasan, and al-Husayn, and the Prophet is rarely if ever encountered without being conjoined to one or more of their number. All their ancestors, from Adam to 'Abd al-Muttalib, were of pure stock, and thus Muslims. Their total immunity from sin is flatly asserted. Meanwhile the quintet itself is responsible for the creation of the following celestial objects: Muhammad for the throne of God, 'Ali for the angels, Fatima for the heavens and earth, al-Hasan for the sun and moon, and al-Husayn for paradise.[1] From the very beginning of Muhammad's ministry, 'Ali is his divinely appointed "Aaron." He was with the Prophet at the Cave of Hira', where revelation first descended; he was included in the prophetic prediction of the monk Bahira; he was a constant witness of all Muhammad's miracles, now grown enormously in number; he and his eleven descendants, the Twelve Imams, are seen as images during Muhammad's Night Journey; 'Ali was Muhammad's partner in knowledge, though not in prophecy; Muhammad had no male issue because this would have voided the divine delegation of authority *(waṣiyya)* from Muhammad to 'Ali; almost all accounts of Muhammad's virtues, or *faḍa'il,* are combined with the virtues of 'Ali; more often than not, 'Ali's various acts are responses to the commands of God.[2]

Majlisi naturally drew quite heavily on his own Shiite tradition of the *Sira,* where 'Ali's role, as we have seen earlier, is pivotal. But he gave it all a final architectural shape, capping that tradition with a halo of miracles and lights, and anchoring it in scholastic polemic derived from the Qur'an and Shiite Hadith. With al-Majlisi the pendulum would swing as far as it would go in the premodern period in the direction of sacrality and the numinous. In the modern period, I hope to show that the pendulum will swing back to Muhammad's humanity.

Two poems in praise of Muhammad, of outstanding popularity throughout the Muslim world, bracket the premodern and modern periods and are often printed together in modern editions. Between them they kept alive—and still keep alive—a legacy, derived ultimately from Sufi devotions, of love for the person of Muhammad, a love that would help to bring back to prominence in modern times the image of the Prophet as a human paragon. The image of the humanity of Muhammad had been increasingly engulfed by the cosmic and supernatural constructions of his life as in al-Qadi 'Iyad, for instance, and ultimately and most spectacularly in al-Majlisi. In the modern period, the human Muhammad was destined, for reasons that will become apparent in the following pages, to reemerge in a variety of guises. But let us now turn to the poems.

The first poem is arguably the most famous celebration of Muhammad in Arabic poetry: the poem called *Al-Burda* ("The Mantle") by the Egyptian Sufi master Muhammad ibn Sa'id al-Busiri (d. 1296). It has 160 lines *(abyat)*, and like many pre- and early Islamic odes begins with a section on *ghazal* (amatory poetry) and longing for the beloved, then follows this up with a confession of the poet's guilt and sin, which in turn leads into the main theme, the love of Muhammad:

> *He is the beloved, whose intercession is hoped for*
> *From every horror one is plunged in . . .*
> *Like the sun that appears small from afar*
> *But blunts the eye when closely beheld . . .*
> *His majesty is such that he, a single man*
> *Appears, when you approach him, as though*
> *amidst an army and courtiers.[3]*

This is followed by a section on the miracles of the Prophet's birth and mission, then comes to the Qur'an:

> *Grant me leave to describe his wonders that appeared*
> *Like the fires of hospitality seen by night on mountain-tops.*

Pearls gain in beauty when strung together
But lose none of their esteem when single . . .
Its verses contain meanings like waves in their profusion
But superior to them in beauty and value.
Countless their wonders and numberless
No matter how often recited, never fatiguing.[4]

The poem ends with a formal entreaty or supplication *(tawas-sul)* addressed to Muhammad by the repentant sinner:

I waited upon him with a hymn of praise, seeking to be rid
Of the sins of a lifetime of poetry and waiting upon others.
For sins had garlanded me with fearful consequences
And I appeared like the animals garlanded for sacrifice.
I obeyed the temptations of youth in both my callings
Reaping nothing but wickedness and regret.
What a loss my soul suffered in its commerce!
It failed to exchange this world for the next, it failed even to bargain!
But if I commit a sin, my allegiance at least is not severed
To the Prophet, nor is my rope cut away . . .
Far be it from him to deny his favors to one who seeks them
Or turn away in disgrace one who desires his shelter.[5]

The Western reader might detect in this poem, with its universal themes of love, sin, repentance, and intercession, certain affinities with the religious poetry of John Donne or George Herbert. But this hymn of praise to Muhammad, revealed to al-Busiri, we are told, in a dream, has always had a mass following in the Muslim world. True, the radical conservative Ibn Taymiyya suspected that the poet was exalting Muhammad to the point where he was coming uncomfortably close to treating him like the Divinity, but time went on to draw a halo of near sanctity around this poem and to endow it with magical healing properties.[6] In al-

Busiri, Muhammad appears as a liege lord and intercessor, the sinner's primary hope for ultimate salvation. No matter how grave the sin, the love of Muhammad is confidently expected to cancel it.

The second poem, called *Nahj al-Burda* ("In the footsteps of *al-Burda"), is by the Egyptian Ahmad Shawqi (1868–1932) upon whom the title "Prince of Poets" was bestowed during a pan-Arab cultural festival in 1927. It is a slightly longer poem of 198 lines but generally follows the same topical structure and headings as its illustrious predecessor, and the same meter and rhyme. It opens with a similar amatory prelude:

> *A white antelope, standing on the plain between willow and mountain*
> *Sanctioned the shedding of my blood, in sacred months.*
> *Fate struck a lion with the eyes of a doe*
> *O denizen of the plains, hurry to aid the denizen of the den!*[7]

The lion and the antelope, the poet and his beloved, the pursuer and the pursued exchange roles. This reversion prepares for the next major theme, the reversals of life itself, in turn joyous and miserable. The poet bewails the sinful soul of his youth, then turns to ask for forgiveness:

> *Though my sins may be too grave to forgive, yet a hope I cherish*
> *Before God, places me with the best of protectors . . .*
> *When I lower the wing of humility I shall ask him*
> *For grace of his intercession, and little do I ask!*
> *I cling to the gate of the "Prince of Prophets" and whoso*
> *Holds the key to God's gate must prosper . . .*
> *Muhammad, chosen of God and His mercy!*
> *The object of God's desire, of creatures and spirits!*[8]

Thus far, not one single verse of Shawqi's poem would have been unfamiliar, in sentiment or diction, to the verses of al-Busiri.

Approaching its last section, however, Shawqi's poem begins here and there to allude to the poet's contemporary concerns until, toward the end, it faces modern Christian Orientalist attacks on Muhammad and answers them directly. We will later see how the challenge of the Orientalists would haunt the modern *Sira*. But the poetry of Shawqi dramatizes this new Muslim worry, which would have been totally alien to al-Busiri.

This final section begins with the theme, which we will later detect in modern *Sira*, that just before the advent of Muhammad the world was plunged in hopeless tyranny, ignorance, and debauchery. Then Shawqi turns to what seems like a reminder to contemporary Christians that pious men of their own past recognized the truth of Muhammad:

> *When Bahira saw him he said: "We recognize him*
> *From what we have learnt of names and signs" . . .*
> *Granting him shade, and deriving shade from him*
> *Was a cloud, humped by the best of rain showers.*
> *It was a love of the Messenger of God, instilled in the hearts*
> *Of men recluse in monasteries, and hermits on mountaintops.*[9]

Now comes the Christian charge:

> *They say: "You conquered, but the Messengers of God were not sent*
> *To kill souls nor did they come to shed blood."*
> *This is ignorance, misrepresentation, sophistry!*
> *You conquered with the sword after you had conquered with the pen . . .*
> *Evil, confronted with good, renders one incapable*
> *Of checking it, but confronted with evil, it recedes . . .*
> *Had Christianity not had its protectors, brandishing their swords*
> *It would not have benefited from its clemency and mercy . . .*
> *It is the adherents of Jesus who have now readied all instruments of war*
> *And we have readied nothing but a state of weakness.*[10]

What Shawqi had in his sights here was the Missionary-Orientalist complex, this being the cultural expression of a wider political and economic process of penetration of the Islamic world by the West. That Muhammad was a prophet of the sword was of course an old charge, as also was the Muslim rebuttal, and echoes of these polemics can be traced back in their most vivid form to the Crusades.[11] In the nineteenth century, these charges were given a new twist by the adherents of the Missionary-Orientalist complex, now armed with evidence derived from original Muslim historical sources to bolster their claims that Muhammad's was a violent religion. The other new twist in this polemic is the obvious military and political superiority of Western Europe and its direct mastery over wide swathes of the "House of Islam." Who is the violent party now, asks Shawqi?

In many ways Shawqi's poem prefigures the specter that haunts modern *Sira.* How do we best defend our beloved Prophet from an all-out Western assault on both his religion and his personal character? On the other hand, how can we retell his life in a manner that accords with the "spirit of modernity"? These are the sorts of issues that we propose to examine in more detail in the following pages.

In the middle of the nineteenth century, two works appeared that, more than any others, were to haunt Muslim writers of the *Sira* in the modern period. Their two authors were British and their works excited a great deal of interest, first in British Indian Muslim circles and later throughout the rest of the Muslim world. Indeed their influence on Muslim writers of the *Sira* can still be glimpsed today, whenever that modern *Sira* takes on the task of assessing or challenging the lives of Muhammad produced by Western "Orientalists" and "missionaries."

The first work is Thomas Carlyle's celebrated *On Heroes, Hero-Worship and the Heroic in History*, a collection of six lectures delivered in London around the year 1840 on eleven "heroes" subsumed under broad headings such as "The Hero as Divinity," "The Hero as Poet," "The Hero as Priest," and so forth.[12] Under the heading "The Hero as Prophet" Carlyle selects "Mahomet" and proceeds, in the best tradition of European Romantic historiography, to an analysis of the "Great Man" to be detected in his person and his mission. Almost at once Carlyle's intense fervor leads him to dismiss out of hand any talk about Muhammad's imposture, lack of sincerity, forgery, violence, or sensuality. The reader is to understand that these charges were commonplace in that day and age, but a free and fair judgment would decree that all these charges were untenable. How could God so misguide those millions who revere him and follow his religion?[13] Like all other "Great Men" Muhammad was sincere and "original," appointed thus by a mysterious force called "Nature" from whose bosom this "fiery man" was cast up. His "great and fiery heart" had brought forth a message of "denial of self" that all humanity can embrace, including "us," that is, Carlyle's British audience.[14] Did Muhammad propagate his religion by the sword? Well, says Carlyle, Christianity did not exactly disdain the sword when once it acquired one. Muhammad may not be the "truest" but he surely is a "true prophet."[15] From the time of its publication to the present, Carlyle's portrait of Muhammad is found widely referred to in modern Muslim *Sira*, where it is cited as an example of a "fair" or "honest" Western voice amidst the prevailing Western anti-Muhammadan and anti-Islamic onslaught.

Recalling the passage in Shawqi's poem, discussed above, about Islam and the sword, readers may well have noted its similarity to the Carlylean countercharge against Christianity. Carlyle was a contrarian, intent on shocking his audience almost as much as enlightening them, and there is a playful note in his introductory remarks where he says he chose Muhammad because he was free to speak about him, there being no danger of "any of us becoming Mahometans."[16] As a contrarian, Carlyle was at least as keen on preaching his moral values to his own society as he was to revamp the image of Muhammad. What he most liked about Muhammad, he tells us, is his "freedom from cant," a compliment to the Prophet but also, surely, a barb aimed at contemporary British society.[17]

Nevertheless, this vehement and unusual rehabilitation of Muhammad by a major Western man of letters would leave a lasting effect on the imaginary horizons of modern Muslim *Sira.*

The second work, Sir William Muir's *The Life of Mohammad,* appearing in 1861, was a different kind of portrait altogether. Muir (1819–1905) was an accomplished Arabist who built his biography on the four founding fathers of the *Sira,* in addition to numerous quotations from the Qur'an by way of historical illustration. The work commences with an introduction on the sources and lays down certain principles of selection. Prominent among them is the view that the Qur'an must be accepted as a primary, valuable, and datable source for the life of Muhammad. When he comes to what he calls the "Tradition," namely, of biography, the principle is to accept as genuine most of the reports that place Muhammad in a bad light, there being no reason for Muslim scholarship, otherwise hagiographical, to have kept them in the "Tradition" were it not for their commonly admitted accuracy.[18]

In following these broad principles of historical reconstruction, Muir built up an impressive and graphic vignette of the Prophet, pruned of miracles. Every historical brick in this narrative rests on textual support from the founding fathers, to the point where it often appears to be a skillful and smooth epitome of them. It is precisely because of its deadly accuracy that Muir's *Life* was found so distasteful by Muslim readership.

For Muir, there were two Muhammads, a Meccan Muhammad whom he by and large approved of, and a Medinese Muhammad whom he by and large did not. The Meccan Muhammad is often described as "tender" and "magnanimous," as "the mastermind" of the age, as simple in his habits, as "modest and pure in manners," respected and honored by his fellow men.[19] But in addition to a long string of virtues, Muhammad was described as "highly strung and nervous" by temperament, and the idea of divine revelation may well have come to him from his frequent "ecstatic states." The Medinese Muhammad, on the other hand, slowly unveils his vices: his cruelty, sensuality, and his "unnatural and revolting" legislation, especially in such areas as divorce.[20]

In Chapter 37 of the work, devoted to a sort of balance sheet, Muir summarizes Muhammad's "person and character." The earlier virtues are again on display and more are added, such as the Prophet's qualities of leadership, his eloquence and poetical genius, his just and temperate exercise of power, and his unswerving faith in the One God and in victory. But there are "darker shades" to this appraisal. The earlier vices are trundled out and new ones are added: a ruthless satisfaction in the execution of enemies, a craftiness and deceptiveness toward his foes, dastardly assassinations of opponents, messages from heaven to justify personal or political conduct; he is characterized as a man prey to sexual passion, a preacher of a religion of the sword. If all this is set against Muhammad's achievements such as his abolition of idolatry, strict monotheism, compassion toward the weak, brotherly love, and so forth, it will be found, says Muir, that these achievements, notable though they may be, came at a costly price. Muir's parting shot is devastating: "The sword of Muhammad and the Quran are the most stubborn enemies of Civilization, Liberty and Truth which the world has yet known."[21]

Muir's *Life* has a distinct moral and judgmental voice, no less intense than Carlyle's fervor. But where Carlyle claims Muhammad for his rostrum of Romantic heroes, Muir's is the stern voice of the Victorian missionary. Where Carlyle was soothing, Muir's lengthy bill of indictment was a stark challenge to Muhammad's followers, thus setting the agenda for most modern Muslim *Siras*, especially of the polemical variety. Many of Muir's charges were of course familiar to Muslim writers versed in the medieval heritage of theological debates with non-Muslims. But in Muir these charges were embedded in a carefully constructed historical narrative and would reignite an old and smoldering fire of polemic, coming as they did under the lengthening shadow of European colonial expansion.[22]

If we adopt the mid- to late nineteenth century as our point of departure for the study of modern Muslim *Sira*, we will find that it was Indian Muslim scholars who first undertook to respond to the new breed of European lives of Muhammad, dramatically initiated by Carlyle and Muir.[23] This is not entirely surprising; Muir had spent most of his working life in India. More to the point, however, in the eighteenth and nineteenth centuries Muslim India had produced a galaxy of religious thinkers and reformers who were arguably the most original in the Muslim world of that age. One star in that galaxy was Shah Waliullah (d. 1762), a writer of very wide religious interests, and deeply grounded in Hadith, theology, philosophy, especially of the al-Farabi school, mysticism, and several literary traditions.[24] His great work, *Hujjat Allah al-Baligha* (God's Crowning Argument), is an overview of Islamic ethics, the intention being to reveal the hidden or spiritual levels of meaning in Muslim belief and practice. This, of course, had been done before, most notably by al-Ghazali in his *Revival of Religious Sciences*, and al-Ghazali was indeed a major influence. However, Shah Waliullah, living in a time and place far more complex in its intersectarian makeup, brought to his ethical system a greater awareness of the universal morality to be found in all religions. In addition to founding Muslim ethics on universal social interest *(masalih)*, on God's mercy, on nature and reason, and on a sort of vitalism that animates creation and dictates right and wrong, Shah Waliullah frequently appealed to what all earlier nations and religious communities had arrived at by way of consensus as to what constitutes moral behavior.[25] His work is remarkable for the extent to which he sets out what he takes to be the natural psychic and moral principles that govern human behavior and shows how these principles are consummated in Islamic revelation. This universalism enabled him to draw up, at the very end of his work, a short *Sira* that, somewhat like that of Ibn al-'Arabi, saw Muhammad as the ultimate model of human perfection.

In his chapter on the *Sira,* Shah Waliullah allows himself little room for historical detail. It is a *Sira* made up almost entirely of Muhammad's miracles: the miraculous birth, the opening of his breast, the Night Journey, the angels that join Muslim battle ranks, the feeding and watering miracles, and so forth, but they all receive a figural interpretation. Thus:

> As regards the opening of his breast, that was in reality the triumph of angelic lights and the consequent extinguishing of the flame of nature and its obeisance to what overflows upon it from the Sphere of Holiness. As to his riding upon the animal *Buraq* [on the Night Journey], it was in reality his rational intellect gaining mastery over his spirit, that is, its animal perfection. So he sat firmly upon *Buraq* just as his rational soul gained full mastery over his animal spirit. His night journey to Al-Aqsa Mosque took place because that is the site where appeared the laws of God and the focus of activity of the Highest Assembly as well as the object of desire of all prophets, thus becoming as it were a sky light to the Heavenly Realm. His meeting with other prophets there and the listing of his virtues as against theirs was in reality their coming together by reason of their

link to the Sphere of Holiness where what distinguished him from among them all became perfectly clear . . . Brought a bowl of sour milk and one of wine [during his celestial journey], he chose the milk. Gabriel said: "You have been guided to natural disposition *(fitra)*. Had you picked up the wine, your community would have slipped into error." Thus it was he who united his community and caused them to triumph. The choice of sour milk was the choice of natural disposition whereas the choice of wine would have meant choosing the pleasures of this world.[26]

In these and similar passages of his short *Sira*, Shah Waliullah was reviving a tradition of allegorical reading of the Qur'an and Hadith expounded by Ibn al-'Arabi and his school. Muhammad's life was determined at every turn by the "Sphere of Holiness" *(Hazirat al-Quds)*, a primary concept in the structure of Ibn al-'Arabi's thought.[27] Nevertheless, Shah Waliullah was also an embattled reformer, much concerned with the revival of Muslim political institutions, especially the caliphate, and Muslim public ethics, especially jihad.[28] Thus both Muhammad's prophetic status and his public acts and regulations grant him and his community a distinctive role in human affairs, because of their perfect accord with common human interests and universal reason.[29] Equally, they impose a duty upon Muslims to defend their religion and heritage against their enemies.

In the work of Shah Waliullah and other celebrated reformers who followed, one detects the emergence of an impressive edifice of Indian Muslim thought rearmed with the polemical skills to take on modern Western detractors of Muhammad such as Muir. For wide sectors of the Indian Muslim elite, who otherwise held a favorable view of British justice, it must have been particularly galling to have to contemplate these unjust assaults on their beloved Prophet. A recent scholar speaks, in a slightly different context, of the "ambivalence of Indian Muslim discourse in the aftermath of the [1857] Rebellion."[30] But this ambivalence, i.e., a sense of patriotism, rooted in religion, versus admiration for certain aspects of British culture and learning, seems if anything to have greatly honed the polemical edge of the *Sira* written in Muslim India in the late nineteenth century.

Between 1872 and 1902, there appeared successive editions of a work on the *Sira* that finally carried the title *The Spirit of Islam or the Life and Teachings of Mohammed* by the celebrated Indian Muslim thinker Syed Ameer Ali (1849–1928).[31] It is really two works in one: a *Sira* in Part I and a defense of the religion in Part II. The *Sira,* which concerns us more directly, is written with passion and considerable elegance, and, although haunted by Muir, Ameer Ali is conscious of the fact that there are other British and European writers expounding on Islam who are more balanced in their judgment, and he frequently refers to them in his footnotes. But he also positions himself as one who wishes to contribute to the possible diffusion of Islam in the West, and to spell out those aspects of the life and teachings of the Prophet that modern and liberal Europe can best absorb.

Muhammad makes his first appearance in this *Sira* as a "teacher of mankind." To justify this epithet there immediately follows a short history of great civilizations before Muhammad. A bleak picture emerges of a world plunged in "disintegration," "depravity," and "chaos" from which even Arabia itself, with its "free air," does not escape. That sort of world needed a "deliverer," one who would lead mankind from darkness to light. The blanket condemnation of the pre-Muhammadan era was to become an important theme in modern *Sira* existing uneasily with the other theme of Arabia as the most appropriate locus of divine revelation.[32]

As his *Life* moves forward, Ameer Ali's grand design is revealed. Borrowing a Carlylean diction, he proceeds to turn the judgmental narrative of Muir inside out. In answer to Muir's argument regarding the survival, ergo authenticity, of anti-Muhammadan stories, Ameer Ali says that it is the very sweetness, sincerity, and nobility of Muhammad's character that render suspect all tales that cast him in an evil light. Such stories, which we have referred to previously as the antibodies of the *Sira,* had of course received answers in al-Qadi 'Iyad and other writers of the premodern period, and Ameer Ali would redeploy many of their arguments in his trumpet blast against Western detractors. Not satisfied with mere defense of the Prophet, he moves forward to show in detail how Muhammad's mission can be proven to be more rational and pragmatic, thus more progressive, than that of all other prophets. All this is echoed in a style of superlatives: never had the world seen his like; never were the highest attributes of the human mind combined in any other figure; no fairy tales had ever been woven round his personality. Toward the very end of the work there occurs an assertion that seems to be a direct retort to Muir's parting shot that Muhammad was the enemy of Civilization: Ameer Ali states that all Muhammad's public achievements and personal qualities serve to "affiliate him with the modern world."[33]

How does Ameer Ali rebut the by now familiar catalogue of the Prophet's failings? Against the charge that Muhammad degraded the status of women, he argues that this is refuted by the high status and position of Khadija and Fatima. To the charge of insincerity and opportunism he responds that Muhammad's followers would have abandoned him at once had they detected any sign of backsliding on his part. Was the incident of the "Satanic Verses" a serious lapse of faith? Even if it were, Muhammad quickly and freely confessed that lapse and repented. What of his cruelty, for example, at the massacre of the Qurayza? That, says Ameer Ali, must be regarded as done "in perfect consonance with the laws of war as then understood by the nations of the world." Equally if not more savage acts of war had been committed in Jewish and early Christian histories. There is even a short appendix on the incident when Muhammad, about to execute an enemy, angrily answered his plea for mercy, based on his having a young daughter, by consigning her to hellfire *(nar)*. Ameer Ali argues that the word *nar* refers in that context not to hellfire but to the name of her tribe — *Nar* with a capital *n*, so to speak. Thus Muhammad consigns the little girl to the mercies of her tribe rather than to hell. Once these and similar charges are dismissed, we are left with Muhammad the great teacher of humanity, mercy, and justice, and the prophet most in accord with the spirit of modernity.[34]

Ameer Ali's *The Spirit of Islam* cast a long shadow across the twentieth century and remains to the present day an elegant and potent defense of the life and achievements of the Prophet. One of its numerous admirers was Muhammad Iqbal (1877–1938), the eminent poet-philosopher of Indian Islam and a pan-Islamic figure. The work that signaled Iqbal's reputation in the Muslim world at large was *The Reconstruction of Religious Thought in Islam,* a title that refers back to al-Ghazali and, although much smaller, has the same grand objective of remodeling Muslim life and thought.[35] With Ameer Ali, Iqbal shares an ultimate ambition: not solely to defend Muhammad but to position Islam itself as the ideal religious and spiritual solution to the ills of the world, perceived to be increasingly materialistic. But compared to Ameer Ali, Iqbal was far more thoroughly grounded in Western philosophy, especially British and German idealism of the late nineteenth century, and his views of prophecy and the Prophet reflect the depth of his readings in that philosophical tradition.[36]

Iqbal begins his work with a sort of survey of contemporary philosophical figures and schools and states that it is the Qur'an that most closely agrees with Alfred North Whitehead's description of the universe as a "structure of events possessing the character of a continuous creative flow." From here Iqbal moves to prophecy, where he defines the prophet as a mystic who descends from the heights, unlike the mystic pure and simple who wishes to remain on the heights. That is the true significance of Muhammad's Night Journey. It follows that "the desire to see his religious experience transformed into a living world-force is supreme in the prophet."[37] Prophecy itself is defined by Iqbal as

[a] type of mystic consciousness in which "unitary experience" tends to overflow its boundaries and seeks opportunities of redirecting and refashioning the forces of collective life.[38]

Then by spanning both the history of revelation as well as its ultimate end, Iqbal seeks to show how Muhammad fulfilled that mission most perfectly:

The Prophet of Islam seems to stand between the ancient and the modern world. In so far as the source of his revelation is concerned he belongs to the ancient world; in so far as the spirit of his revelation is concerned he belongs to the modern world . . . In Islam prophecy reaches its perfection in discovering the need of its own abolition.[39]

Unlike Ameer Ali, Iqbal does not deign to engage in polemics against Orientalist or missionary assaults, and where he occasionally meets with such a charge, for example, that Muhammad was a "psychopath," he dispatches it with sarcastic contempt.[40] Indeed Iqbal seems in many places to be at least as involved in a *Western* philosophical debate on science and religion as he is in any defense of Islam.

Both of these writers went further than any previous Muslim had gone before. They had carried the discourse on Islam and Muhammad and placed it inside the context of European culture.

They were concerned, not so much with Muhammad versus Europe but rather with Muhammad *and* European modernity. There are few modern Muslim *Siras* that come near Ameer Ali's elegance of exposition and polemical skills, and few modern Muslim discussions of prophecy that match Iqbal's profound reading in Islamic and Western philosophy and thought.

The expansion of the British Empire in Asia and Africa in the nineteenth century acted to draw the Muslims living under its direct or indirect influence closer together in sentiment and determination. Inside India, a new Islamic historiography attempted to retell Indian history in a manner that drew Muslims and Hindus closer to each other, while beyond the Indian frontier pan-Islamist figures such as Jamal al-din al-Afghani (d. 1897) were preaching the ever more urgent need for Muslim unity.[41] When Egypt fell under a British protectorate after 1882, the arena of pan-Muslim nationalist discourse expanded and English slowly became a Muslim lingua franca. The turmoil accompanying these dramatic events was noted in Europe, where in the late 1890s several European chancelleries engaged the services of their leading Orientalists in order to report on the extent and significance of what European powers perceived as a threatening "resurgence" of Islam.[42]

Turning our attention to nineteenth-century Egypt we find little by way of *Sira,* or of theological thought more generally, to compare with the Indian record. The contrast between these two Islamic intellectual zones becomes stark when one compares Ameer Ali's *Life* with a roughly contemporaneous work from Egypt, Rifa'a al-Tahtawi's *Nihayat al-Ijaz fi Sirat Sakin al-Hijaz* (A Most Concise Life of the Inhabitant of al-Hijaz). This latter work, published posthumously in 1874, was written by one of Egypt's most famous reformers, historians, observers of Europe, and heralds of "modernity."[43] But al-Tahtawi's *Sira* is to all intents and purposes medieval in structure, argument, and style. A modern cataloguer would not be far wrong in classifying it as an epitome of Ibn Sayyid al-Nas or of al-Suhayli. Against the antibodies of the *Sira,* al-Tahtawi adopts positions familiar from the classical repertoire: the Prophet's sinlessness, the faith of his ancestors, the Devil as the sole actor in the incident of the "Satanic Verses," and so forth. There is hardly a single recognition of the relevance of the contemporary world, and nothing on Muhammad in European scholarship, and nothing on Muhammad and modernity.[44] By contrast, Ameer Ali's *Life,* with its eloquent polemic, seems to belong to a totally different age.

In fact, it was not until the first half of the twentieth century that we begin to see in Egyptian *Sira* some of the sophistication and breadth that we have seen in Indian Muslim scholarship of the late 1800s. The stage is set for this development in the writings of Muhammad 'Abduh (1849–1905), a disciple and colleague of Jamal al-din al-Afghani, and especially in his *Risalat al-Tawhid* (Treatise on God's Unity) of 1897.[45] In the last part of that work 'Abduh deals with prophecy and with the significance of Muhammad's achievements. It is not so much the novelty of his ideas as much as the freshness of voice and orientation that sets this work apart—apart, that is, from the medieval treatment of the *Sira* by al-Tahtawi and far closer in spirit to the kind of theology and prophetology that was being produced in Muslim India. It could well have been Afghani in his capacity as pan-Islamic middleman and facilitator of ideas that propelled 'Abduh onto the path of modernity, by which is meant here recognition of the overwhelming relevance of the contemporary world and the need to meet its challenges.

'Abduh's views on prophecy owe much to the Mu'tazilites, to the Muslim philosophers, and to Ibn Khaldun, for instance, in his arguing that the prophetic soul is one that rises by natural degrees to the highest levels, or that prophecy itself is made necessary by God's wisdom and mercy, by man's sociability and need for laws, and that prophecy is historically more effective than pure reason as the basis of social peace and happiness.[46] But 'Abduh would also argue, in an obvious reference to his own times, that prophetic religions set down broad ethical principles but have no truck with "details of livelihoods" and the "secrets of the sciences."[47] He was thus among the first Muslim thinkers to combat what one might call the preemptive view that was popular among traditional scholars: that all the sciences of modernity are already prefigured in the Qur'an and the lore of the Prophet. When he comes to deal with Muhammad's legacy, 'Abduh once more owes much to predecessors when tackling themes such as the decadence of the pre-Muhammadan world, or else to a Mu'tazilite such as 'Abd al-Jabbar when arguing that Muhammad's *human* achievement, against overpowering odds, is the truly miraculous element of his life.[48] Buried inside this brief account of Muhammad, nonetheless, is a message addressed to 'Abduh's contemporaries: the call to fight against deadening custom and blind emulation. One cannot of course deny the role of divine agency, but for 'Abduh the real lesson to be learned from Muhammad's life is that the Prophet is an ever-present, life-size model for the renewal of rational thought and a precursor of the fight against superstition, tyranny, and false authority.

'Abduh would leave behind him an influential body of disciples and followers who were among the most celebrated intellectual figures of Egypt in the first half of the twentieth century: Rashid Rida, Mustafa Lutfi al-Manfaluti, Muhammad Farid Wajdi, 'Abbas Mahmud al-'Aqqad, and 'Ali 'Abd al-Raziq, some of whom also wrote biographies of the Prophet. In the thirty or so years before World War I, Egypt moved gradually from beneath the Ottoman Empire and into the European orbit of influence, acquiring among other things a relatively free press. This freedom of expression in turn attracted a large and important community of Arab intellectuals from other regions of the Ottoman Near East, many of whom played a principal role in creating or vivifying that press. In the press and the literature of those thirty or so years, there were two overriding concerns: Egypt's political future and its cultural orientation. The first concern centered on nationalism, the second on definitions and formulas of intellectual and social progress. Muhammad 'Abduh's life appears to have spanned both these preoccupations. The first part of his life was caught up in political turmoil while the last part saw him engrossed in the reform of Muslim education and thought.[49]

Swirling all around in the Near East of the nineteenth century was a novel climate of ideas to which the term *Nahda* (Awakening) was later given. The *enfant terrible* of that *Nahda*, or Renaissance, was Ahmad Faris al-Shidyaq (1805–1887), an itinerant, iconoclastic, anticlerical journalist, a brilliant and witty observer of Europe, and a grand master of the Arabic language.[50] Al-Shidyaq had little to say on Muhammad but much to report on the current state of Muslims, whom he often castigated for rigidity of thought and reluctance to engage in technical occupations. He also made much of the justice and liberty practiced by early Muslim rulers as compared to the tyranny of modern rulers.[51] But al-Shidyaq's main contribution probably lay in developing a neoclassical Arabic style, transparently pure yet easily able to interact with the vocabulary of European economic and political hegemony. As a pioneer journalist, he was instrumental in moving Arabic from the madrasa to the marketplace.

'Abduh had his disciples; al-Shidyaq created a new voice. Their legacy was a certain kind of "modernism," a thing more easily cited than defined yet inescapable for the historian of ideas. Where *Sira* is concerned, it was the period between the two world wars that witnessed the emergence of "modernist" biographies of Muhammad, many of whose features remain with us to the present day. Common to all of them is the image of Muhammad as a modern hero, rallying his community to the standard of reason, progress, liberty, and justice—in other words, whatever the "modern age" demanded of its heroes.

In the 1920s the Egyptian intellectual scene was rocked by two books that appeared within two years of each other. First, in 1924, came 'Ali 'Abd al-Raziq's *Al-Islam wa Usul al-Hukm* (Islam and the Principles of Government), subtitled "A Study of the Caliphate and Government in Islam." It was a short treatise, barely a hundred pages long, but with a central and hard-hitting argument: Muhammad had not instituted any particular form of government, the caliphate was entirely a Muslim invention, and modern Muslims were totally at liberty to choose any kind of government that suited them, consonant with reason, "modernity," and self-interest. At a stroke, 'Abd al-Raziq had driven a wedge between Muhammad and the later political history of his community. Reducing the Prophet to a mere teacher of ethics, 'Abd al-Raziq held that the Prophet had little or nothing to say about constitutional issues.

Although by no means a biography of Muhammad, the work appeared in the eyes of its critics to have somehow demeaned the Prophet's achievements. Was Muhammad now to be demoted to the status of other prophets, for example, Jesus, who had simply preached a message of love and decency and little else? Had he not built a model state in Medina? The alarm bells in conservative circles must also have rung in part from fear that the "Orientalists" and "missionaries" were now within the gates. Europe had begun to seduce the minds of Muslims—and what Muslims! 'Abd al-Raziq was an insider, an Azhar graduate, and a religious judge to boot.

Second, in 1926, came Taha Husayn's (1889–1973) *Fi al-Shi'r al-Jahili* (On *Jahili* Poetry).[52] This too was a short treatise, and even less directly concerned with *Sira*. Its main argument was that pre-Islamic or *Jahili* poetry had by and large been fabricated in Islamic times, since most of it reflects an Islamic way of life and thinking. The work set off another storm of criticism and incited the ire of the state and its courts. The reason that conservative circles reacted with such violence was that Taha Husayn, another insider, seemed to have pulled the rug out from under the early history of Islam, employing apparently newfangled, Europe-inspired techniques of internal and historical criticism. The linguistic, theological, and historical dimensions of Islam appeared to be in danger. If the poetry of the pre-Islamic period was suspect, how could any trust be placed in the long and hallowed tradition of Qur'anic exegesis, lexicography, history, and other Muslim sciences, all of which were deeply rooted in that poetry? If one admitted fabrication on such a scale, might not the Qur'an itself, the *Sira*, and early history be next in line?

These two explosive works, written by two timid men, would set the scene for a new canon in *Sira* writing. In the decade between the early 1930s and early 1940s, there appeared in Egypt six lives of Muhammad, and between them they established the foundations for the modern discourse on the *Sira*. Any study of *contemporary* Muslim biographies of Muhammad needs to acquire its bearings from that "canon" and period.[53]

These six works were written under the cloud of controversy generated by 'Abd al-Raziq and Taha Husayn, and all were animated by an expressed desire for a modern *Sira*, written in a modern style, for a modern audience and intersecting with the standards set by modern European scholarship. A full account of the intellectual atmosphere surrounding these lives of Muhammad cannot be given here, but the increasing popularity of fiction with the reading public must doubtless have contributed to the literary form of these biographies, while the gradual takeover of Egyptian culture and literature of that period by a bourgeois mentality determined their ideological horizons. Let us now examine these lives in more detail.[54]

Two of the above-mentioned six lives of Muhammad belong in one basket, quite a distance from the other four, by reason of their dramatic and fictional nature. The first work is a play entitled *Muhammad, Upon Whom Blessings and Peace* (1936), by the celebrated Egyptian playwright Tawfiq al-Hakim (ca. 1900–1987). In his brief introduction, al-Hakim expounds his aim as follows:

It is customary in books of *Sira* for writers to narrate at length, analyzing, commenting, defending and rebutting. But when I first thought of the idea of this book . . . I asked myself the following question: To what extent can that traditional method evoke clearly before us a picture divorced to some extent from authorial interference? A picture of what actually took place, or was actually said, without the addition or subtraction that may reveal the author's intention? It was then that it occurred to me to write a *Sira* in this unusual manner. So I turned to authoritative works . . . and extracted from them what actually happened or was actually said . . . in an attempt to make all this immediately present to the reader's imagination, as though it were happening before his very eyes . . . If, following this work, it becomes clear to people how great the picture really was, its greatness comes from its very essence, not from the defense of a zealous writer, or the rebuttal of a biased author.[55]

Al-Hakim does not keep his promise. He takes liberties with many scenes of the *Sira*, introduces several "attendants and others" in the form of a shepherd here and a Bedouin there, and brings in Qur'anic passages for dramatic effect. Although divided into numerous acts and scenes, complete with stage directions, the play is unsuitable for theatrical performance, not least because of the problem of an actor playing the role of Muhammad on stage. Addressed to readers, it is a very laborious read, and any dramatic effect it might have is dissipated in short and bitty scenes. If al-Hakim hoped to project a picture of the *Sira* onto the imagination, he ends by blurring it in a sort of dramatic effluvium. Yet his is an interesting literary failure. It is a staging of the *Sira* that discards the narrative form in order to capture its supposedly original and dramatic impact and so to elevate it above polemic and zealotry.

The second is the much more famous work of Taha Husayn entitled *'Ala Hamish al-Sira* (On the Margins of the *Sira*), which first appeared in 1933.[56] This too is the *Sira* as a literary genre, an attempt to recast the *Sira* as a historical novel, ostensibly to make it palatable for modern readers. The assumption is that the premodern *Sira* alienates and obscures Muhammad's true image:

These pages are not intended for scholars or historians . . . Rather, it is an image that flashed through my mind as I read the *Sira*, which I quickly recorded. These pages recover for people certain aspects of ancient literature which have escaped them or grown too difficult for them to understand. Today, people read what contemporaries write for them by way of modern literature in their own or in one of a number of foreign languages currently widespread in the East. This literature is found easy, accessible and entertaining whereas ancient literature is difficult to read and even more difficult to understand and enjoy.[57]

For Taha Husayn, "living literature" has the capacity to entertain and inspire perennially, and just as modern French playwrights find in the Greek dramatic heritage endless themes for their inspiration, so too will we find in our own Arabic-Islamic past much to inspire us today. It is especially important for the country's youth to reconnect with their ancient literary tradition, and with the *Sira* in particular. To potential critics who might complain that he has taken too many liberties with the facts of the *Sira*, Taha Husayn responds with a defense of the value of entertainment and a direct "address to the heart."[58] So now the *Sira* is to be recast as a novel, a form that allowed the author to explore the contingencies of historical fiction.[59] If one measure of its success is its continued popularity—there have been more than thirty editions so far—it must surely rank as a best seller. But its literary merit is not so obvious.

Taha Husayn structures his work in episodes chosen for their dramatic quality and flitting back and forth in time. Typical is a chapter called "Temptation," wherein the Prophet's father 'Abdullah meets a temptress, Fatima, on his way to consummate his marriage with Amina, the Prophet's mother. In classical *Sira* writers, the issue was, as we saw before, theological: whether 'Abdullah was, or could have been, guilty of lust. In the hands of Taha Husayn, the episode is spun out across eighteen pages where Fatima pours out her passion to a faltering 'Abdullah, then turns him away when he comes back to her after the consumation. Taha Husayn is not concerned with theological propriety but with youthful passions and their consequences. It is Fatima the temptress rather than 'Abdullah who is at center stage, as a woman first liberated then chastened by passion.

But the diction, neoclassical, is heavy-footed, internal monologues are long and frequent, the continuous tense *(muḍari')* predominates, and the sentiments are melodramatic, reminiscent of what one might call the Manfaluti style.[60] Here is the temptress pouring out her love for 'Abdullah to her confidantes:

Do you know how a flower thrills to the touch of the dew at dawn? This is how I thrilled when touched by the love of that youth. Do you know how a flower longs for the dew-drop when sunshine spreads and intensifies as the day advances? Thus do I long for that youth as daytime separates us. Do you know how a flower falls passionately in love with the dew-drop when covered by approaching night, as it senses the chill of evening and realizes that the dew will soon descend? Thus have I fallen in love with that youth as dawn is breaking.[61]

Taha Husayn's characterization tends to assume the form of moral or cultural personification, and the cast of characters is so long that, strangely for a *Sira,* it almost edges Muhammad out. One chapter, called "The Nursemaid," seeks to capture the love between Muhammad and his nursemaid, Umm Ayman, who once granted him the maternal affection he so missed as an orphan:

Then God perfects His grace upon the orphan, choosing him for what He intended for him by way of honor, and the ability to shoulder heavy burdens. But neither good fortune nor bad, neither rest nor exertion distracted him from that mother of his. Listen to him speaking about her to his companions and uttering those words full of filial piety, tenderness and loyalty: "She is all that remains of my family!" Consider how he took care to make her live and enjoy life, careful that her portion of happiness in this world be no less than the fortune of other free women. Look at how he seeks a husband for her and says to his companions: "Whoever desires to marry a woman of paradise, let him marry Umm Ayman." O noble and tender mother! You bestowed on your son, when young, all you could grant him of love and affection . . . Can you bear to be separated from him? No indeed. Here she is, leaving Mecca as an emigrant to God and His Messenger.[62]

The middle part of the work, volume 2 of the three-volume set in modern editions, is largely devoted to the story, entirely extra-*Sira*, of a Greek philosopher called Callicrates who lived in the Christian era, had read Plato's *Phaedo*, was torn by divergent loyalties to Caesar and Christ, and by the attractions and repulsions of philosophy. All this is put into a dialogue between Callicrates and a friend called Androcles. Enter a monk who at some length convinces Callicrates to join him in monastic life in expectation of a miraculous event that would demonstrate the limits of reason.[63] It is now Bahira who announces to the monk and the philosopher that he had witnessed the coming of the expected one, Muhammad. The philosopher heads toward Arabia and eventually transmogrifies into Subayh, one of the so-called *hunafa'*, men of pure faith who prefigured the Prophet.

The object of this long and tedious fable is to highlight the homage that Hellenistic culture had paid to the religion of Muhammad, a theme familiar from classical *Sira* through the lives of converts such as Salman al-Farisi and Suhayb al-Rumi.[64] The intellectual journey of Callicrates/Subayh was a lengthy variation on that theme, designed to emphasize the debt that Islam owes to Greek philosophy, and also to entrench Christianity as a harbinger of Muhammad's faith. The work ends with a volume largely devoted to Abu Sufyan, the obdurate enemy of Muhammad, who is diagnosed psychologically as consumed with envy, followed by short portraits of Muhammad's uncles and cousins as models of loyalty.

When we set Taha Husayn alongside Tawfiq al-Hakim as two literary recasters of the *Sira*, we should remember that the dramatic genres that they pioneered did not have too many takers in later times. The classical *Sira*, as it had developed by about the seventeenth century, was already heavily "dramatized," and imposing the play or novel form on it ran the risk of overornamenting it, of turning it into baroque. This may well be the reason that both works, though still in print, seem sadly dated, marooned in a particular day and age. The barely concealed moralizing tone in both works and the endless internal monologues and apostrophes in Taha Husayn are in some ways more alien to modern sensibility than is the *Sira* of the premodern period. Both writers had intended to "modernize" the *Sira;* both ended by congealing it in the literary, Europe-inspired fashions of their day.[65] From the point of view of the history of the *Sira,* both these works were dead ends. Nonetheless, their authors were both attempting to respond to a vitally important question: how best should the *Sira* be served up to a modern audience?

The remaining four works in this new canon of Egyptian *Sira* writing owe a great deal to Ameer Ali, and many of them refer admiringly to his work. In the beginning decades of the twentieth century, Indian Islam had continued to produce lives of Muhammad in a vein similar to that of Ameer Ali, sometimes even more strident in tone. Thus in the "Life of Muhammad" appended to his *Translation of the Holy Qur'an,* Hafiz Ghulam Sarwar describes Muhammad as the "pole-star of the world of spirituality," the "light of God," and the "liberator of all mankind." Then again,

> As a child, as a youth, as a husband, as a father . . . ruler . . . trader . . . servant of God . . . loyal friend . . . benefactor of enemies . . . worshipper . . . guide . . . custodian . . . judge and peacemaker and lover of all mankind without distinction, he has set us an example the like of which is not to be found in the history of mankind.[66]

Better known is Maulana Muhammad Ali's *Muhammad the Prophet,* a work in thirty-two chapters that follows the chronological divisions of the classical *Sira*.[67] But the author's gaze is fixed on Europe and its Orientalists and also on the deficiencies of Christianity as a world religion, and Islam and the Prophet's suitability to play the role of a universal religion of peace. It is a work that defends Muhammad against Western caricatures while advancing his claims to lead mankind to its salvation. Like Ameer Ali's, many of Muhammad Ali's arguments crop up again in the four Egyptian lives of Muhammad. The affinities binding India to Egypt in the field of Muhammadan scholarship are by now, that is, the 1930s, at their most evident.

The remaining four lives of Muhammad (by M. A. Jad al-Mawla, Muhammad Husayn Haykal, Muhammad Farid Wajdi, and 'Abbas Mahmud al-'Aqqad) are tied to each other by a number of common concerns that, with some overlap, may be summarized under four categories.

The first concern is to defend Muhammad's life against distortion by "Orientalists" as well as Muslim "zealots" and "reactionaries." Both groups often go unnamed. Where they are named, it is Muir who dominates the horizon, his *Life* still very much a brooding presence some seventy years after its publication. To the other side stands the "fair-minded" Carlyle, who acts as a foil to Muir. Accordingly, one strand among these biographies divides the Orientalists into "biased" and "fair," while another strand attempts to engage seriously with them, regarding their methodology as an offshoot of European scientific thought.

The arguments used to defend Muhammad against the usual charges of lust and violence are the least impressive because they are by and large recycled from modern Indian biography or from premodern *Sira*: The antibodies of the *Sira* are simple fabrications;[68] the acts of cruelty are nothing compared to European examples;[69] and all the marriages of Muhammad are explicable and justifiable on moral or political grounds.[70] The most controversial of his marriages, to Zaynab, is explained as a solution to either a domestic or a socio-legal problem, but in no case does it impugn the purity of his character, which, once established, renders all accusations of lust implausible.[71]

The second concern is to prune Muhammad's life of superstitious accretions and, in the process, to address the question of the Prophet's miracles. This in turn is overshadowed by the larger issue of how divine intelligence and wisdom can relate to modern science. This last issue is once again very topical in our contemporary world, centering on sciences like evolutionary biology and cosmology and their relationship to so-called intelligent design.[72] The Egyptian biographers of the 1930s were grappling with similar dilemmas, and many were to come down firmly on the side of Intelligent Design. Jad al-Mawla phrases the question as follows:

> When asked for a miracle, Muhammad would tell his questioners: "Let the cosmos suffice you for a miracle. Look at the earth for it is a miracle of God's handiwork, and proof of His existence and majesty" . . . He would direct the gaze of his enemies to the cosmos to prove that God has mastery over all things, that no place is bereft of any of His signs which scientists of the present age call force and mass, but in which they see nothing sacred . . . It is to be wondered at that they ignore this dimension, for without it no science can come to exist. There can be no true science without knowledge of God and firm belief in His power. By itself science is false prattle, or, as some Western scholars have phrased it, a rotting chunk of wood, a drooping plant.[73]

This godless science seems to have seduced some of the author's contemporaries. If they are told that some Europeans are planning a journey to the moon, they say:

It is science that produces miracles, and scientific discoveries reveal wonders. But told that the Prophet was made to ascend to heaven, they become agitated and their weak spirits reveal their malice and atheism. We will therefore address them in a language which, were they to hear it from their European masters, they would accept, though they possess neither their knowledge nor the capacity to rival them.[74]

Having reviewed certain current "scientific" theories such as hypnotism and proven to his satisfaction that such phenomena "demonstrate" the superiority of "spirit" to "matter"; having also shown that scientific theories successively undermine one another, Jad al-Mawla concludes by arguing that Muhammad's mission put an end to the age of wonders and marked the beginning of the age of reason:

So his miracles spanned both ages, while the most august, greatest and most lasting of them all, the Qur'an, was appropriate for his own age and for all subsequent ages, being the fittest of all.[75]

There is no need to point to the conceptual confusion in such analysis. A modern reader is more impressed with the passion of the argument than with its internal coherence. But there can be no mistaking the intellectual turmoil generated by the urgency to defend the miracles of the *Sira* against the march of modern science, seemingly relentless, atheistic, empirical, and now, indeed, colonial. The author appears to be arguing that if science cannot explain the whole of reality, then the miraculous, alias spiritual, realm must be accepted as plausible.

M. Farid Wajdi is painfully aware of the difficulties involved in writing a *Sira* in an age of science. This necessitates a new type of *Sira* that steers clear of both empty rhetoric and scientific skepticism:

There are plenty of logical proofs for the truth of prophecy and the possibility of revelation. But a modern mentality finds it difficult to be convinced by them. Materialist philosophy has raised numerous doubts concerning prophecy, and denied the existence of the spiritual realm . . . In broaching this subject, we intend to investigate it from three points of view: (1) Is there in this sensible world proof for the existence of a knowledge, among certain creatures, that occurs through inspiration in the heart and not through the senses, and independently of rational investigation? (2) Does science itself acknowledge the existence of purely human events that demonstrate the existence of an occult connection between the soul and the world beyond? (3) Can science acknowledge the existence of a spiritual realm above that of matter which in turn leads to the possibility of prophecy and inspiration?[76]

A long, meandering disquisition follows on "inspiration" among animals and "genius" among humans, all of which, by way of hypnotism and other phenomena, leads to the conclusion that many scientists nowadays do indeed admit the existence of the spiritual realm.[77] Once this is granted then the *Sira* of Muhammad can be shown to be the most extraordinary of all phenomena of that realm and historically the most useful to mankind in its message.

For M. Husayn Haykal, the challenge of science assumes a different form, that is, the challenge of writing a "scientific" biography in accordance with explicitly Western standards of "objectivity." In his view, most defenders of Muhammad did not follow the "scientific method" whereas many Orientalists unfairly and unscientifically made use of the "absurdities" of the *Sira* to cast aspersions on the personality of Muhammad. In other words, neither the Muslim nor the anti-Muslim bigots had truly practiced the "scientific method," and filling that gap was the chief purpose of Haykal's biography.[78]

But in Haykal too we encounter a number of explanatory difficulties. For instance, the monk Bahira episode is dismissed as a "story"; the miracle of the opening of Muhammad's breast is unacceptable, one of its narrators being a two-year-old; the temptation of 'Abdullah is not a story one needs to linger over, since all that a historian can be "comfortable with" is that 'Abdullah was a handsome youth and therefore a possible target of temptation. On the other hand, the twelve-year-old Muhammad is depicted lyrically, and without support from the *Sira,* as gazing with his "beautiful eyes" on the vistas of Syria or listening to the recitation of pre-Islamic odes, and wondering where the truth lies in all of this; the description of his married life before his mission is purely speculative; and the incident of the "Satanic Verses" is rejected as being unworthy of a truthful person inspired by God. Haykal's reader is never quite sure what constitutes "comfort" for a "scientific historian." For him, miracles are suspect and are totally unnecessary when one possesses the Qur'an. Nevertheless, even if it is pruned of miracles, a great deal remains in the *Sira* that borders on the supernatural, attaching itself to the very fabric of the narrative. Dismantling these supernatural elements proved to be quite a complex task for Haykal and his colleagues. And does the "scientific method" allow for speculation where the historical record is silent?[79]

The third principal concern of these biographers is to situate Muhammad's record in world history, and to compare it with the record of other religions, chiefly Christianity. We have seen how Indian Muslim biographers had drawn a bleak portrait of the history of pre-Muhammadan nations and cultures, the intention being to highlight the need for the coming of a deliverer or savior. World history could thus be neatly divided into an age of darkness and an age of light. We have also seen that these authors' need to establish this sort of dividing line between depravity and goodness would tend to wrap Arabia itself in a pall of gloom, even though there is much in the *Sira* and the Hadith that extols the virtues of Arabia as the home of final prophecy, and praises Arabians as the purest in soul of all mankind.

In two of our biographers, the condemnation of the pre-Muhammadan period is sweeping. As Jad al-Mawla phrases it:

> The era preceding the coming of Muhammad was distinguished by the fact that the whole world was overlaid with a thick cloud of polytheism, ignorance, vice and injustice, whereby evil replaced morality and wicked men assumed power over the nations. In consequence, there emerged the absolute necessity for the appearance of Muhammad, who then carried out the greatest reform of society ever undertaken by a human being, before or after him.[80]

For Wajdi, any attempt to rehabilitate pre-Islamic Arabia, turning it into a land ready to receive revelation, must be resisted as unhistorical and as tending to denigrate the achievement of Muhammad, which is depicted as occurring in a totally hostile and depraved Arabian environment.[81] By contrast, Haykal, who sticks close to his traditional sources and accepts the historicity of the Qur'an without question, grants a high place of honor to pre-Islamic Mecca. True, the Arabians were pagans, but their list of virtues is long: love of liberty, chivalry, courage, generosity, kindness to guests and neighbors, magnanimity, and forgiveness.[82] At issue in these contrasting images of the cradle of Islam is the world historical significance of Muhammad's mission. For some, a historical rupture is imperative if that mission is to be considered truly universal and unique. For others, for example, Haykal and Taha Husayn, historical continuity emphasizes what Muhammad had in common with the cultural heritage that preceded him.

All, however, wanted to position Muhammad on the map of world history. All of them found him incommensurable, as in the following passage from Jad al-Mawla:

> If we count the great kings, skilful statesmen, experienced commanders, orators, men of eloquence . . . men of wisdom, both legislators and non-legislators, prophets and reformers, founders of great kingdoms and states, we find him [Muhammad] to be the greatest of kings, the most rational of statesmen, the wisest of legislators, the most courageous of commanders, the most pious of believers, the greatest reformer of ideas and manners . . . He learnt all this from no human being. Rather, his genius burst forth in one surge when his prophecy appeared . . . Behold all these European states with their cavalry and infantry, sciences and arts, inventions and fleets, tanks and planes, wealth and culture, schools and hospitals! All are incapable of fighting your religion or diverting the sweep of its current . . . all over the world.[83]

The rhetoric here is quite typical of the instinctive, almost knee-jerk reaction of many of these biographers to the perceived assault of European power and the militant Christianity that came with it. Christianity is judged to be inadequate as a universal religion for the following reasons:

> To begin with, it is built on a dogma for which there exists no rational proof and which can only be accepted on faith in an age enveloped in skepticism. Secondly, it is built on asceticism and an other-worldly ethic, whereas social life does not tolerate this . . . Thirdly, it is a religion which abrogates the most important basis of legislation, namely, to repel aggression with force and punish criminality in order to avert harm.[84]

The fourth main concern of these biographers is to bring some "modern" notions of psychology to bear on the personality of the Prophet. Here, it may well have been Muir's attempt to use Victorian psychology to describe Muhammad's personality, for instance, referring to his "ecstatic states" or his "highly strung and nervous temperament," that prompted a Muslim counter-attempt at psychological analysis. We have seen how these and similar psychological diagnoses were contemptuously dismissed by writers such as Muhammad Iqbal. It was now the turn of Muslim biographers to rebut the charges of hysteria or psychological abnormality, and to redraw Muhammad's portrait using largely Western-inspired categories of psychology and science. Was he, for instance, an epileptic? This, argues Haykal, flies in the face of all that modern science has told us regarding what occurs in a true epileptic fit, wherein the victim has no recollection whatever of what transpired during the fit. Muhammad, on the other hand, would recover from his trances of inspiration with perfect recollection of what had been revealed to him.[85]

But the key to understanding Muhammad's personality is his "genius," a concept first developed in Wajdi and then detailed in al-'Aqqad. His genius is intimately bound up with his prophetic persona and with divine inspiration. Both prophecy and inspiration are, according to Wajdi, amenable to "scientific" explanation, but genius is inexplicable. Long extracts from modern Western scientists are adduced to prove all these assertions. When he comes to Muhammad's earliest and agonizing encounters with divine inspiration, Wajdi says that an "experienced psychologist" must be summoned to assist the investigation. What concerns the Wajdian psychologist is this:

That figure which appeared to Muhammad and spoke to him: was it a mental image or a genuine external reality? For the psychologist knows that certain types of nervous disease, especially hysteria, can induce the appearance of phantoms before patients. But such phantoms can only disturb the patient leading him to madness or some such, whereas the image that appeared to Muhammad would guide him to the good, keep him on the straight path and provide him with speech to be transmitted to his people for their guidance.[86]

So Muhammad's case is far different from normal hysteria. Once this diagnosis is refuted, the psychologist can only "fall upon his knees" and acknowledge divine inspiration. Therefore, Muhammad's achievements, given their historical context, and worldwide consequences, must be attributed to the "greatest genius" in history.[87]

The "genius" theme is picked up by al-'Aqqad, who was to write a series of biographies entitled "The Genius of So and So." Like Wajdi's work, al-'Aqqad's *The Genius of Muhammad* is thematic rather than chronological in treatment.[88] At its heart is a concept of genius that is never explicitly defined but that involves, in Muhammad's case, surpassing excellence in many and various fields at once. In structure though not in content the inspiration for this theme seems to have come from Carlyle. Like Carlyle's heroism, Muhammad's genius is compartmentalized: as military leader, politician, administrator, diplomat, sage, orator, and then as friend, father, husband, master, inspired worshipper, and man of consummate manners. To prove his genius in a given field, al-'Aqqad typically cites one or two incidents in the *Sira* and follows this up with a rhetorical flourish: did the world ever witness such skill, morality, courage, pragmatism, love, and so forth? Whatever the quality of Muhammad under consideration may be, al-'Aqqad pays homage to it as the most sublime human example and the one most consistent with logic, common sense, or human decency. If at certain

moments of his life Muhammad appears to have revealed human
weakness, for example, in his *schadenfreude* following the Battle of
Badr, this is because, when all is said and done,

> Muhammad was a living human being, with an impassioned
> soul, subject to the motivations of life, not some emaciated asce-
> tic, a monk in a cell who divests his emotions of all motives and
> feelings . . . His genius as military leader is a genius acceptable
> by the norms of war, by manliness, by the laws of God and man,
> by civilization at its most advanced, and by friends and foes
> alike.[89]

In many of his pronouncements and actions Muhammad was a
forerunner of the most modern advances in such areas as public
health, public policy, freedom of thought, and so forth. Here too is
another aspect of his genius, namely its perennial value to
mankind, its ever-living relevance to all times and places. Al-
'Aqqad's principal purpose in writing, however, is not to extol the
merits of Muhammad's religion but rather to

> explain the psychological motives which inspired Muhammad
> to act and behave as he did. Doubtless, these motives were in
> total agreement with every religious commandment or prohibi-
> tion, but innate goodness is one thing, commanded goodness is
> another. It is [Muhammad's] innate goodness that we intend to
> explain in all that we have set forth. For example, in discussing
> Muhammad's treatment of his servants we were not concerned
> with detailing the commandments of Islam in this regard . . . but
> rather to prove Muhammad's superiority to all other masters,
> a superiority [of character] that is not applicable to those
> who are satisfied with mere obedience of religious command-
> ments.[90]

When one scans this cluster of Egyptian biographies of the 1930s, one's first impression might be that they are characterized by strident rhetoric, arguments passionate in their polemic, a view of the past that puts into the shade all human history before Muhammad, a style that is overly lyrical and lavish with comparatives and superlatives. It may well be that in a period in which many of the authors could not openly attack the imperial power or its native surrogates, attacking the "Orientalists" and the "missionaries" was an indirect form of religious or national protest. In such an age, Muhammad's symbolic importance as leader, hero, genius, and unifier gains new urgency. The burning political issues of the day, such as the struggle for independence, the morality of politics, religion, and science, and the status of women lie just below the surface of these biographies, and Muhammad's example is the ever-living and manifest guide.

Nevertheless these biographers of Muhammad are acutely conscious of the need for a new and modern *Sira*. This new *Sira* needed to be rescued from the doldrums into which conservative religious scholars had submerged it, from the realm of superstition to which modern science seemed to have consigned it, and from the hostile nit-picking of Western Orientalists. With Tawfiq al-Hakim and Taha Husayn the new *Sira* was given dramatic or novelistic form in order to bring it closer to contemporary literary sensibilities. With the others, a strictly chronological or historical treatment gave way to a thematic treatment in order to drive home more powerfully the lessons and examples of Muhammad's life, to be examined, as in Wajdi's subtitle, "in the light of science and philosophy."

The Liberator

By contemporary *Sira,* I mean the *Sira* produced in the Muslim world after World War II and approximately up to the present day. It should be pointed out straightaway that this is a *Sira* that has not, on the whole, received the widespread and enthusiastic welcome that its immediate predecessors in the first half of the twentieth century received. No *Sira* of this more recent period has yet achieved the iconic status of Ameer Ali's *Spirit of Islam* or Muhammad Husayn Haykal's *Hayat Muhammad,* or even the chatty and spirited *Genius of Muhammad* by al-'Aqqad.

This at least seems to be the judgment of one of the most charming and astute of contemporary Muslim authors, Husayn Ahmad Amin (b. 1931). In a work impishly entitled *Dalil al-Muslim al-Hazin ila Muqtada al-Suluk fi al-Qarn al-'Ishrin* (A Guide to the Forlorn Muslim as to Proper Conduct in the Twentieth Century),[1] whose internal rhyming parodies medieval titles, the author casts a cold eye on certain aspects of modern Muslim thought and practice and finds much to bewail, criticize, and mock. What concerns us here is chapter two of his work, headed "Reflections on the Evolution of *Sira* Writing in East and West."

Amin begins by praising the relative objectivity of early Muslim *Sira*, which is the result, among other causes, of a profound admiration for the personality of the Prophet and the authors' concern to hand down to posterity a complete account of all his sayings and acts, great or small. Hence they recorded all the details of his life without any embarrassment or exclusion. Piety dictated total fidelity in transmission and a commitment to truth, conventions that are not far removed from those of modern positive historiography. To these early biographers, Muhammad was a human being, like them, although of course divinely inspired. However, as time went on, the *Sira* began to deviate from its pristine origins, and as Islam came into direct contact with other religions, Muhammad was increasingly pitted against other superhuman religious figures, and a new and more miraculous Muhammad began to emerge. Thus, a decline set in after the age of the founding fathers, and hagiography overshadowed the *Sira*. The image of Muhammad "as flesh and blood" was fading, to be replaced by a more "popular" image of a supernatural hero and miracle worker. Amin thinks that the apogee of *Sira* writing was reached with Ameer Ali, who initiated the disturbing tendency toward a style of polemics and apologetics by falling into the "trap," perhaps unintended, set for Muslims by European biographies of Muhammad:

> This apologetic style springs from a sense of danger . . . and an inferiority complex towards Europeans. Even worse is the fact that the defense [by modern Muslim *Sira* writers] of Muhammad and Islam rested entirely on exclusively western ethical standards, as if these were beyond all question, or as if what was required was merely to prove how Islam and the moral character of Muhammad agree with these standards . . . Hence these modern *Sira* writers are concerned to show how Islam elevated the status of women . . . and how it tempered the

severity of slavery, how it encouraged the pursuit of knowledge . . . and the building of hospitals; how it fought against
racial discrimination and established the bases of social justice—O Socialists, you are their *imam!*[2]

He then pours scorn on the manner in which Muhammad's
multiple marriages are explained by "political or social necessities"
and how modern scientific advances are said to have been anticipated in the Qur'an. Meanwhile the true greatness of the classical
Sira and many of its stories are either forgotten or unknown to
most contemporary biographers of the Prophet. Haykal's biography, while preferable to other works, has nevertheless resulted in
setting up a barrier between the modern reader and the early *Sira.*
The saddest result of this encounter between Islam and the West
in the field of *Sira* is the manner in which Muslims "bloat with
pride and self-confidence" when their Prophet is praised by
Westerners and Orientalists or resort to "defamation and slander"
when up against his detractors. But neither praise nor defamation
should affect us, for those Westerners who praise Muhammad often do so from atheistic or contrarian motives while those who dis-
parage him often lack a genuine understanding of seventh-century
Arabia.[3]

What kind of *Sira* then should contemporary Muslims write?
Amin writes:

It is high time in my view that a new *Sira* be written in the
Muslim world, a *Sira* which does not defend, apologize or is
shy; a *Sira* that does not suppress the facts or invent them . . .
one that does not expunge "what some people find objectionable" . . . a *Sira* that evokes an entire historical era, recreating its
ethical standards, environment and norms, so that the Prophet's
personality can appear clearly in its context . . . written by an
author not lacking in manly courage or shackled by a complex

of inferiority, proud of his religion, confident of his Prophet; a *Sira* worthy of Waqidi and Tabari, were they to be writing in this day and age.[4]

This bold, thoughtful, and witty dissection of the whole tradition of *Sira* writing up to the twentieth century in both East and West comes from a writer widely regarded as the darling of Muslim "liberals," a thinker deeply grounded in both his own as well as European literature. While his faith in historical "facts" might be a bit credulous and some of his conclusions may be questionable, his portrait of the modern *Sira* will serve us here as a template against which to assess contemporary Muslim biography. How justified is Husayn Ahmad Amin's scathing verdict on the twentieth century?

The postwar era in many Muslim countries was one of state building amid the anguished pangs of independence. It was an era when nationalist identities were being reformulated, when powerful socioeconomic ideologies such as socialism, Marxism, and liberal capitalism were competing in the Muslim marketplace. In many Muslim countries, the army came forward as a savior from the politics of corrupt elites, widely seen as relics of colonial days. Political parties with a specific Islamic program had already appeared in the last few decades of colonial rule and became powerful competitors of other groups when independence was finally attained. The "men on horseback" were not unsympathetic to the Islamic groups. But unlike the medieval military sultans whom in some cases they consciously attempted to emulate, these people had limited room for maneuvering, and they juggled their options between nationalism, Islamism, and powerful Western intrusion with often disastrous consequences. In the field of Islamic history

writing, it was, and still to some extent is, an era of heroes, mar-
tyrs, and villains, when the sense of history became exceptionally
vivid, thus populating history with myth. In modern Islamic political discourse the glorious past was everywhere, inspiring, catego-
rizing, agonizing, judging. As the new Muslim states began to take
shape, the Muslim intelligentsia of colonial days, like the colonial
elites in general, were in retreat. Many were suspected of obse-
quiousness, of being too deeply tainted by the cultural agenda and
horizons of the former colonial powers. The "New Intelligentsia"
of postcolonial days sought more radical solutions to the problems
of society and culture, finding this radicalism either in their own
Islamic past or else in some form of nationalist or socialist program. Islamic writers such as Sayyid Qutb (d. 1966) in Egypt
were far less ready to interact with non-Muslim culture; indeed,
they were responsible for popularizing a theme, already found
here and there in early twentieth century *Sira*, that the West was
the home of "materialism" and the East the home of the "spirit."
This baleful distinction continues to thrive in some contemporary
Muslim scholarship. More apparent too is an essentializing discourse, a tendency to speak and write in terms of generalities
called "Islam" and the "view of Islam" on such and such a problem,
compared to earlier views, which had been more nuanced in their
phrasing.

Since the 1950s and 1960s of the last century, radical intellectuals, both Muslim and secular, have suffered from intermittent
and often brutal persecution at the hands of military regimes.
Many of these intellectuals were to find refuge in the West, where
they were able to express their views in relative freedom. Those
who remained behind often had to make their peace with the military regimes, with the result that their impact on their societies became less effective than it would have been in the earlier part of the
century. Indeed, in some Muslim countries, the word "intellectual"
itself has acquired a pejorative connotation.

Open any daily newspaper in the Arab world today and you will find a critique of the role of the intellectuals who are regularly maligned as cowardly, irrelevant, or servile. It is in some such context that the new *Sira* of the second half of the twentieth century might be placed. Muhammad was inducted into the political debates of the Muslim world and both Islamists and secularists attempted to turn him into an ideological champion of one coloring or another. A chronological or historical *Sira* was no longer the preferred means of dealing with his life; instead, works on the *Sira* have tended to align Muhammad brusquely to some current mood or ideology, ignoring the awkward anachronisms in their path, and to adopt a broadly thematic approach to his life.

In most of these contemporary biographies, Muhammad advances to occupy the center of the volatile political arena. He is wrenched from his historical context and plunged into the midst of the modern world. This is a tendency apparent since the time when Indian Muslim biographers began to cast him as a figure of universal significance, and the theme was picked up by Egyptian biographers, who proceeded to turn him into their contemporary. Muhammad is now a hero of freedom, justice, Socialism, the class struggle, revolutionary action, egalitarianism, democracy, national or Islamic unity, and other desirable political goals. He speaks to us today primarily as a statesman and social reformer, and much is made of the lessons he has to teach us: how to run a state, how to reform its institutions, indeed how he anticipated such modern institutions as the parliament, the constitution, and even the intelligence services.[5] Only a small minority of contemporary biographers are unhappy about his wholesale modernization and the transformation of his mission into statesmanship, but even the few writers who criticize that image as antihistorical go on to dress him in modern garb as, for instance, a "humanist."[6] However, it appears that this modernizing image of him is, for the time being at any rate, predominant. Why look elsewhere for guidance and inspiration when our own hero is alive and well and living in our hearts and minds, if only we can free him, Prometheus-like, from the chains of tradition and superstition?

Given his paramount political role, the "ever" and "never" style becomes, if anything, more shrill in these contemporary biographies. There is hardly any biography that does not proclaim that such and such an act or episode in the *Sira* was unique or unprecedented in world history. The prose is frequently gushing and strewn with dots, while internal monologues and apostrophes continue a trope first popularized by Taha Husayn.[7] But alongside the political Muhammad there is also the Muhammad of the heart, an apostle of mercy, love, truth, beauty, justice, nobility, and concern for the common man. This last quality is much in evidence, not surprising in the "Age of the Common Man," and associated with the need, expressed by some biographers, to represent Muhammad to Muslims and non-Muslims alike.[8] In this process of representation, the "Orientalists" of the first half of the century are less visible in the second half. The word is now largely a metaphor, used indiscriminately to designate any and all detractors of Muhammad.[9] There is little evidence that these writers are cognizant of the latest trends in Orientalist studies in the West, as were many of their predecessors. With few exceptions, these *Siras* are addressed primarily to other Muslims.

The ever/never style aggravates the darkness-before-Muhammad theme. In other words, the era of Muhammad is frequently depicted as a completely new era of world history; there is a clean break with everything that came before it. This is particularly well marked in Shiite biographies, where it sits somewhat uneasily with the view that a luminous line of sacred ancestors linked Muhammad back to Isma'il.[10] It is as though true and accurate history, history properly so called, began with Muhammad, and all earlier history is dark in both the moral and archival sense. Why Shiite *Sira* in particular should draw such a conspicuous line between the two eras is not immediately clear. It may be a continuation of the earlier Shiite biographical tradition of radically recasting the *Sira*. Among Shiite biographers, the *Sira* is commonly regarded as replete with superstition and too partisan to Sunni narrative in its verdicts on early Muslim heroes, as, for example, in the works of Haykal and company, where the towering stature of 'Ali is ignored.[11]

On miracles, contemporary *Sira* has little to add to its immediate predecessors. As noted above, one common view of the earlier *Sira* of the twentieth century was that the distinction between science and miracle was not by any means insuperable. Certain "phenomena" of modern science, for example, hypnotism, cannot be explained "scientifically." Therefore such miraculous events as Muhammad's Night Journey must be allowed as possible, indeed they must be undeniable given they have been attested to in the earliest sources. But science and miracle are not comfortable bedfellows in these biographies. In the same work one may encounter the view that the opening of the breast incident is "beyond the capacity of reason" alongside the view that "Muhammad, whether infant, child, youth, mature man or old man, never, in any of his states or any stages of his life, transcended the norms of the universe or the laws of nature."[12] Or else one might encounter a very anti-miracle *Sira* that seeks to prune the narrative of all its antibodies and yet alludes to hypnotism and space travel in connection with the Night Journey.[13] Some *Siras*, written from a Sufi perspective, admit Prophetic miracles without question and even the charisms *(karamat)* of saints as confirming the miracles of Muhammad, yet they also make allowances for a symbolic interpretation of them.[14] Other *Siras* ignore or reject Muhammad's miracles completely or else assert that the truest miracle of all is

"Muhammad's very personality which combined all perfections and reached the ultimate pinnacle in every perfection."[15] Connected indirectly to Muhammad's miracles is the issue of his sincerity. Here, some earlier arguments are rehabilitated, or else new emphasis is added. We hear echoes of early views in such arguments for his sincerity as the one that holds that Muhammad could never have sustained a pretense to prophecy for he would quickly have been exposed by his followers. Indeed, he gained nothing but trouble from being a prophet. The fact that he spontaneously chose to expose his own embarrassments to public view in such incidents as the *'Abasa* verses of the Qur'an, where God reprimanded him for his irritation when a blind and poor believer interrupted his conversation with a rich man, or the *Ifk* incident, which threw doubt on 'A'isha's chastity, can only mean that he was utterly sincere.[16] The argument is also made that Muhammad's sincerity is proven by his total unawareness that the divine mission was about to descend upon him, and by his reluctance thereafter to claim supernatural powers.[17] Further testimony to his sincerity is the fact that he always insisted on his humanity and on not being praised beyond what is normal.

If, at this point, we revert to Husayn Ahmad Amin's low view of modern *Sira*, set out above, we shall find little to disagree with. True, there is a feverish attempt in many contemporary *Siras* to inject a journalist's style into the narrative in order to make it more palatable to modern taste, but there is little that one can call an original breakthrough in interpretation or presentation. Thus, a loudly trumpeted modern *Sira*, Khalil 'Abd al-Karim's *Fatrat al-Takwin fi Hayat al-Sadiq al-Amin* (The Formative Period in the Life of the Truthful and Trustworthy [Prophet]),[18] is devoted to the fifteen or so years of Muhammad's marriage to Khadija before the descent of revelation. We have seen before that this is the period in his life about which the sources are most silent, thus setting a formidable challenge to any writer of the *Sira*, ancient or modern.

Our author plunges into the fray armed already with a number of assumptions that he will insert into the narrative whenever he thinks they are needed. The result is speculative to the extreme. This, that, and the other event must have happened, or must have happened in this or that way.[19] The underlying assumption throughout is that Khadija played an absolutely pivotal role in Muhammad's life. It was she who "must have had her eye on him" from his early youth, and was therefore the true "mother" of Muhammad and of Islam, and it was she who readied him for the prophetic experience. This is all expressed in a repetitive, pompous, pseudoclassical Arabic, and in the course of the narrative the author will point out, in case his reader has not noticed, his subtle use of language and phrasing. It is a work that in many ways exposes and illustrates the shortcomings of contemporary *Sira*, especially where it is at its most conjectural or else most anxious to put a new or original spin on Muhammad's life, regardless of evidence.

But in this somewhat bleak landscape, two biographies stand out: Ma'ruf al-Rusafi's *Al-Shakhsiyya al-Muhammadiyya* (The Muhammadan Personality) and 'Ali Dashti's *23 'Aman* (23 Years).[20] They deserve separate scrutiny.

The name Ma'ruf al-Rusafi (1875–1945) conjures up a whole era of Iraq's cultural history in the first half of the twentieth century. Politician, journalist, teacher, and poet, al-Rusafi lived a troubled, insecure, often destitute life spanning the end of the Ottoman Empire and the years of British domination of Iraq.[21] A proud and fearless man, he was a merciless critic in prose and verse of personalities and policies he disapproved of and tireless in pressing upon his contemporaries the paramount value of the freedom of thought. This was to bring him at many times into direct conflict with government and conservative religious scholars, and there is little doubt that his principal sympathies lay with the so-called "free thinkers" of classical Islam, such as Abu Bakr al-Razi, Abu'l 'Ala' al-Ma'arri, al-Mutanabbi, and their ilk. Although deeply grounded in traditional Arabic literature, religious and otherwise, al-Rusafi felt that Islam had fallen victim to superstition, which needs to be fought with a heavy dose of skepticism. His biography of Muhammad, he knew, would bring him many enemies, but he seems to have regarded it as his own most important contribution to a new and more critical search for "the truth" *(al-haqiqa)* in the history of Islamic origins.[22]

The subtitle of al-Rusafi's biography is *Hall al-Lughz al-Muqaddas* (Solving the Sacred Riddle). A reader will soon discover that the principal object of analysis is not so much the *Sira* itself but the personality of Muhammad. This is where the "riddle" lay and where al-Rusafi intended to direct his search. His list of targets is long and varied, taking in both the Qur'an and the *Sira,* and he attacks them with astonishing vigor. But his very first target is history, which he dubs "the home of lying . . . in which a few atoms of scattered truth are intermingled." The very process of historical transmission can be shown, through ordinary, everyday examples, to be hopelessly flawed. This should make us wary of Ibn Ishaq's narratives and of the narratives of the classical *Sira* in general. Hadith fares no better, and its overreliance on *isnad* for authenticity renders its historical content wide open to attack on grounds of implausibility. Al-Rusafi believes that it is the conflict and contradictions among historical reports that have caused Islam to splinter into sects.[23] Therefore, if we wish to learn about Muhammad as he really was, we have only two safe resorts: the Qur'an — regarded as an accurate historical source — and reason. All other narratives must be subjected to these two criteria before we can accept them.

What follows is a lengthy demolition job, the likes of which had not been seen in Islamic literature since the days of Abu Bakr al-Razi and his famous attack on prophecy in the early tenth century.[24] For al-Rusafi, the Qur'an is the speech of Muhammad, a man of great intelligence and imaginative power. His gifts enabled him to transform his inspiration *(wahy)*, in reality a process of intense contemplation, into what became the Qur'anic text. It was Muhammad's independence of thought that produced the idea of his own prophethood, and not some divine intervention. To understand Muhammad, one must understand his "subconscious mind" *('aql batini)* and recognize that his so-called inspiration was no more than a series of psychological responses to changing needs, personal and public. At times, argues al-Rusafi, there is a disparity between the Qur'an, a subconscious depository of Muhammad's deepest desires, and what one knows of the logic and good sense of Muhammad himself. Thus, when the Qur'an denies that a foreigner is teaching Muhammad because the teacher's *tongue* is foreign, how can this be accepted as a logical defense against the *existence* of that person or the *possibility* that he could have taught the Prophet? In his ordinary pronouncements, Muhammad was too intelligent to make such mistakes.[25]

The Qur'an comes in for a lengthy reappraisal. Its verses, while occasionally supremely eloquent, are not uniformly so. Had such defects of eloquence been spotted in other works, the classical critics would not have spared them. Some Qur'anic verses are unworthy of divine eloquence, and al-Rusafi at times suggests his own amendments to improve expression and sense. Other verses simply make no sense or contravene reason and logic. But it is Muhammad's personality, whether in the Qur'an or in *Sira*, that takes the brunt of the analysis.[26] Was Muhammad illiterate? Clearly not. And what of his early life before his mission? This is enveloped in total darkness, except for perhaps four or five incidents. All his miracles must be rejected as contravening the explicit pronouncements of the Qur'an or as risible nonsense.[27] How did they come about? Let us take for instance the well-known miracle of the tree stump that moaned in longing for him when he abandoned it for a pulpit:

> We stated above that Muhammad had a wide-ranging and powerful imagination whereby if he imagined any matter, it would be as if he saw it and touched it with his hand, speaking of it as if it were a palpable truth . . . This longing of the stump for Muhammad is in fact Muhammad himself longing for the stump and not the stump for Muhammad. The longing issues, in reality, from his own wide and powerful imagination.[28]

And so it goes. The Night Journey? A mere dream. Was Muhammad a poor man? Evidently not, especially not after the *Hijra*. And what of his marriages? They all took place according to his own desires, not for political or compelling reasons, as many modern writers allege, while his undoubted sexual energy was an aspect of his nervous energy. Did Muhammad occasionally display a spirit of vengeance? Yes, for instance at the Battle of Badr. Did the sword play a part in the spread of the faith? The sources leave us in no doubt that this was the case.[29]

Al-Rusafi's Muhammad is thus a man of intense intelligence and imagination yet one whose achievement lies completely within the realm of human possibility:

> If someone says: "If all human beings are like Muhammad in relation to the unity of absolute existence, how and why was Muhammad singled out so that his speech would be the speech of God and his acts be God's acts?" I respond: "Muhammad was not singled out for this but all those who are gifted with profound understanding are likewise singled out when they divest themselves from partial existence and dissolve into total, absolute and eternal existence. Whoever is capable of this can be

like Muhammad and can claim what Muhammad claimed, provided he divests himself from his partial existence and dissolves in the unity of absolute existence."[30]

Muhammad then is a Sufi superhero of the monist variety, who was able to experience the divine and merge himself in "absolute unity," coming out of that experience with a sacred scripture that time proceeded to hallow, together with its author. How this portrait tallies with al-Rusafi's other view that Muhammad's "subconscious mind" channeled his desires remains unclear. If Muhammad was indeed a superior sort of Sufi saint who managed to "dissolve" himself in the absolute unity of existence, and divest himself of "partial existence," would such a person be likely to transfigure his own carnal desires, for instance, in his controversial marriage to Zaynab, during the dissolution process? Would not a Sufi saint be more likely to "dissolve" his own desires first? But that is precisely what al-Rusafi's Muhammad succeeded in doing. The transfiguration of desire is his greatest religious achievement while his political and social accomplishments, his uniting of a whole nation in justice and freedom through sheer determination and a wonderful intelligence, are his true miracle. But given the general tenor of the work, such remarks on Muhammad must be taken with a grain of salt. This bold, original, and iconoclastic *Sira* has yet to leave its impact on modern scholarship inside and beyond the Muslim world. It issues from a skeptical or agnostic current of thought with ancient roots but one that is represented in more modern times by thinkers like al-Shidyaq, Shibli Shumayyil (d. 1917), Farah Antun (d. 1922), and the early Taha Husayn. But in his *Sira* al-Rusafi owed most to his own unswerving belief in total freedom of thought. In a rare reference to other *Siras* of his day he curtly dismisses Haykal for lack of originality and freedom. How can he be free when the Azhar towers over him with its turbans, eyeing him with anger if he deviates from the prescribed path? Without freedom of thought, hypocrisy becomes the order of the day.[31]

The life of the Iranian 'Ali Dashti (1896–1982) holds several parallels with that of al-Rusafi.[32] After a religious education in his native Iran and later in Iraq, he abandoned a clerical career for one in journalism, and he frequently landed in jail for his antigovernment views. Like al-Rusafi, he was for a time a prominent member of his country's parliament, and eventually of the Iranian senate, where he was known as a progressive reformer. But he continued also to gain fame as a novelist, essayist, and literary critic. In his later years Dashti turned to Islamic subjects, but his *Sira*, too bold for the censors of those days to stomach, was first published anonymously in Beirut. Mystery surrounds the last few years of his life under the new Islamic Republic in Iran, although he appears not to have played, or been allowed to play, any significant role in the new regime.

Dashti begins his *Sira* somewhat conventionally. This "extraordinary man," Muhammad, has not yet received an "objective" biography, for ideology and prejudice have wrapped it in myth, as has also the hallowing passage of time. Like al-Rusafi, Dashti quickly dispatches all accounts of Muhammad's miracles, regarding them as contrary to the letter and spirit of the Qur'an. His Night Journey, for instance, is simply a "journey of the spirit" of which many examples can be found among visionaries. The miracle of trees and boulders greeting him in the earliest days of his mission is to be understood as voices within him, while the angel Gabriel is a mere symbol of ambitions long held in his "unconscious." And besides, if such tales are accepted as miracles, why did he not produce a single miracle when dealing with the

Quraysh, when he needed it most?[33] And was Muhammad sinless *(ma'sum)*, a common Shiite and Sufi view of him? Not at all, as evident from the incident of the "Satanic Verses." Indeed, in the Qur'an, Muhammad never attempted to hide his weaknesses. It was the Muslims of later days who masked his normal human failings, and these Dashti dismisses as *plus royaliste que le roi.* Was he a lover of women? Quite obviously, indeed he lusted after them, while the massacre of the Qurayza tribe showed his occasional bent for violence.[34]

Like al-Rusafi, Dashti posits a Muhammad in continuous psychological interaction with the Qur'an, described by him as "prophetic eloquence." Whether any of it is inspired or not, the reader is not informed, but there are several instances in the Qur'an where the speaker *must* be Muhammad and not God, for example, the Opening Chapter *(al-Fatiha),* which is a prayer *to* God. Again, if God is omnipotent, how can He abrogate His own words as in the question of the abrogating and abrogated verses *(al-nasikh wa'l mansukh)?* The explanation must lie in Muhammad's own "unconscious," which constantly intruded into "revelation." And is it appropriate for the Creator to curse Abu Lahab (Q. 111)? And what of these Qur'anic creatures called the *jinn?* Is this God accommodating Hijazi folklore or has it more to do with Muhammad's own beliefs?[35] These are all instances in which it can be shown that there was a "mix-up" between God and Muhammad, and it is only through accepting this fact that one can understand the Qur'an. This latter Dashti regards, unsurprisingly, as nonmiraculous either in style, content, or manner of collection. The real "miracle" of the Qur'an is that it empowered Muhammad and led people to obey him. Above and beyond such issues is the fact that neither the existence of God nor the necessity of prophecy can be scientifically demonstrated.[36]

But the upside to all this psychologizing and demythologizing is that, according to Dashti, we can thereby obtain a fairer image of Muhammad's true greatness. By totally rejecting the supernatural accretions of his *Sira*, we gain a clearer idea of his essential humanity and "genius," for such accretions can only demean him. His love of women is nothing to be ashamed of, for this does not detract from his mission, especially since he never violated the rights of others. As for his occasional cruelty, this is inevitable in state building.[37]

In al-Rusafi and Dashti, we have two oddly parallel and extremely bold reworkings of the *Sira*. The humanizing of the Prophet has gone as far as the pendulum can swing. The man Muhammad remains the extraordinary genius who brought unity and power to Muslims, but his achievement and status can only be lessened when we envelop them in superstition. What the reader misses in these two biographers is any sense of what Muhammad stands for as regards his community. Is he a role model for that community, as in all previous biography, and if so how? Neither of these authors is primarily concerned with the lessons that the *Sira* can teach us. Their target, assiduously pursued, is the radical pruning of Muhammad's image from generations of credulity, charlatanry, and prejudice.

Conclusion

In the early years of the eleventh century, Miskawayhi, a state secretary in Iraq, a man of learning and wide philosophical interests, sat down to write a compendium of history entitled *The Experiences of Nations*, which he intended to be of purely functional and pragmatic use to the ruling elites. He therefore excluded from it all events or narratives that smacked of the miraculous and supernatural, for these in his view were of no practical use in the running of states. Wherever one detects the hand of God in history, one is to assume that no earthly political or military value or lesson can be derived from such intervention. What we are left with are distilled human "experiences" that a statesman can ponder upon and practice when needed.

When Miskawayhi comes to Muhammad's life, it is above all his military expeditions *(Maghazi)* that constitute the "human stratagems" that are useful to statesmen. But even here, it is primarily the Battle of the Ditch, with its novel use of a ditch to deter cavalry attacks, which holds lessons for future commanders. On the other expeditions, Miskawayhi pronounces the following verdict:

We had made it a condition at the very beginning of this work that we would only include such narratives as may hold a valuable stratagem for the future or a cunning trick that took place in wartime or elsewhere, so that it may be something to ponder and learn from for one who undertakes anything similar in future . . . For this reason, we have omitted to mention most of the Prophet's *Maghazi* since they all took place through divine success and support combined with abasement of his enemies. But no experience can be usefully deduced from this, nor any cunning trick or any human stratagem.[1]

Here then is an early attempt by a Muslim historian to make sense of the *Sira,* to see how and where it might be most useful to the governance of Muslim societies. The line that Miskawayhi draws so distinctly between sacred and profane history is unprecedented in the premodern period since it consigns almost the whole of the *Sira* to meta-history and Muhammad himself to the realm of faith. Miskawayhi was writing very much against the grain, in an age when the *Sira* was being pruned of its antibodies and made ready for use—legal, moral, political, and so forth. Dismissing the *Sira* from his history in such a curt fashion had much to do with what some scholars have called the "humanism" of Miskawayhi, his intellectual allegiance to Hellenistic political philosophy, wisdom literature, and, especially, ethics. The relevance of the *Sira* to the totality of human conduct was being spelled out by his contemporaries; that indeed was becoming the norm among biographers of that age. The irrelevance of the *Sira* was the exception.

Reprising the ages of the *Sira* suggested near the beginning of this work into an early age of awe, a middle age of canonization, and a modern age of polemic, one might also plot the evolution of the *Sira* in terms of its relevance, implicit or explicit, to Muhammad's community. In the first age, his life was largely represented as a monument to inspire the community and a record to put alongside the records of other prophets. Its practical relevance to social needs was not immediately obvious. In the second age, his life was shorn of its loose ends, ironed out, compared favorably to the lives of other prophets, and made explicitly relevant to the community's needs, social, legal, and otherwise. In the third age his life became embedded in polemic and made to pass the tests of modern science and logic or else to serve ideological ends. Muhammad is not merely relevant to our needs: he is indeed our contemporary. Against this background, Miskawayhi's view that the *Sira* is devoid of any practicable relevance appears all the more startling.

I have highlighted his views because, from the viewpoint of the history of ideas, it is important to know what a particular intellectual tradition spawned at its margins, what its critics and opponents were doing on its wings. Before Miskawayhi, Abu Bakr al-Razi had launched an all-out assault on prophecy, while in our own day and age Ma'ruf al-Rusafi and 'Ali Dashti have raised concerns about the *Sira* that many conservative believers would find deeply objectionable. When we add to their number the poets and writers who did not directly deal with *Sira* but who nevertheless critically reflected on the significance of issues such as divine inspiration and revelation, we find a vibrant current of thought that constantly questioned the dominant Islamic narrative of Muhammad's life, its significance and its relevance. It is imperative to underline this diversity of thought at a time when Muslim culture is too often pictured as monolithic, univocal, and even, in the horrific phrase of V. S. Naipaul, "wounded."

The *Sira* as a whole is in point of fact a diverse narrative archive. In the hands of master biographers it was also a frank and critical record. Except perhaps in its earliest beginnings, the authors of the *Sira* have demonstrated throughout its history a willingness to spell out their reasons for accepting the versions of events that they chose to accept as also the versions they chose to ignore, combat, or abbreviate. In fact, a detailed study of such reasons would be an important addition to our knowledge of Islamic epistemology. So too could the *Sira* be used to illumine the "social imaginary" of Muslim societies, the way they constructed their common expectations, most often conveyed through narrative.[2]

A canon of *Sira* writing has no doubt emerged across time made up of, say, the four founding fathers, al-Qadi 'Iyad, Ibn Sayyid al-Nas, the *al-Sira al-Halabiyya,* and, in modern times, Ameer Ali and Muhammad Husayn Haykal. But we must remind ourselves of the by now fairly widespread view among cultural historians that what often became part of the canon was once uncanonical, that these works are classics precisely because they "challenged the commonplaces of their period."[3] These works were also, of course, inter-textual, constantly referring to each other, constantly refining and retelling each other's stories. As a result of this interaction, a few "problematic" issues in the life of Muhammad floated to the surface of the *Sira* and have remained since. Two of these issues were to become uppermost in the minds of the biographers: was Muhammad a violent man, a man of the sword? And was he a lustful man? We have seen above some of the ways in which these questions were answered, but it is important to stress that these "problematic issues" were spawned by the *Sira* itself long before they were gleefully deposited in Muslims' laps by the Orientalist West.

A recent scholar has argued that "in early religion, we primarily relate to God as a society" and that relating to him as individuals occurs at a later stage of development.[4] Setting aside the many refinements of the concept of individualism, can one argue that this distinction between relating socially and relating individually is a useful manner of distinguishing the ways in which Muslims related to Muhammad? Did they first relate to him as a society and later as individuals? I am not sure that this thesis can be demonstrated where Muhammad is concerned. It seems altogether too neat.

However, it may contain a fertile question that one can raise relative to the permutations of the *Sira* outlined in the present work. Can one argue that in its long history the *Sira* oscillated between a social and an individual response to the life of Muhammad? I believe a shift of emphasis can be shown to have occurred between Muhammad the builder of the community and, later on, Muhammad the beloved intercessor of the individual believer. But since that shift, the pendulum of images has swung back and forth, as the *Sira* continues to thrive in what I have called Muslim ideality, by which is meant the manner in which that *Sira* conceived of a society and an individual true to the example of its Prophet.

INTRODUCTION

1. For details, see my *Arabic Historical Thought* (Cambridge: Cambridge University Press, 1994), pp. 207–10. See also Michael Cooperson, *Classical Arabic Biography* (Cambridge: Cambridge University Press, 2000), chapter 1.
2. Ibn Sa'd, *Al-Tabaqat al-Kubra* (Beirut: Dar Sadir, 1957–58), 1:366.
3. Hermione Lee, *Virginia Woolf* (London: Vintage, 1997), p. 529.
4. Julian Barnes, *Flaubert's Parrot* (London: Picador, 1985), p. 35.
5. My primary debt in this section is to three outstanding studies of biography: Ira Bruce Nadel, *Biography: Fiction, Fact and Form* (London: Macmillan, 1984); Reed Whittemore, *Whole Lives: Shapers of Modern Biography* (Baltimore: Johns Hopkins University Press, 1989); and Peter France and William St. Clair, eds., *Mapping Lives: The Uses of Biography* (Oxford: Oxford University Press, 2002).
6. Al-Qadi 'Iyad, *Al-Shifa*, ed. 'A.M. Amin (Beirut: Dar al-Kutub al-Ilmiyya, 2002), 2:116.
7. Ibn Sa'd, 1:364.
8. Al-Tabari, *Dhakha'ir al-'Uqba fi Manaqib dhawi al-Qurba* (Baghdad: Dar al-Kutub al-'Iraqiyya, 1947), p. 5.
9. On Carlyle, see especially Whittemore, *Whole Lives*, pp. 11–45.
10. On the *Dictionary of National Biography*, see Whittemore, *Whole Lives*, pp. 47–78.
11. On Freud, see Whittemore, *Whole Lives*, pp. 79–116; Malcolm Bowie in France and St. Clair, eds., *Mapping Lives*, pp. 177–92.
12. On Freud's *Leonardo*, see Whittemore, *Whole Lives*, pp. 83ff.
13. The *Sira* of Ibn Ishaq exists in English translation: see Alfred Guillaume, *The Life of Muhammad* (Oxford: Oxford University Press, 1955); the most readable translation of a Hadith collection is James Robson, *Mishkat al-Masabih* (Lahore: Ashraf,

1963–64). On Ibn Ishaq, see my *Arabic Historical Thought*, pp. 34–39. On the rise and development of the concepts *Sunna, Sira,* and *Hadith,* see Wael Hallaq, *A History of Islamic Legal Theories* (Cambridge: Cambridge University Press, 1997), chapter 1.

14. Al-Qadi 'Iyad, *Al-Shifa,* 2:61.

I

1. Cf. similar passages at Q.13:32, 15:11; and 43:7. **NOTE:** All references to the Qur'an are in the Standard Egyptian edition of 1924. All translations are my own.

2. Cf., e.g., Hosea 9:7. **NOTE:** All biblical references are to *The Jerusalem Bible* (London: Darton, Longman and Todd, 1968).

3. Cf. similar passages at Q.21:5; 27:36; and 69:41.

4. Cf. Q.26:109, 127, 145, 164, 180 (earlier prophets).

5. One of the latest and most balanced treatments of this question is in Sebastian Guenther, "Muhammad, the Illiterate Prophet: An Islamic Creed in the Qur'an and Qur'anic Exegesis," *Journal of Qur'anic Studies* 4, no. 1 (2002): 1–25. See also Khalil Athamina, "Al-Nabiyy al-Ummiyy: An Inquiry into the Meaning of a Qur'anic Verse," *Der Islam* 69, no. 1 (1992): 61–80.

6. An echo perhaps of Luke 7:33.

II

1. The *Sahih* of Muslim is arguably the most rigorous of the six classical *Sahih* collections. Unusually for such collections, it has an important introduction on method, which is discussed in my *Arabic Historical Thought*, pp. 39–43.

2. Ibn Qutayba, *Ta'wil Mukhtalif al-Hadith,* ed. F. Z. al-Kurdi (Cairo: n.p., 1908), p. 51. The text has been consolidated. Ibn Qutayba proceeds to show how apparently contradictory or implausible hadiths can be reconciled.

3. Years later, she falls off her horse and is killed during the invasion of Cyprus, where her shrine exists to this day.

4. There is an extensive discussion of Muhammad's likes and dislikes and their effect on later Muslim taste and practice in Annemarie Schimmel, *And Muhammad Is His Prophet: The Veneration of the Prophet in Islamic Piety* (Chapel Hill: University of North Carolina Press, 1985), pp. 32–45, especially at pp. 43–45.

5. A similar story is told of Hind, the mother of the future caliph Mu'awiya, in Khara'iti (d. 938), *Hawatif al-Jinnan* in Ibrahim Salih, ed., *Nawadir al-Rasa'il* (Beirut: Mu'assasat al-Risala, 1986), p. 199; it is a patently pro-Umayyad yarn.

III

1. For a recent discussion of the problem of authenticity, see Harald Motzki, ed., *The Biography of Muhammad: The Issue of the Sources* (Leiden: Brill, 2000).

2. The stroke sign (/) between some names indicates redactions of the original works by later authors. Thus Ibn Sa'd redacted the original work by his master al-Waqidi, and Ibn Hisham performed the same task on Ibn Ishaq.

3. The *isnad* is the chain of transmitters' names; the *matn* is the substance of the report itself.

4. See the citation from Origen, *Contra Celsum*, in Karen L. King, *What Is Gnosticism?* (Cambridge, Mass.: Belknap Press, 2003), p. 289, 93n.

5. For a discussion of this use of history, see my "The Battle of the Camel: Trauma, Reconciliation and Memory" in A. Neuwirth and A. Pflitsch, eds., *Crisis and Memory in Islamic Societies* (Beirut: Orient-Institut, 2001), pp. 153–63.

6. Ibn Sa'd, *Al-Tabaqat*, 1:20.

7. Ibn Ishaq, *Sira*, ed. M. Hamidullah (Rabat: Ma'had al-Dirasat, 1976), para. 16.

8. Ibn Ishaq, *Sira*, para. 23.

9. See, e.g., Luke 3:15.

10. For the earliest classical collection of these stories of Arabian *kuhhan*, mysterious voices *(hawatif)* of the *jinn*, and similar phenomena announcing the coming of Muhammad, see Khara'iti, *Hawatif*, pp. 123–99.

11. Salman's story is narrated in full in Ibn Ishaq, *Sira*, paras. 68–69.

12. In al-Tabari, *Tarikh al-Rusul wa'l Muluk*, ed. M. J. de Goeje (Leiden: Brill, 1879–1901), 1:1078, the woman is identified as the sister of Waraqa.

13. Cf. Amos 1:12, where the palaces of Busra are threatened with burning.

14. Ibn Sa'd, *Al-Tabaqat*, 1:102.

15. Some confusion exists regarding the name given to him at birth. In addition to Muhammad, Ahmad and Qutham (see note 36, p. 308, below) are cited in some accounts.

16. Ibn Ishaq, *Sira*, paras. 33–34.

17. Ibn Ishaq, *Sira*, para. 53.

18. Ibn Ishaq, *Sira*, para. 55.

19. Ibn Ishaq, *Sira*, para. 57.

20. Ibn Sa'd, *Al-Tabaqat*, 1:128–29.

21. Ibn Ishaq, *Sira*, para. 53.

22. Ibn al-Kalbi, *Kitab al-Asnam*, ed. W. Atallah (Paris: Librairie Klincksieck, 1969), p. 13.

23. Ibn Ishaq, *Sira*, para. 133.

24. Ibn Ishaq, *Sira*, para. 153.

25. A contemporary biographer of Muhammad, Khalil 'Abd al-Karim, builds his entire case for Khadija's seminal importance in Muhammad's life on the obscurity of this period of Muhammad's life. The result is pure speculation. See further chapter 10, below.

26. Ibn Ishaq, *Sira*, para. 332.

27. Ibn Ishaq, *Sira*, para. 159.

28. Ibn Sa'd, *Al-Tabaqat*, 1:132. Could this be to conform with Qur'an 43:31: {They said: If only this Qur'an had been sent down upon some great man from the two towns [Mecca and Ta'if].}

29. Al-Baladhuri, *Ansab al-Ashraf,* ed. M. Hamidullah (Cairo: Dar al-Ma'arif, 1959), 1, para. 177.

30. Ibn Ishaq, *Sira,* para. 140.

31. Ibn Ishaq, *Sira,* paras. 153–54.

32. Ibn Ishaq, *Sira,* para. 140.

33. Ibn Sa'd, *Al-Tabaqat,* 1:195.

34. Ibn Ishaq, *Sira,* para. 144.

35. Ibn Ishaq, *Sira,* para. 200.

36. Al-Baladhuri, *Ansab* 1: para. 156, where it is also implied that Muhammad's origin name may have been Qutham. For other versions of the origins of the name Ibn Abi Kabshah, see Ibn Manzur, *Lisan al-'Arab* (Beirut: Dar Sadir, 1994), s.v. (sub voce) k-b-sh. Al-Baladhuri, *Ansab* 1, para. 140, reports that "a person in her dream" instructed Amina to call the infant Ahmad or, in another version, Muhammad.

37. Ibn Ishaq, *Sira,* para. 254.

38. Al-Baladhuri, *Ansab* 1: paras. 266ff.

39. Ibn Sa'd, *Al-Tabaqat,* 1:123.

40. Ibn Sa'd, *Al-Tabaqat,* 1:111.

41. Ibn Sa'd, *Al-Tabaqat,* 1:122.

42. Ibn Sa'd, *Al-Tabaqat,* 1:214.

43. Interestingly, this truce was cited by defenders of Egyptian president Anwar al-Sadat during the negotiations at Camp David in 1979 as justifying compromise.

44. Al-Waqidi, *Kitab al-Maghazi,* ed. Marsden Jones (London: Oxford University Press, 1966), 1:113–14.

45. Ibn Sa'd, *Al-Tabaqat,* 1:380–81.

46. Al-Waqidi, *Maghazi,* 1:46. Salama seems to have been a well-known wit: see further remarks by him in *Maghazi* 1:116, which cause the Prophet to smile and to forgive him his earlier vulgarity.

47. Al-Waqidi, *Maghazi,* 1:118.

48. Al-Waqidi, *Maghazi,* 1:121.

49. Ibn Hisham, *Al-Sira al-Nabawiyya,* ed. M. Saqqa and others (Cairo: Mustafa al-Babi, 1936) 3:303.

50. Experts express serious doubts about these letters whenever they are exhibited in some Arab or Muslim country, just as there are doubts about the shirt of Muhammad that Mulla 'Umar of the Taliban once waved at his followers before the fall of Kabul in 2001.

51. Ibn Hisham, *Sira,* 4:250ff.

52. Ibn Hisham, *Sira,* 4:292.

53. Ibn Hisham, *Sira,* 4:304.

54. The *shama'il* genre was probably inaugurated by the famous Hadith master Muhammad ibn 'Isa al-Tirmidhi (d. ca. 892), whose work *al-Shama'il al-Muhammadiyya* had several later imitators.

55. This list is based largely on al-Baladhuri, *Ansab* 1, paras. 831ff.

56. An early reference to the science of *Firasa* with regards to Muhammad's physical characteristics is in Abu Hatim al-Razi (d. ca. 933), *A'lam al-Nubuwwa,* ed. S. al-Sawy (Tehran: Imperial Academy, 1977), p. 85.

57. This list is based on Ibn Saʻd, *Al-Tabaqat*, 1:364–73. The encounter with the terrified man is in Ibn Saʻd, 1:23.

58. Ibn Saʻd, *Al-Tabaqat*, 1:374: {I was given the strength of forty men in copulation.} On women who refused to marry him, see al-Baladhuri, *Ansab* 1, paras 926, 928–29, 936, some of whom met bad ends.

59. Al-Tabari, *Tarikh*, 1:6–7. The passage is discussed in my *Arabic Historical Thought*, p. 74.

60. Any discussion of this issue needs to proceed from the seminal articles of W. Arafat in *Bulletin of the School of Oriental and African Studies* 17 (1955); 21 (1958); 28 (1965); and 29 (1966).

61. The Ansar were a sort of "loyal opposition" during the early Umayyad period (661–750). They must have contributed heavily to the fabrication of the poetry of the *Sira* in an attempt to demonstrate their ancient faithfulness to Muhammad as contrasted with the faithlessness of the ruling dynasty.

62. Ibn Hisham, *Sira*, 3:170. The poet is Kaʻb ibn Malik (d. ca. 673).

63. Ibn Hisham, *Sira*, 4:155–56. A few verses have been omitted. For a full translation of this celebrated ode, see Suzanne Pinckney Stetkevych, *The Poetics of Islamic Legitimacy* (Bloomington, Ind.: Indiana University Press, 2002), pp. 54–60.

64. Hassan ibn Thabit, *Diwan*, ed. W. ʻArafat (Beirut: Dar Sadir, 1974), 1:325.

IV

1. In my general remarks on *Adab*, I plunder heavily from a review of mine that appeared in the *Times Literary Supplement*, March 31, 2000. For a recent discussion of the rise and development of *Adab*, see Roger Allen, *The Arabic Literary Heritage* (Cambridge: Cambridge University Press, 1998), chapter 5.

2. For a suggestive treatment of religious and literary continuities in the ancient Mediterranean world, see Garth Fowden, "Religious Communities," in Glen Bowersock and others, eds., *Late Antiquity: A Guide to the Post Classical World* (Cambridge, Mass.: Belknap Press, 1999).

3. Ibn Qutayba, *ʻUyun al-Akhbar* (Cairo: Dar al-Kutub, 1925–30), p. *Yaʼ*. A famous dictionary of technical terms by al-Sharif al-Jurjani (d. 1413) defines *Adab* as "knowledge of that which guards against all kinds of error"; see Jurjani, *Taʻrifat*, (Beirut: Maktabat Lubnan, 1985), p. 14. *Adab* had clearly become normative in the six centuries separating Ibn Qutayba from al-Jurjani.

4. Ibn Qutayba, *ʻUyun*, pp. *Lam, Mim*.

5. A case in point is the mischievous glee with which al-Jahiz quoted the scandalous verses recited by Ibn ʻAbbas, venerable cousin of Muhammad and traditional "founder" of Islamic religious scholarship—while on pilgrimage, no less! For this, see al-Jahiz, *Rasaʼil*, ed. M. A. S. Harun (Beirut: Dar al-Jil, 1991), 2:92.

6. I consulted four major *Adab* anthologies: Ibn Qutayba, *ʻUyun al-Akhbar*; Al-Mubarrad (d. 898), *al-Kamil*; Ibn ʻAbd Rabbihi (d. 940), *al-ʻIqd al-Farid*; and al-Raghib al-Isfahani (d. early eleventh century), *Muhadarat al-Udaba*.

7. Poverty as both concept and social condition in Islamic history is not studied

enough, but see, recently, Adam Sabra, *Poverty and Charity in Medieval Islam* (Cambridge: Cambridge University Press, 2000), which deals mainly with the Mamluk period.

8. Al-Sharif al-Radiyy, *Al-Majazat al-Nabawiyya*, ed. M. al-Atiyya and others (Damascus: Cultural Mission of Islamic Republic of Iran, 1987), pp. 287–88.

9. For an astute and comprehensive discussion of this whole issue, see Wen-chin Ouyang, *Literary Criticism in Medieval Arabic-Islamic Culture* (Edinburgh: Edinburgh University Press, 1997), chapter 2.

10. Muslim, *Sahih* (Beirut: Dar al-Ma'rifa, n.d.), 7:48–50.

11. Abu'l Faraj al-Isbahani, *Aghani* (Cairo: Dar al-Kutub, 1963), 21:211–12. The poet is Abu Khiras al-Hudhali. Another poet of the same era, al-Hutay'a (d. ca. 662), was equally ambiguous in his feelings toward the new faith. In a famous line, he says that he obeyed the Prophet because he was truthful, but why should one obey Abu Bakr his successor? And will one then have to obey Abu Bakr's son? The sarcasm is palpable; see al-Hutay'a, *Diwan* (Beirut: Dar Sadir, 1981), p. 143, 11.2–3.

12. See, e.g., Ibn Hisham, *Sira*, 4:132; also *Aghani*, 22:303.

13. Abu Zayd al-Qurashi, *Jamharat Ash'ar al-'Arab* (Beirut: Dar Bayrut, 1984), p. 13.

14. Ibn Rashiq, *'Umda*, ed. M. M. 'Abd al-Hamid (Cairo: Mustafa al-Babi, 1934), pp. 8, 18. Two passages are conflated and some words have been omitted. Tabari (d. 923), the great Qur'an exegete, had already advanced the view that only polytheist poets are meant in the Qur'anic verse about poets and demons; see *Tafsir* (Bulaq: al-Matba'a al-Amiriyya, 1905), 19:78–80.

15. Quoted in al-Marzubani, *Al-Muwashshah* (Cairo: Jam'iyyat Nashr al-Kutub, 1924), p. 62. See also the answer attributed to the Prophet's poet Hassan, when asked why he wrote no elegies for the Prophet: "Because I find trite anything that I am inspired with on that subject." See Ibn Abi 'Awn, *Al-Ajwiba al-Muskita*, ed. M. A. Yousef (Berlin: Klaus Schwarz, 1988), p. 25.

16. Al-Raghib al-Isfahani, *Muhadarat al-Udaba'* (Beirut: Dar Maktabat al-Hayat, n.d.), 1:79.

17. Abu'l Faraj al-Isbahani, *Aghani*, 4:145.

18. An exception may be made for the poem called *Nahj al-Burda* by al-Busiri (d. 1296), to be discussed later. There is a full and perceptive discussion of *Banat Su'adu*, and its poet, Ka'b ibn Zuhayr, in Suzanne Pinckney Stetkevych, *The Poetics of Islamic Legitimacy*, chapter 2.

19. Of relevance to this topic is S. S. Agha and T. Khalidi, "Poetry and Identity in the Umayyad Age," *Al-Abhath* 50/51 (2002–2003): esp. 108–11.

20. See, respectively, Jarir, *Diwan*, ed. T. Shalaq (Beirut: Dar al-Kitab al-'Arabi, 1993), p. 51, 1. 25; p. 73, 11. 30–31; p. 95, 11. 87–88; p. 206, 1. 38; p. 497, 1. 19; p. 481, 1. 7.

21. See 'Umar ibn Abi Rabi'a, *Diwan* (Beirut: Dar Sadir, n.d.), pp. 117, 323, 366.

22. See Farazdaq, *Diwan* (Beirut: Dar Bayrut, 1980), 1:159, 1. 11 and 1:297, 11. 12–13 (of our number); 2:312, 11. 11–12, and 2:353, 1. 11 (Swords of Badr); 2:9, 1. 7, 2:89, 1. 6, and 1:348, 1. 2 (best except for Muhammad); 1:266, 1. 2 and 1:286, 1. 3 (judging according to Muhammad's *sunna*); 1:65, 1. 2 and 1:82, 1. 8 (ancestor an intimate of Muhammad); 1:214, 1. 4 and 2:282, 11. 1–2 (had Jesus not announced).

23. Ibn 'Abd Rabbihi, *Al-Iqd al-Farid*, ed. A. Amin and others (Cairo: Lajnat al-Ta'lif, 1940), 5:271.

V

1. Stefan Collini, *English Pasts* (Oxford: Oxford University Press, 1999), p. 56.

2. This distinction is to some extent captured in the name of the two wings. The word "shià" means "party" or "following." The Shià (Shiites), with a capital *S*, refers to the party or followers of 'Ali. "*Sunna*" means normative practice. The Sunnis (Sunnites) are those who emphasize the normative practice of Muhammad and his community. By the late ninth century, both wings had reached one formative stage in their evolution.

3. The celebrated historian Ibn Khaldun (d. 1406) affirms that Shiism began in "excessive" attachment to 'Ali and a "desperate" desire to avenge the death of al-Husayn; see his *Tarikh* (Beirut: Dar al-Kitab al-Lubnani, 1981), 5:364–69.

4. Al-Mas'udi, *Muruj al-Dhahab*, ed. C. Pellat (Beirut: Université Libanaise, 1966–1979), paras. 43–46. For a fuller discussion of this and other accounts of the creation of the world in al-Mas'udi, see my *Islamic Historiography* (Albany: SUNY Press, 1975), pp. 56–60.

5. Some Muslim mystics, not necessarily Shiite, also held similar views regarding the immaculate nature of Muhammad.

6. Al-Ya'qubi, *Ta'rikh* (Beirut: Dar Sadir, 1960), 2:10–11.

7. Al-Ya'qubi, *Ta'rikh*, 2:14.

8. Ibid.

9. There are several other reports in Shiite sources that glorify Fatima; see, e.g., al-Kulini, *Usul al-Kafi*, ed. M. J. Shams al-din (Beirut: Dar al-Ta'aruf, 1998), 1:525–26. Muhammad promises her that she alone among all mankind will be resurrected fully clothed when others will appear nude, highlighting her chastity and virtue.

10. Al-Ya'qubi, *Ta'rikh*, 2:35; compare a typical Sunni account of Abu Talib's fate in Ibn Hazm, *Al-Fisal* (Cairo: n.p., 1899–1902), 4:54, where Abu Talib is in the uppermost reaches of Hell, his sandals barely touching a thin sheet of flame.

11. The ten family heroes here may well be a Shiite version of the well-known Sunni hadith about ten of Muhammad's Companions promised paradise by the Prophet in an incident known as "The ten who are promised paradise" *(al-'ashara al-mubashshara bi'l janna)*.

12. Al-Ya'qubi, *Ta'rikh*, 2:114.

13. Di'bil al-Khuza'i, *Diwan*, ed. 'A. S. 'U. al-Dujayli (Al-Najaf: n.p., 1962), p. 225. See also lines expressing a similar sentiment in *Diwan*, p. 196, where the poet berates the Muslims as a "wretched nation" for ill rewarding the Prophet for his revelations by acting like wolves among sheep toward his family. The term *al-Wasiyy* (the Heir or Delegate) is very frequent in Shiite and non-Shiite works as an epithet of 'Ali; see, e.g., al-Mubarrad, *Al-Kamil*, ed. M. A. F. Ibrahim (Cairo: Dar Nahdat Misr, n.d.), 3:204.

14. Al-Ya'qubi, *Ta'rikh*, 2:112.

15. al-Jahiz, *Rasa'il*, 4:26.

16. Al-Mas'udi has been far better served by modern scholarship than al-Ya'qubi, with two full-length studies devoted to his histories: Tarif Khalidi, *Islamic Historiography: The Histories of Mas'udi*; and Ahmad Shboul, *Al-Mas'udi and His World* (London: Ithaca Press, 1979).

17. Al-Mas'udi, *Muruj*, para. 59.

18. Thus, when Adam grieves after his Fall, God comforts him with the news that from him a light will issue (Muhammad) who will be the seal of prophets but whose progeny, the imams, will fill the world with their call and bring it to its end; see al-Mas'udi, *Muruj*, para. 55.

19. Al-Mas'udi, *Muruj*, para. 1481.

20. In this section I draw on my *Islamic Historiography*, pp. 145–46.

21. See the incisive comments on this subject in Maher Jarrar, *"Sirat Ahl al-Kisa'. Early Shi'i Sources on the Biography of the Prophet,"* in Harald Motzki, ed., *The Biography of Muhammad: The Issue of the Sources* (Leiden: Brill, 2000), pp. 98–153.

22. I am convinced by the arguments of Karen King in her *What Is Gnosticism?* that gnosticism should be viewed as a methodology of interpretation rather than as a "heretical" religious group with clearly defined borders; hence the small *g* in my usage.

23. Al-Tabrisi, *I'lam al-Wara bi A'lam al-Huda*, ed. A. A. Ghaffari (Beirut: Mu'assasat al-A'lami, 2004), p. 27.

24. Extraordinary claims are made for the knowledge of the imams in tenth-century Shiite works of Hadith, as, for instance, in the *Kafi* of al-Kulini, cited in note 9, p. 311, above.

25. One common Shiite designation for the Sunnis was *al-'ammah*, i.e., the plebs, the hoi polloi.

26. Al-Tabrisi, *I'lam*, p. 148.

27. Al-Tabrisi, *I'lam*, p. 83.

28. Al-Tabrisi, *I'lam*, p. 87. A well-known Sunni *Sira* of a later age, in narrating the same incident, claims that the only door left open was the door of Abu Bakr: see Dhahabi (d. 1348), *Sira*, ed. H. Al-Qudsi (Beirut: Dar al-Kutub al-'Ilmiyya, 1988), p. 382.

29. Al-Baladhuri, *Ansab*, paras. 1093, 1095.

30. Al-Baladhuri, *Ansab*, para. 1096.

31. Al-Tabrisi, *I'lam*, pp. 145–46.

32. Al-Tabrisi, *I'lam*, p. 147. In Shiite *Sira*, the favorite among the Prophet's wives was Umm Salama. This preference might stem from the report that she allegedly turned down marriage proposals from Abu Bakr and 'Umar before accepting Muhammad. She is also reported to have been an object of jealousy to 'A'isha and Hafsa: see Ibn Sa'd, *Tabaqat*, 8:86–96.

33. The following ad appeared in the Lebanese daily *Al-Safir* [February 2, 2004, p. 1]: "On the occasion of the Battle of Karbala and the martyrdom of al-Husayn, the Prophet said {The killing of al-Husayn leaves a burning sensation *[harara]* in the hearts of the believers which will never cool.}" Al-Husayn was martyred at

Karbala in 680, some fifty years after the death of his grandfather the Prophet. For the development of Fatima's image, see Verena Klemm, "Image Formation of an Islamic Legend: Fatima the Daughter of the Prophet Muhammad," in Sebastian Gunther, ed., *Ideas, Images and Methods of Portrayal: Insights into Classical Arabic Literature and Islam* (Leiden: Brill, 2005).

34. For details, see my *Arabic Historical Thought*, p. 81; and especially my "The Battle of the Camel" in Angelika Neuwirth and Andreas Pflitsch eds., *Crisis and Memory in Islamic Societies* (see note 5, p. 307, above).

35. One notable exception is Wilferd Madelung, "The Hashimiyyat of al-Kumayt and Hashimi Shi'ism," *Studia Islamica* 70 (1989). For reasons of space, I have ignored the poetry to be found in Shiite *Siras*, a topic of considerable historical interest.

36. Al-Mubarrad, *Al-Kamil*, 3:205 (see note 13, p. 311, above).

37. Al-Isbahani, *Aghani*, 9:14–15. Radwa is a mountain near Medina (see note 11, p. 310, above).

38. Al-Isbahani, *Aghani*, 9:15. A few verses have been omitted. Khayf is a valley near Mecca where Ibn al-Hanafiyya was taken after he was liberated from prison. The story is in al-Tabari, *Tarikh*, 2:693–95.

39. Al-Kumayt, *Al-Qasa'id al-Hashimiyyat*, ed. S. A. Salih (Beirut: Mu'assasat Al-A'lami, 1972), pp. 8–25. These verses are in a long ode from which many verses have been omitted.

40. Al-Kumayt, *Hashimiyyat*, pp. 32–33. Some verses have been omitted.

41. Al-Isbahani, *Aghani*, 7:233–34.

42. Al-Isbahani, *Aghani*, 7:259. The poem goes on to attack the Umayyads and other enemies of the Shiites. *Their* imam is the devil.

43. For his images in biographical literature, see M. Cooperson, *Classical Arabic Biography*, chapter 3 (cited in note 1, p. 305, above).

44. Di'bil al-Khuza'i, *Diwan*, p. 272 (cited in note 13, p. 311, above). The incident referred to concerns the destruction of the idols on the roof of the Ka'ba when Muhammad was still in Mecca, for which see al-Tabari, *Dhakha'ir*, p. 85.

45. Di'bil al-Khuza'i, *Diwan*, p. 307. I preferred the variant readings suggested by the editor of the *Diwan*. For the "People of the Cloak," see Jarrar, note 21, p. 312, above.

46. Di'bil, *Diwan*, pp. 147–48.

47. The poem is in the *Diwan*, pp. 124–45.

48. The so-called Day of the *Saqifa*, or covered patio, is the day following the death of the Prophet when the assembled Muslim notables paid homage to Abu Bakr. For details, see Wilferd Madelung, *The Succession to Muhammad* (New York: Cambridge University Press, 1996), pp. 28–46.

49. Yazid (d. 683) was the Umayyad caliph who ordered the execution of al-Husayn. Ziyad, a few lines below, was his governor of Iraq and the East.

VI

1. Several such hymns are translated and discussed in Annemarie Schimmel, *And Muhammad Is His Messenger*, chapters 7 and 8. This work is fundamental for understanding Muhammad's images in the Sufi tradition (cited in II, note 4, p. 306).

2. Abu Hayyan al-Tawhidi, *Al-Isharat al-Ilahiyya*, ed. W. al-Qadi (Beirut: Dar al-Thaqafa, 1973), p. 80.

3. Abu'l Faraj Ibn al-Jawzi, *Talbis Iblis* (Cairo: Maktabat al-Nahda, 1928), *passim*, but especially pp. 220–21. On p. 353 he even attacks the great al-Ghazali for abandoning jurisprudence and embracing Sufism. The anti-Sufi literature is considerable, and remains inadequately studied.

4. I depend on Marshall Hodgson, *The Venture of Islam* (Chicago: The University of Chicago Press, 1974), 1: 392–409, where his discussion of the origins, history, and nature of Islamic Sufism remains one of his finest in what is otherwise a very fine book.

5. Other etymologies are suggested by Sufi writers; see, e.g., al-Kalabadhi (d. 990), *Al-Ta'arruf li Madhhab Ahl al-Tasawwuf*, ed. M. A. al-Nuwawi (Cairo: Maktabat al-Kulliyyat, 1969), pp. 28–35; and Abu al-Hasan al-Shushtari (d. 1269), *Al-Risala al-Shushtariyya*, ed. M. Idrisi (Casablanca: Dar al-Thaqafa, 2004), pp. 135–37.

6. There is a recent and useful discussion of these traditions in Sarah Iles Johnston, ed., *Religions of the Ancient World* (Cambridge, Mass.: Belknap Press, 2004), pp. 640–56.

7. Al-Ghazali, *Ihya' 'Ulum al-Din* (Beirut: Dar al-Ma'rifa, n.d.), 3:76. The last two phrases are a reference to the opening words of suras 73 and 74.

8. There is a short but valuable description of life inside a Sufi *ribat* in Shushtari, *Risala*, pp. 137–38.

9. The most elegant translation of these early Sufi masters remains Margaret Smith's *Readings from the Mystics of Islam* (London: Luzac, 1972), a work that deserves to be far better known.

10. On 'Ali's special place in Sufi devotions, see Abu Nasr al-Sarraj, *K. al-Luma'*, ed. A. H. Mahmud (Cairo: Maktabat al-Thaqafa, 1998), p. 179. The later Sufis adopted several biblical prophets (prominent among whom was Jesus) and several early Muslim figures as Sufi paragons, concerned no doubt to ward off the charge that Sufism was a *bid'a*, or heresy.

11. Abu al-Qasim al-Qushayri, *Al-Risala al-Qushayriyya* (Beirut: Dar al-Kutub al-'Ilmiyya, 2001), p. 381.

12. Abu Talib al-Makki, *Qut al-Qulub*, ed. B. 'Uyun al-Sud (Beirut: Dar al-Kutub al-Ilmiyya, 1997), 2:140.

13. Abu Hafs 'Umar al-Suhrawardi, *'Awarif al-Ma'arif*, printed in vol. 5:42 ff. of al-Ghazali, *Ihya'*, p. 130.

14. Al-Suhrawardi, *'Awarif*, pp. 130–31.

15. Al-Shushtari, *Risala*, pp. 70, 88.

16. Al-Suhrawardi, *'Awarif*, pp. 134ff. See also al-Ghazali, *Ihya'*, 2:357ff; and al-Shushtari, *Risala*, pp. 130, 141ff. for similar lists of Sufi virtues.

17. Al-Ghazali, *Ihya'*, 1:78.

18. One famous account is by the illustrious Sufi Abu Yazid al-Bistami (d. ca. 877); see its translation in A. J. Arberry, *Aspects of Islamic Civilization* (London: Allen and Unwin, 1964), p. 218ff. Another is the Night Journey of Ibn al-'Arabi in *Al-Futuhat al-Makkiyya* (Beirut: Dar Sadir, 2004), 6:60ff.

19. Al-Ghazali, *Ihya'*, 1:329ff.

20. Al-Qushayri, *Risala*, pp. 274–75.

21. Al-Yunini, *Dhayl Mir'at al-Zaman* (Hyderabad: Da'irat al-Ma'arif, 1954), 4:318.

22. Al-Sarraj, *K. al-Luma'*, p. 37.

23. Al-Qushayri, *Risala*, pp. 8–9.

24. Al-Qushayri, *Risala*, p. 50.

25. Ibn Hanbal, *Musnad* (Beirut: Dar Sadir, 1969), 2:304–5, discussed in al-Qushayri, *Risala*, pp. 114–16.

26. Al-Qushayri, *Risala*, p. 133.

27. Al-Sarraj, *K. al-Luma'*, p. 164. On pp. 158–65, al-Sarraj gives many examples of how the Sufis "uncovered the inner meaning" of Muhammadan hadiths.

28. By far the largest cluster of such *karamat* occurs in Ibn al-'Arabi's *Al-Futuhat al-Makkiyya*. If collected they would be a most valuable contribution to the history of mentalities. Most of these *karamat* were witnessed or experienced at firsthand by Ibn al-'Arabi himself.

29. Al-Qushayri, *Risala*, p. 380.

30. Al-Sarraj, *K. al-Luma'*, p. 491.

31. Ibn al-'Arabi, *al-Futuhat al-Makkiyya*, 6:179.

32. Ibn al-'Arabi, *Rasa'il* (Hyderabad: Da'irat al-Ma'arif, 1942); *K. al-Asfar*, p. 17.

33. Ibn al-'Arabi, *al-Futuhat*, 6:26–27.

34. Ibn al-'Arabi, *Fusus al-Hikam*, ed. A. A. Afifi (Beirut: Dar al-Kitab al-'Arabi, 2002), p. 199.

35. The starting point for an examination of the concept of "Perfect Man" is the difficult but fundamental article by Louis Massignon, "L'homme parfait en Islam et son originalite eschatologique," in *Opera Minora*, ed. Y. Moubarac (Beirut: Dar al-Ma'arif, 1963), 1:107–25. A more recent and simpler treatment is in Annemarie Schimmel, *And Muhammad Is His Messenger*, pp. 134–43. Among Ibn al-'Arabi's disciples, it was 'Abd al-Karim al-Jili (d. 1402) who devoted a whole book to Perfect Man, construing him more narrowly than Ibn al-'Arabi as Muhammad; see *al-Insan al-Kamil*, ed. S. 'Uwayda (Beirut: Dar al-Kutub al-'Ilmiyya, 1997), pp. 207–11.

36. Ibn al-'Arabi, *al-Futuhat*, 3:123 and passim.

37. For "heirs and descendants" see *al-Futuhat*, 6:163; for "deducing the treasure of God's knowledge," see *Futuhat*, 8:151.

38. Ibn al-'Arabi, *al-Futuhat*, 7:278.

39. Ibn al-'Arabi, *al-Futuhat*, 5:215. For a recent discussion of these terms in Islamic philosophy, see M. A. Khalidi, *Medieval Islamic Philosophical Writings* (Cambridge: Cambridge University Press, 2005), pp. xviii–xxiv; see also Peter Adamson and Richard Taylor, eds., *The Cambridge Companion to Arabic Philosophy* (Cambridge: Cambridge University Press, 2005), Index, s.v. soul, world. A follower of Ibn al-'Arabi, Abu Bakr 'Abdullah ibn Shahawar al-Razi (d. 1256) calls Muhammad "The First Emanation" *(al-fayd al-awwal)* and "The Highest Soul" *(al-ruh al-a'la)*;

see his *Manarat al-Sa'irin*, ed. S. 'Abdulfattah (Cairo: Al-Hay'a al-Misriyya, 1999), pp. 35–36.

40. Ibn al-'Arabi, *al-Futuhat*, 5:164. The consequent and necessary superiority of Muhammad's *umma* is asserted also in *Futuhat*, 1:180.

41. Ibn al-'Arabi, *al-Futuhat*, 1:170. In *Rasa'il, K. al-Anwar*, p. 16, Muhammad is said to have assigned to all prophets their proper unchanging stations.

42. For these descriptions, see Ibn al-'Arabi, *Fusus*, pp. 50, 54, 215.

43. Ibn al-'Arabi, *Fusus*, pp. 203, 214–15. At issue is a hadith where Muhammad mentions women first among the delights of the world.

44. Ibn al-'Arabi, *al-Futuhat*, 7:68–69.

45. Ibn al-'Arabi, *al-Futuhat*, 3:30, 299.

46. Ibn al-'Arabi, *al-Futuhat*, 5:116.

47. Ibn al-'Arabi, *al-Futuhat*, 3:295.

VII

1. Ibn Qutayba, *Ta'wil*, p. 12.

2. Ibn Qutayba, *Ta'wil*, p. 51.

3. Ibn Qutayba, *Ta'wil*, p. 75.

4. The term *nazar*, or rational investigation, was indeed a favorite of al-Jahiz.

5. Al-Jahiz, *Rasa'il*, 4:245.

6. A recent and judicious treatment of this genre is in Gabriel Reynolds, *A Muslim Theologian in the Sectarian Milieu* (Leiden: Brill, 2004), pp. 178–83, with an up-to-date bibliography.

7. Al-Jahiz, *Rasa'il*, 3:256–57.

8. Al-Jahiz, *Rasa'il*, 3:240, 257.

9. For excellence of character, see *Rasa'il*, 3:280; for devotion of followers, see 3:281; for the miraculous agreement of opponents, see 3:260–61, 270; for the challenge to match eloquence, see 3:274–77; for Qur'an's matchlessness, see 3:278–80.

10. Ibn Qutayba was something of a Bible expert. His work on the allusions to Muhammad in the Bible is unfortunately lost, but enough fragments of it survive in later works to give a fair idea of its scope and method: see Ibn al-Jawzi, *Al-Wafa*, ed. M. 'Ata (Beirut: Dar al-Kutub al-'Ilmiyya, 1988), pp. 58–67. He may well have benefited from the work done in the area of biblical allusions by an older contemporary and convert from Christianity, 'Ali ibn Rabban, on whom see below.

11. Abu Nu'aym, *Dala'il al-Nubuwwah*, ed. M. Qal'aji (Beirut: Dar al-Nafa'is, 1999), pp. 34–36. Some passages have been omitted.

12. Abu Nu'aym, *Dala'il*, p. 174.

13. Abu Nu'aym, *Dala'il*, pp. 587–88.

14. 'Ali ibn Rabban, *Al-Din wa'l Dawla*, ed. A. Nuwayhid (Beirut: Dar al-Afaq al-Jadida, 1982), pp. 98–99.

15. 'Ali ibn Rabban, *Al-Din wa'l Dawla*, p. 36. Other objections to Islam are due to pride, imitation, upbringing, and stubborn foolishness; but see also p. 48 for further objections by Christians.

16. For the ten proofs, see *Al-Din*, p. 47; for his critique of the Torah and other scriptures, see pp. 99–103; for Muhammad as guarantor of prophecy, see pp. 130ff, 137.

17. Abu Hatim al-Razi, *A'lam al-Nubuwwa*, pp. 195–98. A complete English translation of this work by Tarif Khalidi will appear shortly (2009). 'Ali ibn Rabban has many other allusions: see *al-Din*, pp. 137ff.

18. Ahmad al-Haruni, *Ithbat Nubuwwat al-Nabiyy*, ed. K. al-Haj (n.p.: al-Maktaba al-'Ilmiyya, n.d.). For exposure to enmity, see p. 76; for fear of contradiction, see p. 124; for mastery over the Arabs, see pp. 175–76; for glorious Companions, see pp. 176–78; for excellence of Islam's sciences, see p. 178.

19. The various routes taken by Islamic thinkers to reconcile philosophy to prophecy are discussed fully in Jean Jolivet, "L'idee de la sagesse et sa fonction dans la philosophie des 4e et 5e siecles," *Arabic Sciences and Philosophy* 1, no. 1 (1991): 31–65.

20. See the pertinent discussion of this in Peter Adamson, "Al-Kindi," in *The Cambridge Companion to Arabic Philosophy*, pp. 46–49.

21. Al-Farabi, *Al-Milla*, ed. M. Mahdi (Beirut: Dar al-Mashriq, 1968), pp. 43–44.

22. Al-Farabi, *Ara' ahl al-Madinah*, ed. A. N. Nadir (Beirut: Dar al-Mashriq, 1973), pp. 115, 125.

23. Ibn Tufayl, *Hayy*, ed. A. N. Nadir (Beirut: Dar al-Mashriq, 2001), p. 93. Some phrases have been omitted. For a recent and general discussion of Ibn Tufayl, see M. A. Khalidi, *Medieval Islamic Philosophical Writings*, pp. xxix–xxxiv.

24. For further discussions of philosophy and prophecy, see *The Cambridge Companion to Arabic Philosophy*, p. 313 (al-Farabi); pp. 174–75 (Ibn Tufayl); pp. 320–21 (Ibn Sina). For the views of Ibn Sina, see Michael Marmura, "Avicenna's Psychological Proof of Prophecy," *Journal of Near Eastern Studies* 22 (1963): 49–56.

25. Abu Hatim al-Razi, *A'lam*, pp. 3–4.

26. Abu Hatim al-Razi, *A'lam*, p. 31.

27. Abu Hatim al-Razi, *A'lam*, p. 69.

28. See Dominique Urvoy, *Les penseurs libres dans l'Islam classique* (Paris: Albin Michel, 1996), and S. Stroumsa, *Freethinkers of Medieval Islam* (Leiden: Brill, 1999). A concise treatment of al-Razi's "heresy" is in Aziz al-'Azmah, *Abu Bakr al-Razi* (Beirut: Riyad al-Rayyes, 2001), pp. 9–18.

29. 'Aziz al-'Azmah, *Ibn al-Riwandi* (Beirut: Riyad al-Rayyes, 2002), p. 91. This is an accessible anthology of fragments of his works in later writers. Azmah prefers to read his name as al-Riwandi.

30. For "surgery" see Abu al-Hasan al-'Amiri (d. 992), *Al-I'lam bi Manaqib al-Islam*, ed. A. A. Ghurab (Cairo: Dar al-Katib al-'Arabi, 1967), p. 157. The context is a defense of Muhammad arguing that he fought his enemies only as a last resort. For the prophet as one who cures souls, see Miskawayhi (d. 1030), *Al-Fawz al-Asghar*, (Beirut: Dar Maktabat al-Hayat, n.d.), p. 68.

31. This view was first set forth in a systematic manner by Abu Hatim al-Razi, *A'lam*, pp. 273ff. It was picked up and developed by al-Ghazali, *Ihya'*, 1:52 and passim.

32. Ibn Hazm, *Al-Fisal*, 5:17.

33. See, e.g., Ibn Hazm, *Al-Fisal*, 4:2–31.

34. See, e.g., Abu Hayyan al-Tawhidi (d. ca. 1010), *Al-Muqabasat*, ed. H. al-Sandubi

(Cairo: al-Maktaba al-Tijariyya, 1929), pp. 226–30, reporting the views of Abu Sulayman al-Sijistani (d. ca. 985), a philosopher and guru of Abu Hayyan.

35. For these six stages, see Abu al-Hasan al-Mawardi (d. 1058), *A'lam al-Nubuwwah* (Cairo: Maktabat al-Adab, 1987), pp. 258–67.

36. See M. A. Khalidi, ed., *Medieval Islamic Philosophical Writings*, pp. xxiv–xxix, pp. 84–86 (on al-Ghazali). For a broad-ranging discussion of al-Ghazali's important and original views on prophecy, see Frank Griffel, "Al-Ghazali's Concept of Prophecy: The Introduction of Avicennan Psychology into Ash'arite Theology" in *Arabic Sciences and Philosophy* 14 (2004): 101–44.

37. Al-Mawardi has received considerable scholarly attention, especially his political theory: see, most recently, Patricia Crone, *Medieval Islamic Political Thought* (Edinburgh: Edinburgh University Press, 2004), pp. 232 ff. For 'Abd al-Jabbar, see Gabriel Reynolds as per note 6, p. 316, above.

38. Al-Mawardi, *A'lam*, pp. 105–6. For his other views cited above, see pp. 67ff (Qur'an as greatest miracle); p. 180 (a monotheist from youth); pp. 90ff (his immunity and other miracles).

39. For the reference to al-Jahiz, see *A'lam*, p. 64.

40. For details concerning the origins and development of the debate on miracles, see Tarif Khalidi, *Arabic Historical Thought in the Classical Period*, pp. 151–58.

41. For complementarity of reason and religious law, see 'Abd al-Jabbar, *Al-Mughni*, ed. M. Khudayri and others (Cairo: Al-Dar al-Misriyya, 1965), 15: 26–29, 111–12; for a messenger and his laws, see *Al-Mughni*, 15:95; for best interests, see *Al-Mughni*, 15:97; for absence of conflict, see *Al-Mughni*, 15:117–18; for preconditions of true prophecy, see *Al-Mughni*, 15:171.

42. My remarks on 'Abd al-Jabbar and his *Tathbit* draw heavily on my *Arabic Historical Thought in the Classical Period*, pp. 154–58.

43. See my *Arabic Historical Thought*, pp. 155–56.

44. 'Abd al-Jabbar, *Al-Mughni*, 15:213–15.

45. 'Abd al-Jabbar, *Al-Mughni*, 15:215.

VIII

1. Here is a sample: Yaqut (d. 1228), geographer: ("I thoroughly investigated"); Ibn Abi Usaybi'a (d. 1270), biographer: ("I did not find a comprehensive work"); Ibn Khallikan (d. 1272), biographer: ("easy of access"); Safadi (d. 1363), biographer: ("I left no one out"); Kutubi (d. 1363), historian: ("knowledge of all that passed and all that shall pass until death overtakes me"); Qalqashandi (d. 1418), author of a manual for state secretaries: ("Nothing in my view is more shameful than for persons capable of comprehensiveness to neglect it"); Maqrizi (d. 1441), historian: ("I thoroughly investigated"); Mujir al-Din (d. ca. 1520), historian of Jerusalem: ("A comprehensive history"). This did not prevent some of them from also referring to their works as an epitome *(mukhtasar)* and to describe prolixity as tending to reader boredom, even when their own works were voluminous. This was often no more than a nod in the direction of a common literary conceit.

NOTES

2. One measure of the influence of al-Qadi's work is the important *Sira* of Ibn al-Jawzi (d. 1200) entitled *Al-Wafa bi Ahwal al-Mustafa* (Full Compendium of the Life and Times of the Chosen One), a title which echoes al-Qadi's. In his introduction, Ibn al-Jawzi declares his intention that his work will be a coverage of the life of Muhammad and all that pertains to it "from its beginning to its end." His *Sira* is the first to turn Muhammad's life into chapters, some five hundred in number, arranged under headings in chronological order. The author employs abbreviated *isnad*, and the chapters are deliberately designed for easy reading and consultation. Like al-Qadi, Ibn al-Jawzi will often venture outside the scope of the *Sira* itself to explain, e.g., why many prophets have been shepherds *(Al-Wafa,* p. 139), why trees should come at Muhammad's bidding *(Al-Wafa,* p. 329) or how sorcery is to be distinguished from miracle *(Al-Wafa,* pp. 301–2).
3. Al-Qadi 'Iyad, *Al-Shifa,* 1:155.
4. Al-Qadi 'Iyad, *Al-Shifa,* 1:225–27.
5. Al-Qadi 'Iyad, *Al-Shifa,* 2:97.
6. Al-Qadi 'Iyad, *Al-Shifa,* 2:108. At 2:94, the Sufis are credited with first establishing this view.
7. For forgetfulness, see *Al-Shifa,* 2:94; for magic spells, see 2:113; for joking, see 2:117; for the date season, see 2:116.
8. Al-Qadi 'Iyad, *Al-Shifa,* 2:79. For a recent discussion of the Satanic Verses episode, see G. R. Hawting, *The Idea of Idolatry and the Emergence of Islam* (Cambridge: Cambridge University Press, 1999), chapter 6.
9. For Zaynab, see al-Qadi 'Iyad, *Al-Shifa,* 2:117–18.
10. Al-Qadi 'Iyad, *Al-Shifa,* 2:19–20. Some phrases have been left out.
11. This "school" is the subject of a study by Maher Jarrar, *Die Prophetenbiographie im Islamischen Spanien* (Frankfurt am Main: Peter Lang, 1989).
12. Marshall G. S. Hodgson, *The Venture of Islam* (Chicago: The University of Chicago Press, 1974), 2:31.
13. Ibn Hazm, *Jawami' al-Sira* (Cairo: Dar al-Jil, 1982), p. 147.
14. Ibn Hazm, *Jawami' al-Sira,* pp. 35–36. It is often asserted in classical political writings that forbearance *(hilm)* is the foremost characteristic of a good ruler. It is ascribed here by Ibn Hazm to Muhammad as the first of his many public and private virtues.
15. Al-Suhayli, *Al-Rawd al-Unuf* (Beirut: Dar al-Kutub al-'Ilmiyya, 1996), 1:16.
16. For consistency, see al-Suhayli, *Al-Rawd,* 2:359; for God's wisdom, see 3:246.
17. Al-Suhayli, *Al-Rawd,* 3:241.
18. Al-Suhayli, *Al-Rawd,* 4:50.
19. For his fairness as a suckling infant, see al-Suhayli, *Al-Rawd,* 1:286; for his parents' resurrection, see 1:299; for the son willing to kill his father, see 4:17.
20. Ibn Sayyid al-Nas, *'Uyun al-Athar* (Beirut: Dar al-Afaq al-Jadida, 1977), 1:151.
21. Three recent studies come to mind: Michael Chamberlain, *Knowledge and Social Practice in Medieval Damascus, 1190–1350* (Cambridge: Cambridge University Press, 1994); Everett K. Rowson, "An Alexandrian Age in Fourteenth Century Damascus: Twin Commentaries on Two Celebrated Arabic Epistles," *Mamluk Studies Review* 7 (2003): 97–110; and Robert Irwin, "Mamluk Literature" in *Mamluk*

Studies Review 7 (2003): 1–29. Chamberlain is more interested in the function and praxis of knowledge than he is in literary history. Rowson discusses two works of *Adab* of that century in an attempt to revise a common and negative literary verdict on that age. Irwin provides a broad survey of Mamluk literature and his footnotes contain a good bibliography. Irwin (p. 9) does speak of a literary "renaissance."

22. Unfortunately Chamberlain devotes little space to this: see Chamberlain, *Knowledge and Social Practice*, pp. 95–96.
23. Ibn al-Athir, *Al-Kamil* (Beirut: Dar Sadir, 1979), 2:253.
24. Ibn al-Athir, *Al-Kamil*, 2:286–87.
25. Ibn Kathir, *Al-Bidaya wa'l Nihaya* (Cairo: Matba'at al-Sa'ada, 1932–39), 5:109.
26. Ibn Kathir, *Al-Bidaya wa'l Nihaya*, 3:182–83.
27. In lumping them together with Ibn Kathir, I am avoiding the question of influence, preferring to treat them as part of the same literary mass.
28. Al-Dhahabi, *Al-Sira al-Nabawiyya*, ed. H. al-Qudsi (Beirut: Dar al-Kutub al-'Ilmiyya, 1988), pp. 152–53.
29. Al-Dhahabi, *Al-Sira al-Nabawiyya*, p. 176.
30. Al-Hafiz Mughultay, *Al-Ishara ila Sirat al-Mustafa*, ed. M. N. al-Futayyih (Damascus: Dar al-Qalam, 1996), pp. 138–39.
31. Al-Hafiz Mughultay, *Al-Ishara ila Sirat al-Mustafa*, pp. 414–21.
32. Ibn Qayyim al-Jawziyya, *Zad al-Ma'ad*, ed. M. A. 'Ata (Beirut: Dar al-Kutub al-'Ilmiyya, 2002), 3:160–63. Some passages have been left out.
33. Ibn Qayyim al-Jawziyya, *Zad al-Ma'ad*, 3:163–66.
34. Ibn Qayyim al-Jawziyya, *Zad al-Ma'ad*, 3:192–93.
35. Some modern scholars argue that this tradition was in reality Arabian folk medicine interacting with the newly arrived Greek medical tradition: see, e.g., Manfred Ullmann, *Islamic Medicine* (Edinburgh: Edinburgh University Press, 1978), pp. 5, 22.
36. Ibn Qayyim al-Jawziyya, *Zad al-Ma'ad*, 4:94.
37. Ibn Qayyim al-Jawziyya, *'Iddat al-Sabirin* (Cairo: Maktabat al-Mutanabbi, 1977), pp. 266–69. My thanks to M. A. Khalidi for helping me to understand this passage.
38. Ibn Qayyim al-Jawziyya, *Hidayat al-Hayara* (Beirut: Dar al-Kutub al-'Ilmiyya, n.d.), pp. 87–88.
39. On Bahira, see *Al-Sira al-Halabiyya*, ed. A. al-Khalili (Beirut: Dar al-Kutub al-Ilmiyya, 2002), 1:172; on the opening-of-the-breast incident, see 1:147.
40. On general import, see *Al-Sira*, 1:319; on change in meaning, see 1:525; on nonmention and nonoccurrence, see 2:181; on "befitting" reports, see 1:367.
41. For Salman al-Farisi, see *Al-Sira al-Halabiyya*, 1:270; for the bell, see 1:366–69.

IX

1. For existence as lights before creation, see al-Majlisi, *Bihar al-Anwar* (Beirut: Mu'assasat al-Wafa', 1983), 7:11; for their pure stock and pristine Muslim faith, see *Bihar*, 7:70–76; for their creative activities, see *Bihar*, 7:12–13.
2. For 'Ali as Aaron, see al-Majlisi, *Bihar*, 8:297–98; for Hira', see al-Majlisi, *Bihar*,

7:241; for Bahira, see al-Majlisi, *Bihar,* 7:131–32; for the Night Journey, see al-Majlisi, *Bihar,* 7:162 and 8:400–401; for partnership in knowledge, see al-Majlisi, *Bihar,* 7:716; for delegation, see al-Majlisi, *Bihar,* 7:384.

3. *Sharh al-Burda li'l Busiri wa Nahj al-Burda li Shawqi,* ed. Fathi 'Uthman (Cairo: Dar al-Ma'rifa, 1973), pp. 105–9.

4. Ibid., pp. 117–19.

5. Ibid., pp. 130–31.

6. For an example of its healing properties, see Schimmel, *And Muhammad Is His Messenger,* p. 242 and notes 12 and 13 (in connection with Iqbal).

7. *Sharh, al-Burda,* p. 193.

8. Ibid., pp. 203–5.

9. Ibid., pp. 206–8.

10. Ibid., pp. 221–25.

11. These premodern charges and counter-charges can best be pursued in such works as Norman Daniel, *Islam and the West: The Making of an Image* (Oxford: Oneworld, 2000); John V. Tolan, *Saracens: Islam in the Medieval European Imagination* (New York: Columbia University Press, 2002); and, on the Muslim side, Carole Hillenbrand, *The Crusades: Islamic Perspectives* (Edinburgh: Edinburgh University Press, 1999).

12. Thomas Carlyle, *On Heroes, Hero-Worship and the Heroic in History* (Lincoln/London: University of Nebraska Press, 1966).

13. Ibid., p. 44.

14. Ibid., pp. 45–46.

15. On Christianity, see Carlyle, *On Heroes,* p. 61; on his being a true prophet, see Carlyle, *On Heroes,* p. 43.

16. Ibid., p. 43.

17. Ibid., p. 72.

18. Sir William Muir, *The Life of Mohammad,* revised by T. H. Weir (Edinburgh: John Grant, 1923), p. lxxi.

19. Ibid., pp. 22, 66, and *passim.*

20. For his "ecstatic states" see Muir, *Life,* pp. 7, 200, and *passim.* For divorce legislation, see p. 338. At p. 334, such regulations are described as "offensive to the European ear."

21. Ibid., p. 522.

22. There is a profound analysis of competing Indian historiographies and their encounters with the West in Partha Chatterjee, *The Nation and Its Fragments* (Princeton: Princeton University Press 1993), especially chapters 3, 4 and 5.

23. The intellectual and social background of this Indian response cannot unfortunately be dealt with at any length here, but see the important synthetic study by C. A. Bayly, *Origins of Nationality in South Asia* (Delhi: Oxford University Press, 1998), especially chapters 3 and 4, as also pp. 278–84, which deals with the missionaries, citing further studies on that subject. The earlier work by Aziz Ahmad, *An Intellectual History of Islam in India* (Edinburgh: Edinburgh University Press, 1969), still has value.

24. On Shah Waliullah see *Encyclopedia of Islam,* new edition, s.v. *Al-Dihlawi* (not very

analytical). There are some suggestive pages on him in Schimmel, *And Muhammad*, pp. 221–28, especially his reflections on prophecy.

25. On *masalih* and Muslim law, see, e.g., Waliullah, *Hujjat Allah al-Baligha*, ed. M. T. Halabi (Beirut: Dar al-Ma'rifa, 1997), 1:21 and 2:360; on God's mercy, see 2:298; on nature, reason and vitalism, see 1:33ff; on the appeal to universal categories of morality, see, e.g., 1:93, 100–101, 137; and 2:146. Examples can be multiplied: these concepts do indeed permeate his work.

26. Waliullah, *Hujjat*, 2:365–66.

27. Schimmel, *And Muhammad*, p. 222, defines this sphere as "the angelic plane" and "that sphere in which the events from the highest level of the heavenly realm are reflected." It is clearly a Sufi image.

28. On the caliphate, see Waliullah, *Hujjat*, 2:258–64. On the virtues of *Jihad*, see 2:298–314. At 2:299 he states, "abandoning the *Jihad*, especially at times like these, would be to abandon much good."

29. See, e.g., Waliullah, *Hujjat*, 1:268ff, which argues that there exists a natural need for a final religion that would abrogate all earlier religions but retain what is best in them all.

30. C. A. Bayly, *Origins of Nationality*, p. 113.

31. It appears that as a young man of twenty-three Ameer Ali had published a short work entitled *A Critical Examination of the Life and Teachings of Mohammed* (1872) which, in a first edition of 1890 and then a second of 1902, transmuted into the celebrated *The Spirit of Islam* (1902; repr. London: Darf Publishers, 1988).

32. This ambiguity is detected in Ameer Ali's argument that Arabia was unaffected by the doom and gloom of surrounding cultures as in *The Spirit*, p. xlvi, but also that Arabia had sunk to the "depths of moral degradation" and that Arabs were "effete," "lawless," "depraved," and "sunk in superstition and vice" as in *The Spirit*, pp. 11, 103. By contrast Shah Waliullah takes Arabians to have been possessed of the "most moderate and least affected" of customs and habits: see Waliullah, *Hujjat*, 2:329.

33. For Muhammad and other prophets, see, e.g., *The Spirit*, p. 104. The superlative style permeates the entire work: typical is p. 47, where Muhammad is described as "the grandest of figures upon whom the light of history has ever shone." For Muhammad's affiliation with the modern world, see *The Spirit*, p. 105.

34. For Khadija and Fatima, see *The Spirit*, p. 12, as also Part II, chapter 4, for greater detail on Muhammad and women. For abandonment of followers, see *The Spirit*, pp. 20–21. For the Satanic Verses, see p. 33. For Qurayza, see p. 76, and for acts of similar cruelty among Jews and Christians, see p. 81. For the Appendix on *nar*, see p. 60.

35. Muhammad Iqbal, *The Reconstruction of Religious Thought in Islam* (Lahore: Kapur, 1930). It had its origin in a series of lectures first delivered in 1928.

36. Any study of Iqbal's views on prophecy must begin with Schimmel, *And Muhammad*, chapter 12. Schimmel is particularly good on Iqbal's poetry.

37. Iqbal, *Reconstruction*, p. 124.

38. Iqbal, *Reconstruction*, p. 125.

39. Iqbal, *Reconstruction*, p. 126.

40. Iqbal, *Reconstruction*, p. 190.

41. The new Indian historiography of reconciliation is analyzed with exemplary clarity in Partha Chatterjee, *The Nation*, chapter 5. Al-Afghani pays little attention to Muhammad but in his pan-Islamic writings refers repeatedly to conditions in British India.

42. For this European inquest on a resurgent Islam, see the fascinating study by Marwan Buheiry, "Colonial Scholarship and Muslim Revivalism in 1900" in his *The Formation and Perception of the Modern Arab World* (Princeton: Darwin Press, 1989), pp. 109–26.

43. On al-Tahtawi, see *Encyclopedia of Islam* (new edition), which has a useful bibliography. His *Nihayat al-Ijaz* is volume 4 of his *Al-A'mal al-Kamila* (Complete Works), edited by Muhammad 'Amara (Beirut: Al-Mu'assasa al-'Arabiyya, 1977).

44. For sinlessness, see al-Tahtawi, *Nihayat*, pp. 23–24, 39; for faith of ancestors, see pp. 25, 33–34, 36; for the devil as sole actor, see p. 111.

45. The best modern edition is by Mahmud Abu Rayya (Cairo: Dar al-Ma'arif, 1966).

46. For the ascent of the prophetic soul, see 'Abduh, *Risalat*, pp. 104–7; for God's wisdom and mercy, see pp. 90–91, 112; for sociability, see pp. 93–97; for religion and reason, see pp. 98–99, 103.

47. 'Abduh, *Risalat*, pp. 115–16.

48. For decadence of the pre-Muhammadan world, see 'Abduh, *Risalat*, pp. 123–26; for his human achievement against huge odds, see pp. 133–34.

49. On the Egypt of the late nineteenth century and early twentieth century, see Afaf Lutfi al-Sayyid-Marsot, *A Short History of Modern Egypt* (Cambridge: Cambridge University Press, 1985), and the classic work of Jacques Berque, *Egypt: Imperialism and Revolution* (London: Faber and Faber, 1972). Albert Hourani, *A History of the Arab Peoples* (London: Faber, 1991), pp. 265–349, is a masterly historical survey of this period in the Near East. On 'Abduh, see *Encyclopedia of Islam* (new edition). For 'Abduh's agenda for political reform, see the classic work by Malcolm H. Kerr, *Islamic Reform: the Political and Legal Theories of Muhammad 'Abduh and Rashid Rida* (Berkeley: University of California Press, 1966).

50. On al-Shidyaq's life and works, see *Encyclopedia of Islam* (new edition), s.v. Faris al-Shidyaq, somewhat dated. See now the valuable Introduction to a selection of his works under the title *Silsilat al-A'mal al-Majhula* (Series of Unknown Works), edited by Fawwaz Tarabulusi and 'Aziz al-'Azma (Beirut: Riyad al-Rayyes, 1995). On the *Nahda* in general, see the survey by 'Ali al-Muhafaza, *Al-Ittijahat al-Fikriyya 'ind al-'Arab fi 'Asr al-Nahda 1798–1914* (Currents of Arabic Thought in the Age of the *Nahda*) (Beirut: Al-Ahliyya, 1975), and the more analytical work of 'Afif Farraj, *Ishkaliyyat al-Nahda* (Problematics of the *Nahda*) (Beirut: Dar al-Adab, 2006). Albert Hourani's *Arabic Thought in the Liberal Age* (Cambridge: Cambridge University Press, 1983) remains fundamental.

51. For rigidity of thought, see al-Shidyaq, *Silsilat al-A'mal*, p. 341; for reluctance of Muslims to engage in technical occupations, see pp. 276, 312–13; for earlier rulers, see pp. 223–26.

52. The original and complete text of this work has been reprinted in the journal *Al-Qahira*, no. 149 (April, 1995), which also includes the full and interesting text of the Prosecution's case against the work. The most detailed critique of Taha

Husayn's work is in Nasir al-Din al-Asad, *Maṣadir al-Shiʿr al-Jahili wa Qimatiha al-Tarikhiyya* (Sources of Jahili Poetry and Their Historical Value, 1956; repr., Beirut: Dar al-Jil, 1988), pp. 377–478.

53. For larger issues having to do with the formation of literary canons and periods, see Frank Kermode, *History and Value* (Oxford: Oxford University Press, 1990), pp. 108–27.

54. There are numerous studies of Egyptian culture in the first half of the twentieth century. A useful introductory survey is J. Brugman, *An Introduction to the History of Modern Arabic Literature in Egypt* (Leiden: Brill, 1984). See also the pertinent remarks on the new *Sira* in Antonie Wessels, *A Modern Arabic Biography of Muhammad* (Leiden: Brill, 1972), pp. 1–6.

55. Tawfiq al-Hakim, *Muhammad* (Cairo: Maktabat Misr, 1988), p. 11.

56. The edition of Taha Husayn used here is Cairo: Dar al-Maʿarif 1975–87, in three slim volumes.

57. Taha Husayn, *ʿAla Hamish*, p. *waw*.

58. Ibid., pp. *waw* to *lam*.

59. The filiations of influence for this work might lead back to Michelet, who famously defined history as a "resurrection of the spirit of the past": see Patrick H. Hutton, *History as an Art of Memory* (Hanover, Vt. and London: University Press of New England, 1993), p. 131. Hutton has much to say on the construction of memory in nineteenth-century France. Maxime Rodinson in his wide-ranging and splendid article, "A Critical Survey of Modern Studies on Muhammad" in M. Swartz, ed., *Studies on Islam* (New York: Oxford University Press, 1981), p. 29, signals the influence on Taha Husayn of Jules Lemaitre (1853–1914). The latter had written a work entitled *En marge des Vieux Livres* (Paris: Boivin 1905), consisting of fables inspired by Homer and Virgil. Both the title itself and the subject matter may well have influenced Taha Husayn.

60. For Mustafa Lutfi al-Manfaluti (1876–1924), see *Encyclopedia of Islam* (new edition), and Brugman, *An Introduction*, pp. 83–88. Manfaluti is now mostly remembered for his adaptations, maudlin and lachrymose in style, of French Romantic tales.

61. Taha Husayn, *ʿAla Hamish*, 1:41.

62. Ibid., 1:164–65.

63. Ibid., 2:63.

64. Subayh appears to be an anagram of Suhayb, surnamed al-Rumi, the Byzantine, a well-known Companion whom the Prophet described in a hadith as *sabiq al-Rum*, first to the faith among the Byzantines.

65. For a more favorable view of the literary merit of these two works, see Antonie Wessels, *A Modern Arabic Biography of Muhammad* (Leiden: Brill, 1972), pp. 6–14.

66. H. G. Sarwar, *Translation of the Holy Qurʾan* (n.p, n.d.), p. lxviii; see also pp. lx–lxi. The lecture on Muhammad's life was delivered in 1925.

67. Maulana Muhammad Ali, *Muhammad the Prophet* (Lahore: Ahmadiyya, 1924).

68. Muhammad Ahmad Jad al-Mawla, *Muhammad al-Mathal al-Kamil* (Muhammad the Perfect Model) (1931; repr., Cairo: M. A. Sabih, 1968), pp. 387–401. At p. 52, the author flatly asserts that there are no contradictions in the reports about his life and actions. He is thus the "most historical" of prophets.

69. Muhammad Husayn Haykal, *Hayat Muhammad* (Life of Muhammad) (1934; repr., Cairo: Dar al-Ma'arif, 2002), p. 226; Muhammad Farid Wajdi, *Al-Sira al-Muhammadiyya* (Muhammadan *Sira*) (1939–1944; repr., Cairo: Al-Dar al-Misriyya al-Lubnaniyya, 1993), pp. 166–68.

70. 'Abbas Mahmud al-'Aqqad, *'Abqariyyat Muhammad* (Muhammad's Genius) (1944; repr., Sidon/Beirut: Al-Maktaba al-'Asriyya, 2003), pp. 105–12.

71. On Zaynab, see Jad al-Mawla, *Muhammad*, pp. 255–57; Haykal, *Hayat*, pp. 262–64; Al-'Aqqad, *'Abqariyyat*, p. 106.

72. See, e.g., the review article by Thomas Dixon in *The Times Literary Supplement*, December 22 and 29, 2006, pp. 3–4, which discusses the works of Richard Dawkins, Owen Gingerich, Francis S. Collins, and others.

73. Jad al-Mawla, *Muhammad*, pp. 38–39.

74. Jad al-Mawla, *Muhammad*, p. 129.

75. Jad al-Mawla, *Muhammad*, p. 161.

76. Wajdi, *Al-Sira*, pp. 45–46.

77. Wajdi, *Al-Sira*, p. 59.

78. For Western standards for his biography, see Haykal, *Hayat*, p. 31; for Muslim defenders and Western attackers, see p. 29. Haykal appears to be arguing that the lines between "us" and the "Orientalists" are not that rigid. A "modern" Muslim scholar should see how best one can interact with their methodology, in which there is much that is built on critical principles familiar to Muslims from their own critical heritage. Haykal has been well served by two book-length studies in English: Antonie Wessels, *A Modern Arabic Biography of Muhammad* (Leiden: Brill, 1972), and Charles D. Smith, *Islam and the Search for Social Order in Modern Egypt: A Biography of Muhammad Husayn Haikal* (Albany: SUNY Press, 1983). The first is a close and subtle reading of Haykal's *Hayat*, and the second is a general biography which deals with *Hayat* at pp. 113–25.

79. For Bahira, see Haykal, *Hayat*, p. 107; for the opening of the Prophet's breast, see pp. 104–5; for 'Abdullah's temptation, see p. 101; for the twelve-year-old Muhammad, see p. 107; for married life with Khadija, see pp. 116–17, 122. Haykal devotes many pages to similar speculation, especially where the traditional sources are silent or meager. For "Satanic Verses," see p. 145.

80. Jad al-Mawla, *Muhammad*, p. 66. The universal gloom includes Arabia and Mecca: see pp. 56–64.

81. Wajdi, *Al-Sira*, p. 118. He appears to believe that this rehabilitation of Arabia is connected to Arab nationalist sentiment.

82. For the historicity of the Qur'an, see Haykal, *Hayat*, pp. 32, 87 (*contra* Muir) and *passim*; for the "honorable status" of Mecca, see pp. 83–99; for the virtues of Arabians, see p. 79.

83. Jad al-Mawla, *Muhammad*, pp. 169–70.

84. Wajdi, *Al-Sira*, p. 100. The author concludes that the religion of Muhammad is the most universal and the one most conforming to reason and human nature.

85. See, e.g., Haykal, *Hayat*, pp. 47–49.

86. Wajdi, *Al-Sira*, p. 90. The charge of hysteria is further refuted on pp. 92–93.

87. Wajdi, *Al-Sira*, pp. 94, 104.

88. On al-'Aqqad's life and works, see Brugman, *An Introduction*, pp. 121–38. More particularly on his *Muhammad*, see the valuable comments in Wessels, *A Modern Arabic Biography*, pp. 14–19.
89. Al-'Aqqad, *'Abqariyyat*, pp. 57, 59.
90. Ibid., p. 125. Here Muhammad's "genius" is not very different from Carlyle's hero as a force of Nature.

X

1. The fourth edition (Kuwait/Cairo: Dar Su'ad al-Sabbah, 1992) is used here.
2. Amin, *Dalil*, p. 37. For his admiring views of early *Sira*, see *Dalil*, pp. 32–34; for miracles and hagiography, see pp. 33–37; for his critique of Ameer Ali, see pp. 37–38. Regrettably, I am not concerned here with his perceptive and often very amusing views on the European Orientalist tradition of biographies of Muhammad.
3. For the arguments above, see Amin, *Dalil*, pp. 37–45. Among other things, he takes Muslims to task for their enchantment with Carlyle and his ilk.
4. Amin, *Dalil*, p. 45.
5. For Muhammad as ideological or class hero, see, e.g., 'Abd al-Rahman al-Sharqawi, *Muhammad Rasul al-Hurriyya* (Muhammad, Apostle of Liberty) (1962; repr., Beirut: Al-'Asr al-Hadith, 1986, 1962, pp. 10, 54, 84; 'Aziz al-Sayyid Jasim, *Muhammad: al-Haqiqa al-'Uzma* (Muhammad: The Greatest Truth) (Beirut: Dar al-Andalus, 1987), pp. 16, 41, 45, 97; Muhammad M. al-Fahham and others, *Muhammad: Nazra 'Asriyya Jadida* (Muhammad: A New and Modern Viewpoint) (Beirut: Al-Mu'assasa al-'Arabiyya, 1972), pp. 37, 47, 88, 101–2; Safiyy al-Din al-Mubarakfuri, *Sirat Rasul Allah (Sira* of the Messenger of God) (1976; repr., Damascus/Beirut: Dar al-Khayr, 2001), pp. 211, 238, 245, 255, 471.
6. For a critique of the image of Muhammad as an ideological or class hero, see Mustafa Mahmud, *Muhammad, salla Allahu 'alayhi wa sallam* (Muhammad, Upon Whom Blessings and Peace) (repr. Cairo, 1997: Dar al-Ma'arif, 1970), pp. 8, 10–12, 39; Hisham Ju'ayt, *Fi al-Sira al-Nabawiyya: Al-Wahy wa'l Qur'an wa'l Nubuwwa* (On the Prophetic *Sira:* Inspiration, the Qur'an and Prophecy) (Beirut: Dar al-Tali'a, 2000; 1999), pp. 103, 107; Murtada Mutahhari, *Al-Sira al-Nabawiyya* (The Prophetic *Sira)* (Beirut: Mu'assasat al-Ba'tha, 1990), p. 38. Some *Siras* of the earlier part of the century had argued that the Muslim alms-tax *(zakat)* was an ideal system because it helps the poor without hurting the rich, unlike the "socialists of today" who undermine prosperity and threaten the nation's security: see Muhammad al-Khudari, *Nur al-Yaqin fi Sirat Sayyid al-Mursalin* (The Light of Certitude Regarding the *Sira* of the Lord of Messengers) (1900?; repr., Beirut: Dar al-Ma'rifa, 2004), pp. 81–82.
7. For gushing prose, the dotted style and exclamation marks, see, e.g., Khalid Muhammad Khalid, *Insaniyyat Muhammad* (The Human Aspects of Muhammad) (Cairo: Maktabat Wahba, 1960), and Sharqawi, *Muhammad*; for internal monologues and apostrophes, see 'A'isha 'Abd al-Rahman, *Ma 'al-Mustafa* (With the Chosen One) (Beirut: Dar al-Kitab al-'Arabi, 1980), pp. 27–51; Sharqawi,

Muhammad, pp. 28, 59; Shawqi Dayf, *Muhammad, Khatam al-Mursalin* (Muhammad, Seal of Apostles) (Cairo: Dar al-Ma'arif, 2000), p. 79; 'Abd al-Halim Mahmud, *Dala'il al-Nubuwwa wa Mu'jizat al-Rasul* (Proofs of Prophecy and the Miracles of the Messenger) (Cairo: Dar al-Ma'arif, 1998), p. 21.

8. Khalid M. Khalid organizes his *Insaniyyat* in chapters headed "Mercy," "Justice," "Love," and "People's Problems." 'Abd al-Rahman, *Ma 'al-Mustafa*, p. 333, speaks of Muhammad leading mankind to "truth, goodness and beauty." Alone, I think, among them, Sharqawi speaks of the need to present the *Sira* to Muslims and non-Muslims alike: see his *Muhammad*, p. 11.

9. 'Abd al-Halim Mahmud, *Dala'il*, p. 18, describes the "Orientalists" as being "led by Abu Jahl."

10. For the "darkness" of the pre-Islamic era and the clean break, see, e.g., Muhammad al-Tayyib al-Najjar in al-Fahham, ed., *Muhammad: Nazra 'Asriyya Jadida*, p. 84; Abdul Hameed Siddiqui, *The Life of Muhammad* (Beirut: al-Fath, Dar ca. 1965), pp. 47, 69, 84; Sharqawi, *Muhammad*, pp. 26, 61–62; Mubarakfuri, *Sirat*, pp. 456, 470–71. For Shiite biographies on this theme, see Muhammad Baqir al-Sadr, *Al-Mursil, al-Rasul, al-Risala* (The Sender, the Messenger, the Mission) (Beirut: Dar al-Ta'aruf, 1978), pp. 70–80; Muhammad Taqi al-Mudarrisi, *Muhammad, Qudwa wa Uswa* (Muhammad, Paragon and Model) (Beirut: Dar al-Sadiq, ca. 1960), p. 21; Murtada Mutahhari, *Al-Sira*, pp. 51–52, asserts that a whole period of 273 years was "sinless" in Shiite history. One Shiite biographer, Hashim Ma'ruf al-Hasani, *Sirat al-Mustafa* (The *Sira* of the Chosen One) (Beirut: Dar al-Ta'aruf, 1996), pp. 13–23, allows the Bedouins of pre-Islamic Arabia some nobility of character.

11. Haykal's denial of 'Ali's role is explicitly pointed out in Hashim Ma'ruf al-Hasani, *Sirat al-Mustafa*, pp. 353–54.

12. See, e.g., Hasani, *Sirat*, p. 45, and compare p. 54.

13. See, e.g., Shawqi Dayf, *Muhammad*, pp. 9, 12, and compare p. 17, on the Night Journey.

14. See, e.g., 'Abd al-Halim Mahmud, *Dala'il*, p. 154, where he affirms: "we believe that God breaks natural custom for both prophets and saints *(awliya')*," but at p. 124 speaks too of Muhammad's *Hijra* as a "beautiful spiritual symbol" and at pp. 199–200 of the Night Journey as both a miracle and "an unending journey to God." In this heavily Sufi treatment, Mahmud owes much to earlier works like Yusuf al-Nabhani, *Hujjat Allah 'ala al-'Alamin fi Mu'jizat Sayyid al-Mursalin* (The Proof of God to the World Regarding the Miracles of the Lord of Messengers) (ca. 1900; repr., Beirut: Dar al-Kutub al-'Ilmiyya, 1996), where both miracles and saintly charisms are affirmed at pp. 20, 43, 556.

15. Dayf, *Muhammad*, is possibly the loudest in his rejection of miracles. For Muhammad's perfection, see Mustafa Mahmud, *Muhammad*, pp. 14–15, where the Prophet combines the eloquence of Demosthenes with the poetic genius of Byron, the leadership of Pericles, the wisdom of Luqman (a Qur'anic sage), the military skills of Napoleon, and the legislative judgment of Solon.

16. See, e.g., Ahmad Shibli in al-Fahham, ed. *Muhammad: Nazra 'Asriyya*, pp. 52–55, 64.

17. See A. H. Siddiqui, *The Life of Muhammad*, pp. 71, 75. At p. 81, Siddiqui quotes, for further proof of sincerity, Stanley Lane-Poole's opinion that Muhammad was a "hero to his valet."
18. Cairo: Merit, 2001.
19. See, e.g., 'Abd al-Karim, *Fatrat*, pp. 35–37, 117, 124.
20. Al-Rusafi seems to have finished this work in 1933 but the work itself was first published in Koln, Germany, in 2002 by Manshurat al-Jamal from a manuscript at Harvard University. Dashti's work, which first appeared in Persian circa 1974, was published in Damascus by Dar Petra in an Arabic translation in 2004.
21. On al-Rusafi's life and works, see "Ma'ruf al-Rusafi," *Encyclopedia of Islam* (new ed.).
22. Al-Rusafi, *Al-Shakhsiyya*, p. 16.
23. For history as the home of lying, see al-Rusafi, *Al-Shakhsiyya*, p. 15; for everyday examples of faulty transmission, see the charming story on p. 55; for his critique of Ibn Ishaq, see p. 53; for Hadith, see p. 69; for divergence of history leading to sectarianism, see p. 74.
24. See the fascinating tenth-century debate between Abu Hatim al-Razi and Abu Bakr al-Razi in the former's work entitled *Dala'il al-Nubuwwa* (Proofs of Prophecy) (Tehran: Imperial Academy, 1977).
25. For the Qur'an as the speech of Muhammad, see al-Rusafi, *Al-Shakhsiyya*, pp. 162, 598 and *passim*; for Muhammad's intelligence and imagination, see pp. 77, 95, 140, 157, and *passim*; for prophethood as a self-generating idea, see p. 136; for his "subconscious mind," see p. 115, this being a frequent phrase; for inspiration as a series of psychological responses to changing needs, see pp. 157–59; for the disparity between desire and good sense, see pp. 77–78; for someone teaching him, see pp. 78, 639. Nothing prevents someone from *teaching* him, though a foreigner, what he later could *compose* in Arabic. For other examples of faulty logic, see, e.g., p. 79 on Abraham and Nimrod and p. 696 on Moses and al-Khidr.
26. For disparity in Qur'anic eloquence, see al-Rusafi, *Al-Shakhsiyya*, pp. 458, 461, 614ff; for its defects and classical critics, see p. 570; for verses "unworthy" of God, see p. 567; for his own emendations, see pp. 617ff; for verses that contradict reason and logic, see pp. 616ff. Al-Rusafi on the Qur'an would require a separate treatment.
27. For his illiteracy, see al-Rusafi, *Al-Shakhsiyya*, pp. 166–71; for his early life before his mission, see pp. 101–3; for rejection of miracles, see pp. 402, 737–39.
28. Al-Rusafi, *Al-Shakhsiyya*, pp. 274–75.
29. For the Night Journey, see al-Rusafi, *Al-Shakhsiyya*, p. 200; for Muhammad's poverty, see pp. 336–37; for his marriages, see pp. 408–9 (on Zaynab) and 423; for his sexual energy, see p. 350; for occasional vengefulness, see p. 322; for Islam and the sword, see pp. 207, 608.
30. Al-Rusafi, *Al-Shakhsiyya*, p. 415.
31. For Haykal and hypocrisy, see al-Rusafi, *Al-Shakhsiyya*, p. 600. There follows a line of poetry from Abu al-'Ala' al-Ma'arri, a hero of al-Rusafi, on hypocrisy in religion.
32. For Dashti's life, I rely on the introduction to Dashti, *23 'Aman*.
33. For lack of an "objective" biography and myth-making, see Dashti, *23 'Aman*, pp.

17–20; for miracles as contravening Qur'an, see pp. 26–27, 76–88; for his Night Journey, see p. 24; for trees greeting him, see p. 57; for Gabriel as a "symbol," see p. 54; for failure to produce a miracle while confronting Quraysh, see p. 117. Dashti, *23 'Aman*, pp. 118, 333, calls these biographers "peddlers of miracles."

34. For Muhammad's sinlessness and the Satanic Verses, see Dashti, *23 'Aman*, pp. 65, 107. Dashti argues, p. 108, that the fact that he was *not* sinless actually elevates his status. For Muhammad not hiding his weaknesses in the Qur'an, see p. 217; for biographers being *plus royaliste que le roi*, see p. 218; for love of women, see pp. 195–222; for occasional brutality, see pp. 152, 154, 162–68. Dashti argues that Muhammad in Mecca was Jesus-like but became David-like in Medina.

35. For the Qur'an as "prophetic eloquence," see Dashti, *23 'Aman*, p. 83; for the *Fatiha*, see p. 239; for abrogation, see p. 249; for Muhammad's unconscious intruding into revelation, see p. 243; for Abu Lahab, see p. 239; for the *jinn*, see p. 258.

36. For the "mix-up," see Dashti, *23 'Aman*, p. 237. On p. 236, Dashti asserts that the God of the Qur'an displays many human characteristics. On the eloquence of the Qur'an and its nonmiraculous nature, see pp. 91, 98. On p. 59, Dashti describes its manner of collection as "unnatural," "illogical," and "dull-witted." On the Qur'an empowering Muhammad, see p. 103; on prophecy as unnecessary and God's existence as unproven, see pp. 46–47.

37. For supernatural accretions demeaning his achievement, see Dashti, *23 'Aman*, p. 332. At p. 333, he attacks his own Shiite "myths." For love of women, see p. 197; for cruelty and state building, see p. 154.

CONCLUSION

1. Miskawayhi, *Tajarib al-Umam* (Leiden: Brill, 1909), p. 307. On Miskawayhi's historical thinking, see Tarif Khalidi, *Arabic Historical Thought*, pp. 170–76.

2. I am of course referring to a Charles Taylor phrase.

3. See James Tully, ed. *Meaning and Context: Quentin Skinner and His Critics* (Cambridge: Polity Press, 1988), p. 13. The same point is echoed in Annabel Brett, "What Is Intellectual History Now?" in David Cannadine, ed. *What Is History Now?* (Basingstoke: Palgrave, 2000).

4. Charles Taylor, *Modern Social Imaginaries* (Durham, N.C.: Duke University Press, 2005), pp. 52–67.

Index